D0024749

# *Culture and Customs of Norway*

# Culture and Customs of Norway

## MARGARET HAYFORD O'LEARY

Culture and Customs of Europe

AN IMPRINT OF ABC-CLIO, LLC
Santa Barbara, California • Denver, Colorado • Oxford, England

**Library of Congress Cataloging-in-Publication Data**

O'Leary, Margaret Hayford.
　　Culture and customs of Norway / Margaret Hayford O'Leary.
　　　　p. cm. — (Culture and customs of Europe)
　　Includes bibliographical references and index.
　　ISBN 978–0–313–36248–4 (hard copy : alk. paper) — ISBN 978–0–313–36249–1 (ebook)
　1. Norway—Civilization. 2. Norway—Social life and customs. I. Title.
DL431.O54　2010
948.1—dc22　　　　　　2010016987

ISBN: 978–0–313–36248–4
EISBN: 978–0–313–36249–1

14  13  12  11  10　　1  2  3  4  5

This book is also available on the World Wide Web as an eBook.
Visit www.abc-clio.com for details.

Greenwood
An Imprint of ABC-CLIO, LLC

ABC-CLIO, LLC
130 Cremona Drive, P.O. Box 1911
Santa Barbara, California 93116-1911

This book is printed on acid-free paper ∞

Manufactured in the United States of America

# Contents

# Series Foreword

THE OLD WORLD and the New World have maintained a fluid exchange of people, ideas, innovations, and styles. Even though the United States became the defacto world leader and economic superpower in the wake of a devastated Europe in World War II, Europe has remained for many the standard bearer of Western culture.

Millions of Americans can trace their ancestors to Europe. The United States as we know it was built on waves of European immigration, starting with the English, who braved the seas to found the Jamestown Colony in 1607. Bosnian and Albanian immigrants are some of the latest new Americans. In the Gilded Age of one of our great expatriates, the novelist Henry James, the Grand Tour of Europe was de rigueur for young American men of means to prepare them for a life of refinement and taste. In the more recent democratic age, scores of American college students have Eurorailed their way across Great Britain and the Continent, sampling the fabled capitals and bergs in a mad, great adventure, or have benefited from a semester abroad. For other American vacationers and culture vultures, Europe is the prime destination. What is the new post–Cold War, post–Berlin Wall Europe in the new millennium? Even with the different languages, rhythms, and rituals, Europeans have much in common: They are largely well-educated, prosperous, and worldly. They also have similar goals, face common threats, and form alliances. With the advent of the European Union, the open borders, and the

Euro, and considering globalization and the prospect of a homogenized Europe, an updated survey of the region is warranted.

*Culture and Customs of Europe* features individual volumes on the countries most studied for which fresh information is in demand from students and other readers. The Series casts a wide net, including not only the expected countries, such as Spain, France, England, and Germany, but also countries such as Poland and Greece that lie outside Western Europe proper. Each volume is written by a country specialist with intimate knowledge of the contemporary dynamics of a people and culture. Sustained narrative chapters cover the land, the people, and offer a brief history; they also discuss religion, social customs, gender roles, family, marriage, literature and media, performing arts and cinema, and art and architecture. The national character and ongoing popular traditions of each country are framed in a historical context and celebrated along with the latest trends and major cultural figures. A country map, chronology, glossary, and evocative photos enhance the text.

The storied and enlightened Europeans will continue to fascinate Americans. Our futures are strongly linked politically, economically, and culturally.

# Preface

IN MANY WAYS I have been preparing to write this book for most of my life. I began learning Norwegian at the Concordia College Norwegian Language Village as a young teenager and, after some detours into other fields, got a Ph.D. in Scandinavian Studies. Years teaching at the University of Oslo International Summer School as well as living in Norway both as a student and with my spouse and children has given me the in-depth knowledge of Norway that can only be gleaned by living there. My nearly 35 years teaching courses on Norwegian language, life, and society at both St. Olaf College and the summer school have also provided me with the academic knowledge necessary to write this book.

The structure of the Culture and Customs series has, however, pushed me to research and learn about topics that are not typically included in my courses or other books about Norway. I am grateful to Greenwood for asking me to write this book, thus requiring me to learn about new areas. Until now, little or nothing has been available in English about many subject areas in the book: media, fashion, leisure, marriage and family, and architecture. I have used books in both English and Norwegian from libraries here at St. Olaf and in Norway in addition to a wide range of up-to-the-minute information available on the internet. It is my hope that in addition to the chapters I have written about these topics, the reader will find the bibliography useful. Here I have gathered additional English-language sources—both in print and electronic—for those curious to learn more.

I am grateful to St. Olaf College for its wonderful Rølvaag Library and for the yearlong sabbatical leave that has given me time to research and write. I also would like to express my thanks to my children Kari and Sean and my spouse, Doug, who have read and edited chapters. They and my son Erik have also shown amazing patience with my lengthy stays in Norway both with them and without. My St. Olaf friends and colleagues Todd Nichol, Torild Homstad, and Solveig Zempel have provided valuable comments, advice, and guidance on many chapters. I am so thankful for their encouragement and confidence in me.

# Chronology

| | |
|---|---|
| 1217–1319 | Period of greatness |
| 1274, 1276 | Magnus Law Mender creates laws for countryside and cities |
| 1299–1319 | Reign of Håkon V Magnusson |
| 1319–1343 | Swedish–Norwegian union |
| 1349–1351 | The Black Death |
| 1360–1754 | The Hanseatic League |
| 1380–1814 | Norway and Denmark in union |
| 1388–1412 | Queen Margaret I regent of all three Nordic countries |
| 1397–1521 | Kalmar Union: Norway, Denmark, and Sweden |
| 1468–1469 | Shetlands and Orkneys pawned to the Scottish king |
| 1521 | Sweden, under Gustaf Vasa, withdraws from Kalmar Union, leaving Denmark and Norway in union |
| 1537 | Lutheran Reformation in Norway. Archbishop Olav Engelbrektsson flees. Norway subordinated to Danish rule |
| 1563–1570 | Nordic Seven Years war between Sweden and coalition of Denmark–Norway, Poland, and Lübeck |
| 1588–1648 | Reign of Christian IV |
| 1700–1720 | Great Nordic War |
| 1736 | Confirmation law adopted |
| 1739 | First school law passed, requiring school for all children |
| 1807 | Denmark–Norway enters Napoleonic war, allied with Napoleon |
| 1808 | War with Sweden |
| 1811 | First university established in Norway. Opened in 1813 |
| 1814 | Treaty of Kiel |
| May 17, 1814 | Norwegian Constitution signed at Eidsvoll with Danish prince Christian Frederik elected Norwegian king. Brief war with Sweden, followed by acceptance of union with Sweden under a shared king |
| 1814–1905 | Norway in union with Sweden |
| 1800s | National Romanticism |
| 1821 | Inheritance of noble titles abolished |

| | |
|---|---|
| 1825 | First emigrants leave Norway for America |
| 1845, 1863, 1900 | Poor laws |
| 1848–1851 | Marcus Thrane movement |
| 1851 | Jews permitted to enter Norway |
| 1853 | Ivar Aasen publishes samples of *Landsmaal* |
| 1854 | Daughters gain equal inheritance rights |
| | First train line from Oslo to Eidsvoll |
| 1863 | Unmarried women over age 25 gain same legal rights of majority as adult men |
| 1866–1873 | First great wave of emigration to America |
| 1880–1893 | Second great wave of emigration |
| 1882 | Women gain the right to study at the university and take examinations at all faculties |
| 1883 | Liberal Party (*Venstre*) founded |
| 1884 | Conservative Party (*Høyre*) founded |
| | Parliamentarism introduced |
| | *Nynorsk* becomes an official language |
| 1887 | Labor Party (*Arbeiderpartiet*) founded |
| | Public prostitution banned |
| 1888 | Married women gain majority and right to own property |
| 1889 | Public elementary school for all |
| | Girls allowed to march in May 17 parades for first time |
| 1890s | First laws granting protection to workers and accident insurance |
| 1898 | Universal vote for men |
| 1899 | LO (Labor Union) founded |
| 1900 | NAF (Employers union) founded |
| 1905 | Union with Sweden dissolved |
| 1905–1957 | Reign of Haakon VII |
| 1906–1909 | Concession laws passed regulating foreign ownership of waterfalls |

| | |
|---|---|
| 1907 | Limited voting rights for women |
| 1909 | Bergensbanen railroad constructed between Oslo and Bergen |
| | Illness insurance law passed |
| 1910 | NTH (Norway's Technical College, in Trondheim) founded |
| 1911 | Roald Amundsen reaches South Pole |
| 1913 | Women receive full voting franchise |
| 1914–1918 | Norway neutral during World War I |
| 1919 | Eight-hour workday introduced |
| 1919–1927 | Prohibition against sale of distilled spirits and strong wine, by referendum |
| 1922 | State Wine Monopoly established to control sale of table wine and beer |
| 1920 | Norway becomes member of the League of Nations |
| | Agrarian party (now Center Party) founded |
| 1920–1924 | Postwar economic crisis; stock market crash |
| 1921 | First woman elected to *Stortinget* |
| | Labor unrest and strikes |
| 1922 | Norway's teachers college founded |
| 1923 | Norway's Communist Party founded |
| 1925 | Norway gains sovereignty of Svalbard |
| 1930 | Worldwide economic crisis reaches Norway |
| 1931–1933 | Labor conflict. General lockout 1931, greatest labor conflict ever in Norway |
| 1933 | Christian Democratic Party founded |
| | *Nasjonal Samling* (Norwegian Nazi Party) founded |
| 1935 | Agreement reached between labor (LO) and employers (NAF/NHO) |
| 1936 | Old-age pension law passed |
| 1938 | Unemployment insurance law passed |

| | |
|---|---|
| 1940–1945 | Norway occupied by Germany during World War II |
| April 9, 1940 | Norway invaded by Germany |
| June 7, 1940 | King, Crown Prince, and government flee to London |
| 1942 | Jews arrested |
| 1944 | Russian troops enter north Norway |
| May 8, 1945 | Liberation day |
| June 7, 1945 | King returns |
| | Joint government (Labor, Norway's Communist Party, Conservative, Liberal, Agrarian parties) under Einar Gerhardsen as Prime Minister |
| 1945–1950 | Reconstruction |
| | Rationing of consumer goods (until 1952) |
| 1945 | Norway part of forming of United Nations. Norwegian Trygve Lie is first Secretary General |
| 1946 | University of Bergen founded |
| | SAS (Scandinavian Airlines System) formed |
| | Child benefit payments instituted (*Barnetrygd*) |
| 1947 | State Loan Fund for students established |
| | 18 days of vacation guaranteed (three weeks) |
| 1948–1951 | Marshall Plan aid to Norway |
| 1948 | Norway joins GATT (General Agreement on Tariffs and Trade) and OEEC (Organization for European Economic Cooperation), later called OECD (Organisation for Economic Co-operation and Development) |
| 1949 | Norway becomes member of NATO |
| 1957–1991 | Reign of Olav V |
| 1957 | Norway announces refusal to allow atomic weapons on Norwegian soil |
| 1959 | 45-hour workweek instituted |
| 1960 | Television begins development |
| | Norway joins EFTA (European Free Trade Association) |
| | End of rationing of cars |

| | |
|---|---|
| 1961 | Disability and retraining assistance introduced |
| | Socialist Peoples Party formed |
| 1962, 1967 | Norway applies for membership in European Economic Community |
| 1963 | First non-socialist government since 1935 |
| 1964 | Freedom of religion guaranteed by Constitution |
| 1965 | Pension for widows and mothers introduced |
| 1967 | *Folketrygd* law (Health and Welfare Insurance Scheme) |
| 1968 | Universities in Tromsø and Trondheim founded |
| | 42.5-hour workweek |
| | Youth uprising |
| 1969 | Nine-year required school introduced |
| | Oil discovered in North Sea |
| | District colleges in Kristiansand, Molde, and Stavanger founded |
| 1970 | Norway applies for membership in the EEC (European Economic Community) |
| 1972 | Equal Rights Council formed |
| | Norwegian voters reject membership in the EEC |
| 1973 | Pension age lowered from 70 to 67 |
| | Oil crisis introduces period of economic stagnation |
| | New parties: Anders Lange's Party (later Progress Party), SV (Socialist Left Party), AKP (Workers Communist Party), and The Liberal People's Party |
| | Birth of Haakon Magnus, son of Crown Prince Harald |
| 1974 | *Odelsloven* changed. Males and females have equal inheritance rights |
| | Upper secondary educational reform |
| 1975 | Restriction of immigration |
| 1976 | Law regulating work environment. *Arbeidsmiljøloven* |
| | 40-hour workweek |

| | |
|---|---|
| 1978 | Abortion law passed. Free choice allowed up to 12 weeks pregnancy |
| 1979 | Alta-Kautokeino dam controversy |
| 1980 | Naming laws changed |
| 1981 | Gro Harlem Brundtland first woman prime minister |
| 1987 | Paid maternity leave expanded from 18 to 20 weeks |
| | 37.5-hour workweek |
| 1989 | Paid maternity leave expanded from 20 to 22 weeks |
| 1990 | Constitutional amendment giving the oldest heir the right to inherit the throne, regardless of gender |
| 1991– | Reign of Harald V |
| 1993 | Oslo Accords between Israel and the Palestinians |
| | Paternal quota of childbearing leave reserved for the father |
| 1994 | Winter Olympics in Lillehammer |
| | Norwegian voters reject membership in the European Union for second time |
| 1996 | NTNU (Norwegian University of Science and Technology) formed in Trondheim |
| 2000 | New school law. Children begin first grade in the year they turn six (previously seven) |
| 2001 | Crown Prince Haakon marries Mette-Marit Tjessem Høiby |
| 2003 | Partnership law. Gays and lesbians gain right to registered partnerships |
| | *Stortinget* passes law requiring each gender to be represented by at least 40 percent of board members of publicly owned companies |
| 2004 | Princess Ingrid Alexandra born, daughter of Crown Prince Haakon and Crown Princess Mette-Marit |
| 2006 | Law for 40 percent minimum representation of each gender extended to boards of all corporations, with a two-year transition period. Quota achieved by 2008 |

| | |
|---|---|
| 2008 | Poles overtake Pakistanis as largest immigrant group in Norway |
| 2009 | Gender-neutral marriage law takes effect |
| | Paternity quota extended to ten weeks of 56-week child-bearing leave |

# 1

# The Land, People, and Politics

NORWAY has come a long way since World War II. In 1945, emerging from five years of occupation by German forces, Norway was one of the poorest countries in Europe, with a massive housing shortage, rationing of consumer goods, and a broken-down infrastructure. Today it is one of the richest countries in the world, one of the largest exporters of oil, a promoter of world peace, and a place with a relatively small difference between rich and poor.

Norway is one of the best places in the world to live according to several international lists. For example, the Global Peace Index[1] has ranked Norway first, second, or third since 2007. (The United States was number 83 in 2009, 97 in 2008, and 96 in 2007.) Created by the Institute for Economics and Peace, this index examines 24 indicators, including relationships with other countries, crime, democracy and transparency, education, respect for human rights, and material well-being. The Human Development Index,[2] commissioned annually by the UN Development Programme, ranked Norway first in 2009. This index attempts to go beyond simple gross domestic product per capita, providing a composite measure of three dimensions of human development: a long and healthy life, education, and standard of living. Norway does, however, frequently appear on lists of the most expensive places to live. According to the *The Economist*'s annual Big Mac index, for example, the price of the large McDonald's burger is among the highest in the world.[3]

Norwegians concur with international opinion according to the results of a recent poll taken by Norway's Agency for Public Management and eGovernment. According to the survey, 86 percent of the citizens of Norway agree that their country is a nearly perfect place to live: 94 percent indicate that they are satisfied or very satisfied, with great consistency over the entire country; 88 percent agree that their own municipality is a good place to live; and 80 percent expect to live in the same city three years from now; 70 percent express satisfaction with government services, although 51 percent believe that the cost of such services is high in comparison to the quality; and 58 percent think that money is wasted in the public sector.[4]

Norwegians are immensely proud of their country and yet simultaneously apologize for being such a small country. It is considered unacceptable to have too high an opinion of oneself, as seen in the oft-quoted Law of Jante. According to the law of the fictional village of Jante:

1.  You shall not believe you are something.
2.  You shall not believe you are as good as we are.
3.  You shall not believe you are wiser than we are.
4.  You shall not imagine yourself better than we are.
5.  You shall not believe you know more than we do.
6.  You shall not believe you are greater than we are.
7.  You shall not believe you amount to anything.
8.  You shall not laugh at us.
9.  You shall not believe that anyone cares about you.
10. You shall not believe you can teach us anything.[5]

Former Prime Minister Gro Harlem Brundtland experienced firsthand how Norwegians react if one demonstrates too obvious pride. When discussing Norway's business and sports reputation in her 1992 New Year's speech, she said, "It's typically Norwegian to be good."[6] This gaffe has never been forgotten, and the quote is endlessly used in discussions of Norwegian identity. Yet it is true that Norwegians both expect and experience domestic and international success far out of proportion to its tiny population of fewer than 5 million people.

## LAND[7]

In 2009, *National Geographic* rated the fjords of western Norway at the top of its list of tourist destinations in the world, remarking on "well-preserved Norwegian rural life" in addition to the gorgeous scenery. The *National Geographic* list is "an assessment of authenticity and stewardship, evaluating the qualities that make a destination unique and measuring its 'integrity

Geiranger Fjord. (Photo courtesy of the author.)

of place.'"[8] Its criteria include environmental and ecological quality, social and cultural integrity, condition of historic buildings and archaeological sites, aesthetic appeal, quality of tourism management, and outlook for the future (Figure 1.1).

Norway's latitude is almost identical to the state of Alaska, ranging from 71°11′09″ in the north to 57°57′31″ in the south. The distance by air from the northernmost tip to the south is 1,089 miles, which is only slightly less than the distance between the southern tip of Norway and Rome. The length of the mainland coastline is 15,626 miles. Including the distance of the coastlines of all the islands adds another 36,122 miles. This total is impressive, considering that it is twice the distance around the earth's equator. Norway shares land borders totaling 1,592 miles with three countries, Sweden (1,013 miles), Finland (457 miles), and Russia (122 miles). Its narrowest point is less than a mile across, and the widest point is 268.4 miles.

With an area of 125,013 square miles (mainland Norway and islands), Norway is about the same size as the state of New Mexico. To that you can add the North Sea possessions of Svalbard (23,560 square miles) and Jan Mayen (146 square miles). Norway also has possessions in Antarctica: Bouvet Island, Peter I Island, and Queen Maud Land.

**Figure 1.1**
Map of Norway

During the summer the area north of the Arctic Circle (66°33′39″) experiences the midnight sun, which lasts longer the farther north you go. In the city of Tromsø, it shines from May 20 to July 22. (Even in the south it never gets completely dark at night.) Of course this means a corresponding period of darkness during the winter. In the south, the sun is only up for six or seven hours a day in winter. In Tromsø, the sun does not rise at all from November 25 to January 16. It is not pitch-black during this period, however, because the sun is just beneath the horizon for a time each day, producing a bluish arctic light. On clear days and nights, the darkness is relieved by the moon, stars, and northern lights reflecting on the snow.

Much of Norway is covered with water, with about 7 percent fresh water and glaciers, and 5.8 percent wetlands. The largest lake is Mjøsa, located in southern Norway, north of Oslo. It covers 140 square miles. The longest river is the Glomma, at 373 miles. The highest waterfall is Kjelfossen, at 2,756 feet. The longest fjord is Sognefjorden, on the west coast, which reaches 127 miles inland. Jostedalsbreen is the largest glacier at 188 square miles.

Norway has little arable land, only 3.2 percent, with only about 2.8 percent actually being cultivated. The best farmland is concentrated around the Oslo fjord, north of Oslo near Lake Mjøsa, and south and east of Trondheim. The trend is toward larger farms and more renting of farmland, resulting in a reduction in the number of farms in operation by almost seven farms every single day between 1999 and 2008. During the same decade the amount of

View from Stalheim Hotel over Nærøydalen. Located south of Sognefjorden, this side excursion is usually included in the Norway in a Nutshell tour. (Photo courtesy of author)

land under cultivation was reduced by 94,000 acres. One problematic result of the reduction in farming is that the previously cultivated areas are in danger of becoming overgrown with trees and bushes, blocking the scenic views people are used to. The mild climate and long days of summer allow many kinds of fruit to be grown, especially on the west coast. Apples, plums, cherries, and pears are common. Strawberries are cultivated all over Norway and are especially prized during their short season.

Most of the country is covered by forests (38%) and mountains and plateaus (44%). The mountains in Norway are not particularly high, although the tree line is low because of its northerly location. The highest level of tree growth in southern Norway is 3,937 feet in the Jotunheimen Mountains. Along the coast of northern Norway, it might be at sea level. By comparison, the tree line in Colorado is at 12,000 feet. The two highest mountains are both inland: Galdhøpiggen rises 8,100 feet and Glittertind 8,084 feet, including its permanent snow cap. Although not as high, the mountains lining the fjords of western Norway look especially spectacular because they rise from sea level.

Despite its northerly location, the climate in Norway is surprisingly mild, due in large part to the moderating influence of the Gulf Stream, which flows from the Gulf of Mexico all the way up the coast of Norway. In Oslo, for example, the average temperature ranges from 19.4°F (−7°C) in January to 60.8°F (16°C) in July. These figures are not that different from Tromsø in the far north, where they range from 21.2°F (−6°C) in January to 53.6°F (12°C) in July. The areas of most extreme temperature differences lie farthest from the coast. The record high temperature is 96°F (35.6°C), set in Nesbyen in Buskerud in 1970, and the record low is −60.5°F (−51.4°C), in Karasjok in Finnmark, set in 1886.[9] The most precipitation falls on the west coast because mountain ranges block much of the moisture from reaching the eastern side of the country. The city of Bergen gets 88.6 inches (2,250 mm) a year, while Oslo receives only 30 inches (763 mm).

Norway is the second least-densely populated country in Europe, after Iceland, with about 41.5 people per square mile. According to the Organisation for Economic Co-operation and Development (OECD), only Oslo is defined as predominantly urban, while the areas around Bergen-Stavanger and Trondheim and the area surrounding the urban core of Oslo are defined as intermediate, with 15–50 percent living in rural areas. The rest of Norway is defined as predominantly rural, meaning that more than 50 percent of the population lives in rural areas.

Norway is divided into 431 municipalities and 19 counties, with Oslo considered both a county and a municipality. There is a great variety among municipalities in terms of geography, area, and population. More than half have fewer than 5,000 people, while only 12 municipalities have more than

50,000 inhabitants. The five largest cities are Oslo with 575,000; Bergen, 252,051; Trondheim, 168,257; Stavanger, 121,610; and Kristiansand, 80,109. All are located along the coast.

## TRANSPORTATION

Because of all the mountains and fjords in Norway, transportation has always been a challenge. Roads and railroads were constructed with great difficulty because of the rocky and mountainous terrain, as well as the harsh inland climate. The first railroads were built after 1850, with the first line opening in 1854. It was not until the very end of the nineteenth century and early twentieth century that the long-distance lines were completed. The Oslo-Trondheim line via Røros was opened in 1890, the Oslo-Bergen line in 1909, the Oslo-Trondheim via Dovre in 1921, and the Oslo-Kristiansand in 1938. Construction of rail lines continued during the World War II occupation, with the scenic Flåm line completed in 1941 and the rest of the Oslo-Stavanger line in 1944. The northern route to Bodø was finished in 1962. This is the farthest north one can travel through Norway by train, although a train line from Narvik, which lies farther north, to the Swedish border was completed in 1902. This line was useful to the Germans during World War II for transporting iron ore from the Swedish mines to the ice-free Norwegian port. No additional lines have been built since 1962, although the existing ones have been modernized and tunnels built. All the trains are electric now, and there is a move toward the development of high-speed rail. The railroad system is an example of a public-private partnership. The rail infrastructure is owned by the state, while four companies, both public and private, run the trains. A number of smaller lines have been shut down, and modern and comfortable buses have begun competing for passengers.

Boats have always been vital in Norway, particularly because the harbors and fjords are mostly ice-free all along the coast, thanks to the Gulf Stream. Water was traditionally considered a means of transportation and contact, rather than a barrier. Along the west coast, ferries of various sizes still transport cars and passengers from one side of a fjord to the other, although many ferry routes have been replaced by bridges and tunnels. The most famous passenger line is *Hurtigruta*, the Norwegian Coastal Route, which goes from Bergen all the way to Kirkenes in the north and back in 11 days. At one time the route was plied by working boats, carrying freight and mail in addition to passengers. Now the ships are luxury cruise liners, with comfortable accommodations, delicious food and activities on board, and excursions on land along the way. It is possible to travel a portion of the entire route or to go by boat in one direction and air or land in the other. In addition to this famous route, there are also fast boats of various sizes carrying passengers to destinations in the fjord country of western Norway.

Because of the rough terrain, roads in Norway are difficult and expensive to build. There are major European-network highways that resemble freeways in southern Norway, but in most of the country the standard road has one lane in each direction. Even on freeways the maximum speed limit is only 62 mph (100 km/h). On ordinary highways it is 50 mph (80 km/h). In some places there are single-lane roads with *møteplasser*, or meeting spots, strategically placed along the way. It is up to the drivers to figure out who has to pull over, or perhaps even back up, to allow the other to pass.

Hundreds of tunnels have been built through the mountains providing access by road to towns that previously were only accessible by boat and straightening out some of the many curves. Some of the older tunnels are so narrow that a large tour bus or truck must drive right up the middle. Today Norway has 4 of the 18 longest tunnels in the world, including the Lærdal tunnel, which at 15.2 miles (24.5 km) is the longest road tunnel in the world. Completed in 2000, this tunnel is also an example of the latest in safety technology. To keep drivers attentive during the 20-minute drive, the tunnel has been divided into four sections by creating three large caverns, or mountain halls, 3.7 miles (6 km) from each end and one in the middle. These caverns are illuminated with blue and yellow light, to give one the impression of driving into daylight.[10]

Air transportation is vitally important to Norway. Nearly 50 airports are scattered all over the country. Most of these are owned and operated by the state-owned company Avinor. The largest international airport is Oslo's Gardermoen, opened in 1998 and located 22 miles north of the city.

## People

Norway's population is just under 4.9 million in 2010. Its life expectancy is among the highest in the world: 78 for a newborn boy and 83 for a girl. Norwegians have always considered themselves to be a homogeneous population, sharing language, culture, and values. As we shall see, that is an overly simplified view. Even before the new immigration of the last 40 years, there were significant differences among the inhabitants of Norway: the north and west versus the south and east, urban versus rural, the indigenous Sámi people, as well as immigrants and other minorities. Nonetheless certain values are widely held in the population and are viewed as especially Norwegian.

### Values

One habit shared by many Norwegians is an obsession with determining what is typically Norwegian, whether it be food, words, activities, or values.

In 1998, the then Prime Minister Kjell Magne Bondevik created a commission to examine the values of Norwegians. For three years it interviewed thousands of people, participated in more than 500 public meetings and debates, and received thousands of letters and phone calls. The work of the commission was described in about 8,500 newspaper articles and more than 20 publications. The main goal was to "contribute to a broad value-driven and ethical mobilization in order to strengthen positive values of community and response for the environment and for community."[11] The commission was ridiculed at the time by the media, but even so, its existence indicated a sincere desire to identify the values that underlie Norwegian society.

### Equality, Moderation, and Closeness to Nature

What values do most Norwegians identify with? According to Inge Eidsvåg, writer and former rector of the Nansen Academy, most would recognize equality, moderation, and closeness to nature.[12] Norwegians are fond of pointing out that the Norwegian word for equality, *likhet*, also has the meaning of sameness or similarity. Some would say that not only are people considered to be equal in Norway, but that there is also a strong pressure for conformity. They do, nonetheless, have a society that is more equal than most. Relative to most other countries, the gap between rich and poor is small. There is little poverty, and redistribution of wealth is considered a matter of course. This is not to say that no Norwegians consider themselves to be poor, as poverty is a relative concept and difficult to define. While almost no one in Norway today lacks basic food, shelter, and clothing, life can be difficult for children from relatively poor families. Children feel stigmatized when they cannot afford international vacations or expensive hobbies that their friends enjoy. While there are also homeless people on the streets of Oslo, most are there because of other problems interfering with their acceptance of assistance.

Another illustration of the value of equality is that CEOs of large Norwegian corporations do not receive the enormous bonuses seen in the United States and elsewhere. Grocery store magnate Stein Erik Hagen, attending the World Economic Forum in Davos, Switzerland, recently stated that such extreme disparity in compensation between the top leaders and the average workers would never be accepted in Norway.[13] The distance between the people and the government is also small. It is common to see government officials taking public transportation or drinking a cup of coffee in a café. They often appear in the studio on evening news or debate programs.

### Moderation

The pressure for equality and conformity can also be seen in the moderate lifestyle most Norwegians lead. It is still common for Norwegians—even relatively wealthy and powerful ones—to bring a simple bag lunch, called a *matpakke*, along to work. There is relatively little difference in the homes of middle-class Norwegians and those with higher income. A large percentage of Norwegians owns or has access to a boat and a cabin, and that percentage is increasing. In 2005 there were 375,000 vacation homes, nearly double the number in 1970. Some families even have two cabins, one by the shore for summer use, and one in the mountains for other times. These cabins have traditionally been small and simple, often with no electricity or running water. Using the cabins to get back to nature and live the simple life was part of the charm. These attitudes have been changing, although not without debate. Some wealthy celebrities, like fisheries magnate Kjell Inge Røkke and businesswoman Celine Midelfart, among others, have built extravagant vacation homes, but they have had to endure relentless criticism in the press. Røkke even complained publicly that he has felt bullied, and announced plans to move his operations out of Norway. Other wealthy Norwegians, however, had little sympathy for Røkke's point of view.

The royal family, despite its wealth, has traditionally tried to maintain a low profile and to live moderately. Its members have even sought to set a positive example of moderation and equality. The most famous story involves King Olav. During the energy crisis of 1973, driving on Sundays was banned. Although the king of Norway undoubtedly could have used his car to be driven up to the ski trails, instead he chose to ride public transportation. More recently Crown Prince Haakon and Crown Princess Mette-Marit purchased a modest cabin in southern Norway and planned only minimal improvements. They also built another cabin in the mountains in which they tried to use the latest in green materials and building techniques.

### Closeness to Nature

Not only the rich and royal enjoy nature. Since 1957, the *Allemannretten*, or Public Right of Access, has guaranteed everyone the right to hike, camp, and pick berries anywhere in Norway as long as it is at least 100 yards from someone's house or cultivated field. Hiking and skiing are among the most popular leisure activities. Many of the most admired Norwegian heroes have been outdoor explorers, like Fridtjof Nansen (1861–1930), who explored the Arctic; Roald Amundsen (1872–1928), the first man to the South Pole; anthropologist Thor Heyerdahl (1914–2002); and polar explorer Monica Kristensen Solås (1950–).

Of course none of these ideals is unique to Norway. Nor can one claim that all Norwegians share these values, or live according to them. They are, however, values that would at least be recognized and affirmed by most, even if only to rebel against them.

## DIVERSITY AMONG NORWEGIANS

Not all Norwegians fit the stereotype of being tall, blond, and blue-eyed. In addition to the immigrant population of roughly 10 percent, there are also several minority groups—the Kvens, Forest Finns, Romani, Roma, and Jews—and the indigenous people, the Sámi.

### The Sámi

The Sámi were historically a hunter-gatherer group, but today only about 10 percent make their living from traditional industries such as reindeer herding or fishing. Although the Sámi people are found in Norway, Sweden, Finland, and the Kola Peninsula of Russia, the largest group is in Norway. Because many Sámi are assimilated, their exact number is not known, but the population in Norway is estimated to be about 40,000.

Until after World War II the Sámi were persecuted and prohibited from speaking their language or practicing their religion (shamanism). In the 1800s, many were converted to Christianity by Swedish revivalist pastor Lars Levi Læstadius (1800–1861), and many practice this form of Lutheranism today.

The position of the Sámi improved after World War II, and laws mandating their Norwegianization were repealed. But it was Sámi resistance against the planned damming of the Alta River after 1978 that gave them a political identity. Although the protests were in vain, a new political activism was created among Sámi people. This led to the establishment of the Sámi Parliament in 1989 and the expansion of the use of the Sámi language in education, culture, and government. More information about the Sámi language, literature, and music is found in later chapters.

### National Minorities

Five other groups have official status in Norway as national minorities because of their historical connection to Norway. The Kvens, Forest Finns, Romani, Roma, and Jews have long ties with Norway, but all were stigmatized and discriminated against in the past. To compensate for past mistreatment, organizations representing these minorities now receive state support for special projects, and information about them has been included in the school curriculum since 2006.

### Kvens

The Kvens are the Finnish-speaking minority in northern Norway numbering about 30,000–50,000 people. They arrived as early as the 1700s, but their migration into Norway peaked in 1860, during a time of famine in Finland. They suffered the same persecution as the Sámi during the period from

1850 to the end of World War II. Today about 10,000 still speak their own language, which is closely related to Finnish. The language received official status in 1996.

### Forest Finns

The Forest Finns also came from Finland, mostly between 1575 and 1660. They settled in Finnskogene, along the Swedish border as well as in Drammen and Akershus, which surround Oslo. They are known for their burnt earth farming, which they used until about 1800. They no longer speak Finnish and are generally assimilated into Norwegian society.

### Romani

The Romani, also known as *Tatere* or Travelers, originated in India and have been in Norway for 500 years. These wanderers are spread over the whole world now, and number more than 10 million worldwide. While their numbers are difficult to know precisely, it is estimated that there are around 5,000–10,000 Romani in Norway.

### Roma

The Roma, also known as Gypsies, are a much smaller group than the Romani, numbering about 500. They originally arrived in the 1800s but were banned from Norway from the 1920s until 1956. There has been tension and conflict between the Roma and Norwegians, who feel they are responsible for a disproportionate amount of crime and violence resulting from feuds between Roma clans.

### Jews

Norway has a long history of anti-Semitism, despite the fact almost no Jews lived in the country before the late 1800s. There had, however, been a community of well-assimilated Jews in the joint kingdom of Denmark-Norway since the 1600s, mostly in Copenhagen. When the union between the countries ended in 1814, Jews were banned from entering the kingdom of Norway in the constitution ratified that year. Although this article was removed from the constitution in 1851, due largely to the efforts of poet Henrik Wergeland, relatively few Jews migrated to Norway. Those who did were not particularly assimilated, maintaining separate enclaves in the vicinity of their synagogues. At the outbreak of World War II, only 1,800–2,000 Jews lived in Norway, mostly in Oslo and Trondheim, where they had synagogues. While nearly all of Denmark's Jews were rescued, 49 percent of Norway's Jews died during World War II. (This figure compares to 26% of the Jews in France, 22% in Bulgaria, and 20% in Nazi Italy.)

Problems for the Jews began almost immediately after the invasion of Norway in April 1940. Despite protests of the Norwegian state church, the situation worsened. In October 1942, mass arrests of Jews carried out by the Norwegian police began. On November 26, 1942, Norwegian Jews were sent to Auschwitz on the ship *S/S Donau*. The Norwegian resistance helped nearly 900 Jews escape to Sweden in 1942 and 1943, despite facing the death penalty for assisting Jews. Of the 800 who were deported to Germany, however, only 29 survived.

Upon their return, Norwegian Jews discovered that their property had been liquidated. Many years passed before they received compensation for their losses, although Norway was the first country in the world to complete its restitution work. In 1999, the Norwegian parliament voted unanimously to grant $58 million in restitution: 40 percent of the money was distributed to individuals to compensate them for their losses, and the remaining 60 percent was used collectively to promote Jewish culture and institutions both in Norway and elsewhere. Among other projects, the former mansion of Vidkun Quisling, Nazi collaborator and leader of the wartime Norwegian government, has been rededicated as The Center for Studies of Holocaust and Religious Minorities.[14]

### Immigrants

People have always moved to Norway from other countries, whether voluntarily or otherwise. In the Viking age, it might have been slaves kidnapped from Ireland; in the Middle Ages, it was stonemasons brought from Germany to build churches or missionaries imported from Germany and England to convert the Norwegians. German merchants from the Hanseatic League came to establish trading centers. During the union with Denmark, from about 1400 to 1814, government officials came from Denmark. What little aristocracy there was after the Black Death came from abroad, mostly Sweden and Germany. And as mentioned above, in the 1500s and 1600s a number of Finns came to an area of eastern Norway called Finnskogene, the Finnish Forests. Another group of Finns, the Kvens, came to North Norway in the 1700s and 1800s. During the period of increasing industrialization of the 1800s, Swedes came to help build the railroads and roads. After 1851, a few Jews came to Norway, and a larger number as refugees in the 1930s.

By 2010 approximately 11.4 percent of the population of Norway was of immigrant background: 552,000 people in all, from more than 200 countries. There are 459,000 first-generation immigrants in Norway, and 93,000 people were born in Norway of immigrant parents.[15] There are immigrants living in all municipalities in Norway. Oslo has the largest share, with 160,500, comprising 27 percent of its population. One out of three first-generation immigrants is of Western background. Half of the first-generation immigrants from Africa, Asia (including Turkey), Eastern Europe, and South and Central

America came as refugees. While the level of unemployment is higher than among ethnic Norwegians, the differences are less among those groups who have lived in Norway the longest. Many immigrants have come to Norway in recent years to work as doctors and dentists, in response to a shortage of health personnel. In 2009 one of five general practice doctors was an immigrant, with more than half born in the European Union or the European Free Trade Association area, including the Nordic countries.

### Refugees and Asylum Seekers

While many people have migrated to Norway seeking work or reunion with family members, others have come as refugees. This is also nothing new. Jews came between 1880 and 1920; Germans, both Jewish and other, in the 1930s; Vietnamese and Chileans arrived in the 1970s; and Eritreans, Somalis, Bosnians, and Kosovo Albanians in the 1990s.

Many refugees come under the auspices of the United Nations, under a system of quotas. Others arrive individually, seeking asylum. Norway adheres to international regulations regarding refugee policy.

### Services for New Refugees

A new law enacted in 2004 established a mandatory introductory program for all immigrants receiving public assistance. This program creates an individual plan for each person and includes language instruction, a course on Norwegian society, and assistance with job skills. The program can last two years, or even three, if there are special circumstances. Labor immigrants (not including EU or EEA citizens) also have both the right and the duty to have up to 300 hours of language and culture instruction.

### Issues and Challenges of Immigration

Although most refugees have a higher education level than the average in their home country, they usually end up in unskilled jobs. They are hampered by the fact that they do not speak Norwegian, and frequently their previous education and training is not acknowledged. Many suffer from traumatic experiences in their past, and they may have ambivalent feelings about settling in Norway. Because refugees are settled all over Norway, many suffer from feelings of isolation and loneliness. Frequently asylum seekers must wait months or even years before receiving a response to their application.

These problems will only get larger because the number of asylum seekers is increasing. In 2009, there were 50 percent more entering than in the year before. Because it is impossible for authorities to know how many people will enter Norway seeking asylum, there has been inadequate space for new asylum seekers, and many end up living in tents or barracks.

Other challenges for immigrants include differing opinions on the rights of women. Concerns have been expressed about forced marriages and female genital circumcision among some groups. Unemployment is also higher among immigrants, with a greater percentage on welfare than among the general public. In 2009, only 33 percent of non-Western immigrants were self-sufficient.

Another problem related to immigration is the increase in organized crime that coincided with the expansion of the European Union and opening of borders throughout Europe. A disproportionate percentage of crime involves citizens of Eastern European countries, especially Bulgaria, Romania (the Roma-people, who accounted for 80% of arrests in 2009), and Lithuania. While the majority of the crimes are committed in Oslo, the groups are quite mobile and strike all over the country. They often engage in seemingly innocent activities such as begging, selling flowers and jewelry, or offering card games and shell games to disguise their crimes. Other crimes include theft, drugs, and the stealing of credit card information by skimming. While it is not against the law to engage in prostitution, women from Africa and Eastern Europe are overrepresented on the streets. Laws have been passed outlawing the purchasing of sex, and groups are working to protect these women from exploitation and try to find them alternate employment.

### How Norwegians Feel about Immigrants

There seems to be an increasing level of tolerance and acceptance of immigrants among Norwegians in recent years. Interestingly, people who have the most contact with immigrants seem to have the most positive attitudes. The proportion believing that most immigrants represent a source of insecurity in society has declined by 13 percent since 2002, and the percentage reporting they would find it distasteful having a son-in-law or daughter-in-law with an immigrant background has dropped from 40 percent to 24 percent,

Immigration policy was, however, a hot political issue in the 2009 elections. Questions are being raised as to how many immigrants a small country like Norway can accommodate. Another issue is how soon immigrants should be required to begin work. The United States has been used as an example of a place where welfare benefits are not as generous as they are in Norway and yet certain groups such as the Somalis actually seem to be faring better. The right-wing populist Progress Party (FrP) has made immigration reform an important element of its platform, and has grown tremendously in popularity.

## POLITICAL SYSTEM AND GOVERNMENT

Norway has a social-democratic form of government, where openness, a spirit of consensus, and pragmatism are valued. It remains a country emphasizing care and solidarity, where egalitarian values are arguably more dominant than in other Western countries. Norwegians accept legitimate inequality, where some receive more than others because of greater need. In the long run it is hoped that poverty can be eliminated. Challenges for society include an aging population, increased numbers of disabled people, and the potential for abuse of the generous system of benefits. People grumble over increased pressure in their work lives, with complaints of bullying in the workplace. High rates of absenteeism, from both short- and long-term sick leave, present a challenge to the state budget. The increasing prevalence of drug addition, leading to violence, crime, and overdoses, is another major issue for Norwegian society.

Most Norwegians hold a generally positive view of the state and expect it to take the lead in meeting the challenges of society. The basis of the welfare state is that poverty is a societal problem, not an individual failing. Despite differences among the political parties, popular support for the welfare state remains stable or is even increasing. It is considered the role of the state to protect individuals and families against poverty.

### The Norwegian Constitution (1814)

The Norwegian constitution is founded on three principles: sovereignty of the people, separation of powers, and human rights. The legislative branch is called *Stortinget* or "The Grand Assembly." The word *Ting* comes from Old Norse and was a designation for a Viking-age assembly serving as both court and legislature. The most important duties of the *Storting* are to pass legislation, adopt a budget, determine taxation and spending policies, debate political issues, and supervise the government. Parliamentary elections are held every four years for the 169 seats in the *Storting*: 150 members represent the 19 counties according to geographical size and population and 19 are members at large. Local and regional elections are also held every four years, but two years after the *Storting* elections. The *Storting* cannot be dissolved, and unlike in some parliamentary systems, no new elections can be held between scheduled election years.

While Norway's king has no actual power, he has a number of constitutionally mandated duties, including weekly meetings with the council of state, which consists of the prime minister and all the members of the government. In addition it is the role of the king to receive any resignation from a sitting prime minister and to request a new prime minister form a government. Although some Norwegians would undoubtedly prefer a republic, a majority approves of the role of the royal family. Indeed, an upsurge of popularity followed the birth of Princess Ingrid Alexandra, daughter of the crown prince and princess.

King Harald, Crown Prince Haakon, and Princess Ingrid Alexandra, August 28, 2009. Morten Brun, The Royal Court, Norway. (Photographer and The Royal Court, Norway.)

All Norwegian citizens who are 18 by the end of the year have the right to vote. Non-Norwegian citizens who fulfill the other requirements can vote in local and regional elections, if they have been registered residents the previous three years. In the September 14, 2009, *Storting* election, 76 percent of eligible voters participated. This percentage sounds high, but actually reflects a downward trend in voter participation. Twenty-four parties ran for office, although only eight ran in all nineteen counties. Seven parties had representatives elected to *Stortinget*.

### Direct Elections and Proportional Representation

Voting in elections is done by secret ballot. Ballots consist of lists of candidates from the various political parties, who select and rank candidates at their nominating conventions. All parties except the Progress Party voluntarily ensure that at least 40 percent of the candidates on the ballot are of each gender (60/40 rule). In addition to the seats for the 19 constituencies, there are 19 at-large seats, one for each constituency. The purpose of these additional seats is to even out discrepancies. To compete for an additional seat, parties must obtain more than 4 percent of the national vote.[16] The actual distribution of seats is compared with what would have happened if the country were one big constituency.

Underrepresented parties awarded at-large seats in the constituencies are those that come closest to winning an ordinary seat.

A new government is formed when the prime minister in office has submitted an application for permission to resign. The king then instructs another person to form a new government.

The political parties are divided into two main categories, socialist and non-socialist, although the differences in party platforms are not extreme. The socialist parties currently represented in parliament are the Socialist Left Party (SV) and the Labor Party (DNA). The non-socialist parties are the Center Party (SP), the Christian Democratic Party (KrF), the Liberal Party (V), the Conservative Party (H), and the Progress Party (FrP). Differences in party philosophy generally involve the extent of the role of government in regulating society.

The Socialist Left Party wants stronger political management of society and a radical redistribution of social benefits, and is interested in environmental issues. The Labor Party is a democratic socialist party. It wants to change society through gradual reforms and to level out social disparities. It favors greater state responsibility for education, care of the elderly, and health care. It is the largest party, but does not hold a majority of seats in *Stortinget*.

While the non-socialist parties generally prefer lower taxes and fees, no party supports a reduction in welfare benefits to residents. The Center Party (originally called the Agrarian Party) emphasizes rural Norway and the environment. It addresses issues affecting the primary industries of farming, forestry, and fishing. The party is an enthusiastic supporter of the welfare state and wants to preserve welfare benefits. The Christian Democratic Party stands for basic Christian values. Important issues for this party are education and family policy, a restrictive alcohol policy, and a positive attitude toward the church. The Liberal Party is a socially liberal party. It is interested in both individual rights and society's responsibilities, and supports a state welfare system as well as private business and industry. The Conservative Party, currently the third largest party, believes that a market economy and private ownership are necessary to produce welfare and liberty. Nonetheless, the party is a supporter of the state welfare system.

On the far right, the Progress Party calls itself a classical liberal party, believing in the rights of the individual and freedom of choice. It is interested in lower taxes and duties, the free market, and less centralization of control. It campaigns for less money to be spent on development aid, feeling that poor countries would benefit more from the expansion of market economies, free trade, democracy, and human rights. It also favors a more restrictive immigration policy, where obligations of new immigrants are emphasized in addition to their rights. The Progress Party favors spending more money from the pension fund on Norwegian infrastructure, such as roads, schools, hospitals, and nursing homes, rather than investing most of it in overseas markets. Although it is the second largest party in *Stortinget*, it has never been asked to be part of a government because the other non-socialist parties feel they do not have sufficient shared interests. It also happens to be the only party that supported the U.S. invasion of Iraq in 2003.

The Labor Party dominated post–World War II politics until the mid-1960s. Since then Labor or Labor coalition governments have alternated with non-socialist coalition governments. It is quite common for the Christian Democratic Party, the Conservative Party, and the Center Party, as well as the Liberal Party, to work together. In 2005, the Labor Party formed a coalition with the Center Party and the Socialist Left Party. The coalition called itself the Red-Green coalition and was the first time the Socialist Left Party served in a government. In 2009 this coalition retained power, with Jens Stoltenberg (Labor) continuing as prime minister. In the 2009 election, 67 women and 102 men were elected to *Stortinget*, 39.6 percent women.

There is virtually no corruption in Norwegian government, and Norwegian politicians are held to a high level of ethical behavior. The World Governance Indicators, which aggregate individual indicators for 212 countries and territories, place Norway in the 90th–100th percentile in all of its measures, including political stability, government effectiveness, and control of corruption.[17]

## CRIME AND THE LEGAL SYSTEM

Crime is generally low in Norway, due historically to its geography, climate, scattered population, and limited transportation. While it is always difficult to determine definitively whether rates of crime are increasing or decreasing, it is accurate to say that there has been an increase in property crimes, such as robberies, and economic and environmental crimes. The rates of murder and other person-on-person crimes have traditionally been low. Norway's participation in the Schengen agreement, providing for open borders among the participating nations, however, has made it easier for criminals to arrive from other countries. Drugs, organized crime, bandits, and Eastern European and African prostitutes have been coming to Norway in greater numbers.

There has always been a certain amount of smuggling, especially of alcohol, because of Norway's strict policies and high fees. That has declined, however, following the methanol scandal of the early 2000s when a number of people died from drinking smuggled alcohol containing the poisonous substance. Heroin is smuggled in from Afghanistan and cocaine from Colombia. There is less problem with milder drugs like marijuana, although the amount of methamphetamine is exploding, much of it coming from Lithuania. There is a greater incidence of crime in large cities such as Oslo, but crime, especially family violence, also occurs in rural areas. In some cases, there has been a link between ethnic groups and crime. The Pakistani A-gang and B-gang are killing each other, and motorcycle gangs like Banditos and Hells Angels have been sources of violence.

Two high-profile violent crimes in recent years have captured media attention. The murders of Anne Orderud Paust and her parents, the so-called Orderud Case, occurred in 1999, and the Nokas bank robbery, which resulted in the killing of a police officer, was in 2004.[18] Both the cases had unresolved questions, which have kept them in the public eye years later. They also illustrate an aspect of the Norwegian legal system that differs from the American: appeals can be initiated by the prosecution as well as by the defense. In both the cases, defendants were given harsher sentences after the appeal.

Norwegian police, who are trained for three years, do not routinely carry weapons. They do have guns in their patrol cars, but these are secured. The police themselves do not wish to be armed; they feel that not having weapons encourages them to use other techniques and tools to resolve difficult situations. During police college they are trained in psychology and conflict management.

Prison guards receive similar training in the use of dialogue to defuse conflict situations. Even maximum security prisons appear relatively relaxed, and the guards typically do not wear uniforms. Each guard is assigned prisoners with whom to develop a personal relationship. According to the philosophy of Norwegian prisons, the fact that inmates are deprived of the freedom to come and go as they please is punishment enough. The task of the prison is to rehabilitate and prepare inmates for eventual release into society, not to punish them. While serving their sentences, inmates may receive leaves of absence and education or training. They eat meals communally, may have conjugal visits, and may also have their children visit. Overnight visits are possible for young children, although no children are allowed to live in prison. The opening of a new prison near Halden, Norway, in 2010 received attention in the American press, which described the luxurious facility, as well as the strong relationship between the inmates and the staff.[19]

The minimum age of criminal responsibility is 15. Only a small number of youth between the ages of 15 and 18 are incarcerated in Norway, between 2 and 10 at any given moment. While the goal is to enable such prisoners to be in facilities near their families, to be together with other youth, and not to be imprisoned with adults, it is difficult or impossible to fulfill all these goals because the population of Norway is spread over such a large geographic area.

At the end of 2009, there was a disproportionately large population of foreigners in prisons, with one in three inmates being a foreign citizen, mostly from Nigeria and Romania. Sixty percent of those in temporary custody are foreigners.[20]

## NORWAY AND THE WORLD

The Nobel Peace Prize, which includes a medal, a personal diploma, and prize money, has been awarded by Norway in December each year since 1901. The decision is made by a small, independent committee of the Nobel Institute, appointed by the *Storting*. The choice is based on the stipulation in Alfred Nobel's will, which states that the prize shall be awarded to whomever "shall have done the most or the best work for fraternity between nations, for the abolition or reduction of standing armies and for the holding and promotion of peace congresses."[21] The committee has occasionally been criticized for using the Peace Prize as a tool to encourage what they see as steps in the right direction, as in the 2009 awarding of the prize to President Barack Obama, rather than as a reward for deeds already accomplished.

Because Norway never was a colonial power, it views itself as a small, nonthreatening, peaceful country that can be trusted as a mediator between parties in conflict. Norwegians see promotion of peace and conflict resolution as work that requires a long-term perspective. Indeed many of the close, trusting relationships they have developed around the world stem from the missionary activities of past generations. Since the early 1990s, the so-called Norwegian model has been characterized by a willingness to make a long-term commitment, to involve nongovernment organizations, provide generous aid, and maintain good relationships with international partners including the United States, Russia, and India. Norway has played an important role in peace building all over the world, most notably in the Middle East, between Israel and the Palestinians, in Asia, particularly in Sri Lanka, and in Guatemala, Colombia, and Sudan. The programs continue even with shifts in government because of the strong consensus among all the political parties that it takes time to develop relationships. Practical work is supported by extensive academic peace research. Recently scholars have criticized Norwegian conflict resolution efforts, and questions have been raised regarding the effectiveness of development aid programs.

Norway was a founding member of both the United Nations and NATO, although NATO membership is somewhat controversial. In addition it is a member of dozens of other international organizations, including Schengen and the World Trade Organization, among many others.[22] It views the promotion of peace, fairness, and development, and respect for human rights as central to its own economic and political interests, noting that increased connections between countries have increased interdependence among nations. Norway supports its philosophy with money, spending nearly 1 percent of its GDP on development aid, one of the highest rates in the world. Norway was the first Organisation for Economic Co-operation and Development member to present a comprehensive plan of action on debt relief for developing countries and the first to advocate 100 percent debt cancellation for heavily indebted poor countries.

Norway has not, however, chosen to join the European Union (EU). This decision might seem to contradict the engagement with world events it otherwise displays, but Norwegians believe that they have more influence as an independent broker. Norwegian authorities have applied for membership in the EEC/EU several times, but when the decision was put to a referendum in 1972 and 1994, membership was rejected by the Norwegian voters. Many Norwegians were concerned about sacrificing sovereignty by ceding control of Norwegian affairs to a distant European capital. In addition, they were concerned that Europeans would not understand their particular need for farm subsidies. While the EU is not interested in subsidizing marginal farms, Norwegians choose to do so in order to maintain a population spread over the entire country. Furthermore, the Norwegian fishing community was concerned about the possibility of overfishing if Norwegian territorial waters are opened up to fishing by EU countries like Spain. As a member of European Free Trade Association, however, Norway is a signatory to the European Economic Area agreement. This treaty between the EU and European Free Trade Association grants Norway access to the inner market, but also obligates Norway to follow all of the EU rules and regulations. It also costs Norway a significant amount of money to receive these benefits, which, as a wealthy oil nation, it can easily afford. Ironically, Norway has been one of the first countries to adopt new EU regulations, even though they have no say in the development or adoption of the rules.

## NOTES

1. http://www.visionofhumanity.org/gpi/results/norway/2009/. Accessed 11/30/09.

2. http://hdr.undp.org/en/statistics/. Accessed 11/30/09.

3. *The Economist*, January 6, 2010. http://www.economist.com/daily/news/displaystory.cfm?story_id=15210330&fsrc=nwl. Accessed 1/8/10.

4. Press Release from The Department of Government Administration, Reform and Church Affairs, 1/14/10. http://www.regjeringen.no/en/dep/fad/press-centre/press-releases/2010/citizen-survey-shows-satisfied-users-but.html?id=590343. Accessed 1/17/10.

5. From Axel Sandemose, *A Fugitive Crosses His Track*, 1933. Translation by the author.

6. Gro Harlem Brundtland, "Det er typisk norsk å være god." From New Year's speech 1992. http://www1.nrk.no/nett-tv/klipp/35843. Accessed 12/3/09.

7. Statistics Norway. *Mini Facts about Norway 2009*. http://www.ssb.no/english/subjects/00/minifakta_en/en/. Accessed 12/18/09.

8. http://traveler.nationalgeographic.com/2009/11/destinations-rated/europe-text/13. Accessed 12/1/09.

9. The Norwegian Meteorological Institute. http://met.no/Klima/Klimastatistikk/Varrekorder/Temperatur/. Accessed 12/18/09.

10. http://www.bergen-guide.com/538.htm. Accessed 12/9/09.

11. http://www.besteforeldre.no/Om%20oss/Verdikommisjonens_rapporter.htm. Accessed 12/1/09. Translation by the author.

12. Andreas Aase, "In Search of Norwegian Values," in Maagerø and Simonsen, eds., *Norway: Society and Culture* (Kristiansand: Portal, 2008), p. 13.

13. http://www.aftenposten.no/okonomi/utland/article3489799.ece. Accessed 1/29/10.

14. http://www.hlsenteret.no/Mapper/ENG/page/index.html. Accessed 12/4/09.

15. http://www.ssb.no/english/subjects/00/00/10/innvandring_en/. Accessed 5/7/10.

16. http://www.regjeringen.no/en/dep/krd/kampanjer/election_portal/the-parliamentary-storting-election/determining-the-election-results-who-get.html?id=570018. Accessed 12/4/09.

17. World Governance Indicators. http://info.worldbank.org/governance/wgi/sc_chart.asp. Accessed 1/8/10.

18. The Orderud case is one of the most infamous murder cases in Norwegian history. The Orderuds and their daughter Anne Paust were brutally murdered in their rural home. Later the Orderuds' son and his wife, along with two others, were convicted based on circumstantial evidence. The motive was said to involve ownership of the property. A complicating factor is that Anne Paust, a foreign ministry employee, had been a victim of attempted murder on two earlier occasions. The convictions were appealed, both by the defense and the prosecution, and the defendants received longer sentences. They continue to insist on their innocence. The NOKAS robbery occurred in Stavanger, a small city in western Norway. It was the largest bank robbery in Norwegian history. The robbers were caught and convicted, but the money was never recovered. Later their sentences were appealed first by the defense and later by the prosecution finally to the Supreme Court, where the sentences were increased. The case received further attention when two paintings by Edvard Munch were stolen later that year in Oslo. It is assumed that this robbery was ordered by main defendant David Toska to distract police attention from the NOKAS robbery.

19. http://www.time.com/time/magazine/article/0,9171,1986002,00.html?artId=1986002?contType=article?chn=us. Accessed 5/7/10.

20. http://www.aftenposten.no/nyheter/iriks/article3427491.ece. Accessed 12/17/09.

21. http://nobelpeaceprize.org/en_GB/about_peaceprize/. Accessed 12/29/09.

22. http://www.regjeringen.no/en/dep/ud/Documents/veiledninger/2000/internasjonale-organisasjoner-norge-er-m.html?id=87594. Accessed 1/15/10.

# 2

# History

ALTHOUGH PEOPLE have lived in Norway for at least 10,000 years, it was not until the Viking age, around 800 CE, that the inhabitants began to think of themselves as Norwegian, living in a place called Norway. They distinguished Norway from surrounding places, like Sweden and Denmark, although they did not conceive of it as a modern nation-state. The name Norway probably derives from the Northern Way, referring to the coastal route made possible by the shipbuilding techniques developed during the Iron Age.

Although almost nothing was written during this period, information on the Vikings comes from archeological evidence as well as the Icelandic sagas, which were only written down in the 1200s. In addition some contemporary sources, such as the Arab Ibn Fadlan and the wealthy and powerful north-Norwegian Ottar provide information. Ottar's report to the Anglo-Saxon King Alfred of England in the 880s was recorded in Old English. He told Alfred that he lived in the northernmost area of Norwegians, which we recognize as somewhere in southern Troms county. By Ottar's time, Norwegians spoke a common language and had a common religion.

## VIKING HISTORY

The Viking age is usually considered to have begun in 793, with the looting of the Lindesfarne monastery off the northeast coast of England. It was, at any rate, an event that brought the Vikings to the attention of other Europeans. The sudden explosion of Viking activity had a number of causes. The empire of Charlemagne had collapsed in the 800s, which left a power vacuum in

Europe and provided a perfect opportunity for the Vikings to strike. The Vikings had developed advanced technology for building fast, flexible, and maneuverable ships, enabling them to sail both on the seas and on rivers. And while the Vikings are best known for their plundering, they were also active traders and settlers.

These Viking traders or raiders headed in various directions. The Norwegian Vikings headed west, toward England, Scotland, and Ireland, then onward to Iceland and Greenland where they established settlements, and Vinland in North America where they stayed more briefly. They also settled in the Orkneys, the Shetlands, the Hebrides, and the Isle of Man, as well as in northern Scotland and Ireland. They settled in northwest England, capturing the city now known as York, where significant Viking archeological finds have been made. The city of Dublin was founded by Vikings in the 840s and was under Nordic control until 1171. The largest Viking cemetery in Europe is located there. In their journeys, the Vikings traded their furs and fish for spices, fabrics, precious metals, ceramics, glass, and other goods they did not produce at home, as well as for slaves. They also came in contact with Christianity, and a number of Vikings were baptized, including kings Olav Tryggvason and Olav Haraldson. They produced remarkable metalwork, wood carving, and weavings, which have been found at archeological sites.

Until late in the Viking age, Norway was not one unified country, but rather a collection of petty kingdoms. Assemblies called *tings* created an early structure for maintaining law and order. The word *ting* is in fact the origin of the name of Norway's parliament, *Stortinget*. The early *ting* was attended by all the free men, and later developed into representative *tings*, including Gulatinget in western Norway and Frostatinget in Trøndelag.

According to the Sagas, Harald Fairhair was the first to unite Norway into one kingdom when he won the Battle of Hafrsfjord around 890. As the saga goes, the beautiful Gyda of Valdres rejected his offer of marriage, telling him she would not marry him until he became the king of all Norway. He vowed that he would not cut his hair until he had achieved this goal, hence his (perhaps ironic) name. But his area of control was really only a portion of Norway, located in the south and west. Beyond that he was dependent on the loyalty of his sons and other petty kings.

Harald Fairhair's death was followed by a period of unrest and war, with his sons battling each other for power. The king of Denmark was also interested in gaining control over Norway. North of Harald's territory, around Trondheim, was the home of the powerful Earls of Lade. They preferred a Danish king to a Norwegian one because an absentee king meant they could run things as they liked. In 995, however, Harald's descendent Olav Tryggvason entered the scene and won support from many of the chieftains. He forcibly attempted to impose Christianity upon the population. He was unsuccessful, however, and was eventually defeated by his enemies, who allied themselves with kings of the Swedes and the Danes. He fell at the battle of Svolder in 1000.

Fifteen years later Olav Haraldson returned to Norway after living most of his life abroad, where he had been baptized. He also claimed descent from Harald Fairhair and was known as Olav the Stout and later as Saint Olav. He met little resistance because both the Danish king and the Earl of Lade were off fighting a war in England. Olav was the first king since Harald Fairhair to control the entire country. He had Christianity declared the legal state religion at the *ting*, and used the sword against any who refused to accept the new religion. Although as we have seen, he was not the first to introduce Christianity to Norway, he used it as a tool to consolidate his power. In 1028 a large army sent by the powerful King Knut, who at the time was king of both Denmark and England, forced Olav to flee to Russia. He returned two years later, but fell at the battle of Stiklestad, near Trondheim. His followers smuggled his body away from the battlefield and buried it near the Nid River in Nidaros, known today as Trondheim. Rumors of miracles began to be reported, and the body was exhumed. According to the sagas, it was in perfect condition, his cheeks were ruddy, and the hair, beard, and nails had grown. He is considered the patron saint of Norway. It is believed that his body is still buried in the environs of Nidaros Cathedral in Trondheim, but the exact location is unknown.

Olav's status actually helped the kings who followed because it was an advantage to be able to claim descent from Norway's eternal king. As a result, a period of peace and equilibrium followed for the next century. Christianity gained influence over new laws. Infant baptism was required, and the law specifically forbade the killing of deformed babies. Eating meat during Lent was not allowed, and the use of thralls, or slaves, declined under Christianity. Marriage came to be seen as a sacrament. Men were now discouraged from having mistresses, but women lost the right to divorce their husbands. The power of the king, as head of the church, was strengthened, and cities began to be founded, both as trading stations and as the administrative seat of the king.

The high Middle Ages, from 1130 to 1319, was a period of great population growth. Many new farms were cleared in the wilderness, especially in eastern Norway. It became increasingly common for farmers to rent their land, rather than own it. One reason for this situation is that any new land that was cleared for farms belonged by definition to the king, so the farmer became the tenant of the king. These tenant farmers had status as free men. The years 1130–1217 are called the period of civil wars, but this time was really an extended conflict between various men claiming the throne and the powerful landowners who supported them. At that time rules of royal succession allowed any male descendent of the king to claim the throne, whether a legitimate son or not. During this unrest the church increased in power, especially after 1152–1153, when Rome granted Norway its own archbishopric, with its seat in Nidaros (Trondheim). The conflict finally ended in 1217, when the warring parties agreed on Haakon IV Haakonson as king.

Norway now entered into what has been called the period of greatness, which lasted from 1217 to 1319. During this time a number of monumental buildings were constructed and reconstructed, including the cathedral in Nidaros, the original sections of Akershus Fortress in Oslo, Haakonshall in Bergen, and the archbishop's residence in Nidaros. Many churches were built, both stave churches and stone churches, with altarpieces, crucifixes, baptismal fonts, and other religious art. Snorri Sturluson, in Iceland, wrote his history of the Norwegian kings, and King Magnus Lawmender codified the laws. Although Norway lost Scotland, the Hebrides, and the Isle of Man, it gained control over Iceland and Greenland.

Entering the late Middle Ages, which lasted from 1319 to 1536, Norway's population reached a high point, with between 60,000 and 70,000 farms. It had a powerful king with a well-organized state. But by the end of the Middle Ages, Norway was under Danish rule, with the state in tatters and the population cut in half. There are several explanations for this dramatic decline, including a worsening of the climate. One major catalyst, however, was the Black Death, which first raged from 1349 to 1351. It is thought to have entered Norway via ships calling in Bergen. Rats from the ships carried fleas whose bites infected people. The clergy were especially hard hit, probably because they were involved in caring for the sick. Even after 1351, there were other outbreaks of plague approximately once a decade until 1500. These outbreaks decimated the population. While it cannot be proven that the plague affected Norway's population more severely than elsewhere in Europe, it is probably true that it had a greater effect on the economy because of the larger number of independent farmers whose agricultural production was lost when they died. The loss of farmers also meant a decline in revenues both for the aristocracy and the crown. The aristocracy was so diminished that by the 1500s it had almost entirely died out.

Ultimately, the survivors benefited from the Black Death. They had greater access to farmland, and actually saw an improvement in their living standard because they could afford to eat more animal protein like milk products, eggs, meat, and fish. The church increased its power and wealth, becoming the largest landowner, with nearly one half of the land in Norway.

The German traders of the Hanseatic League stepped into the vacuum in the fish trading industry resulting from the Black Death. They established an office in Bergen around 1360 as well as so-called factories, or trading stations, in Oslo and Tønsberg. Rostock, Germany, was the mother city for Oslo, while Lübeck,

Germany, served that role for Bergen. The Hansa in Bergen gradually took over the entire area of the harbor now called Bryggen, and soon there were more than 1,000 single German men living and working there. They had their own enclave and lived under their own laws, having little contact with the surrounding Norwegians. While the existence of the Hansa may have inhibited the development of an urban bourgeoisie in Norway, it did provide a market for dried fish and other Norwegian wares in exchange for imported goods. The office in Bergen lasted until about 1754.

In 1380 King Haakon VI died, leaving behind his widow, Margrete and their 10-year-old son, Olav. Five years previously Margrete's father, King Valdemar of Denmark, had died, leaving the Danish throne to Olav. The death of Olav's father made him king of both Denmark and Norway, although it was actually Queen Margrete who served as regent. When Olav died at the age of 16, she managed to be chosen regent in Norway, Sweden, and Denmark. In 1397, Margrete called the most powerful men in all three countries to Kalmar, where they elected her nephew, Erik of Pomerania, king. The seat of power of the resulting Kalmar Union moved to Copenhagen, where Margrete retained real power until her death in 1412.

In a rebellion led by Gustav Vasa, Sweden pulled out of the union in 1523, but Norway and Denmark remained in the union until 1814, a time referred to by some as the "four hundred years night." Although Norway and Denmark were supposed to have equal status in the union, Norway remained subordinate to Denmark. Its Council of the Realm was dissolved, and the Norwegian church lost its autonomy with the imposition of the Lutheran Reformation the next year. The King was now head of the church and the largest landowner, Danish nobility was permitted to take office in Norway, and the last remnants of the Norwegian written language disappeared. Technically Norway was now a province of Denmark, although Norwegians never considered themselves to be Danish, and the Norwegian spoken dialects lived on.

The 1600s and 1700s were a difficult period in Norway. The birth rate was high, twice as high as today, but infant mortality was also great, as were hunger and disease. Houses were drafty and dirty, with a hearth in the middle of the floor. There was no chimney, and the smoke escaped through a hole in the ceiling. Nevertheless, the population increased. The farmers also got the opportunity to buy land from the crown and nobility, who needed to raise money to pay for the wars they were waging against Sweden. By 1800, the majority of farmers owned their own land. During this period, however, there was also an increasing number of cotters, who were allowed to farm a small piece of land in exchange for rent and labor for the landowner. In addition to the farmers and the cotters, there was a third group of servants, who were often the children of the cotters. They worked on farms in exchange for room, board, and clothing.

During the union with Denmark, Norway frequently was drawn into wars against Sweden or other countries on the continent. These conflicts affected Norway badly because most imports, such as badly needed food, were shipped through Copenhagen. During the Napoleonic Wars, Denmark allied itself with France. This led to a British blockade, isolating Norway from Denmark. This blockade led to a shortage of goods and great privation in Norway. Because of the difficulties involved in administering Norway from Copenhagen, a Norwegian commission was appointed to govern Norway. In addition, the Danish king was forced to submit to some Norwegian demands, including one for a Norwegian university.

Napoleon was defeated, of course, leaving Denmark-Norway on the losing side. In 1814, Denmark ended its alliance with France. Acquiescing to the terms of the treaty of Kiel, Denmark transferred Norway to Sweden to compensate for Sweden's loss of Finland to Russia. Norway was to join a union with Sweden, but be allowed to retain the same laws, rights, and freedoms as they had enjoyed under Denmark. The Norwegians were not willing to accept these terms, however, and were unhappy about being transferred to Sweden without their consent. The governor of Norway in 1814 happened to be Prince Christian Frederik, nephew of the Danish king and heir to the Danish throne.

Taking advantage of the fact that the Swedish armies were still engaged in fighting down in Europe, he encouraged the Norwegians to elect representatives to assemble at Eidsvoll to declare Norway's independence. There is little doubt that Christian Frederik expected to be chosen King of Norway, and then to reunite Norway with Denmark later when he inherited the Danish throne. The 112 representatives consisted of businessmen, independent farmers, civil servants, and military officers. All were males over the age of 25, and nearly half were under 40. Because of the short time between the summons and the meeting, no representatives came from north Norway. Approximately, two thirds of the representatives were in favor of Christian Frederik as king. The remaining third, the unionists, felt that a union with Sweden was inevitable and that negotiations with Sweden were essential to preserve Norway's best interests. Initially the royalists prevailed, and in a little over a month a constitution was written that was heavily influenced by Enlightenment ideals, including those found in the American and French constitutions. On May 17, 1814, the new constitution was signed, and Christian Frederik was elected king of a free and independent Norway.

Christian Frederik's reign did not last long. As soon as Karl Johan of Sweden returned from the Napoleonic Wars, he gathered troops on the southern border between Sweden and Norway. There was never significant fighting, and the campaign lasted only two weeks before Christian Frederik capitulated.

When the ceasefire was signed in August of that year, Karl Johan declared his willingness to accept the May 17 constitution as a basis for negotiations, rather than the Treaty of Kiel. Under pressure from Sweden, the Norwegian parliament accepted the union, but waited until November 4 to elect Karl XIII of Sweden as king of Norway. The two countries were now united in a personal union under one king. King Karl XIII was bound by the terms of the Norwegian constitution; Norway would have its own bank, parliament (*Stortinget*), and government. The king would not be allowed to declare war without *Stortinget*'s consent, nor could he appoint Swedish civil servants to posts in Norway. Only four years later, Karl Johan became king, Karl XIV. To underscore the fact that Karl Johan was king of two different countries, two different coronations were conducted, one in Stockholm and one in Trondheim.

## UNION WITH SWEDEN

The early years of the union with Sweden were characterized by a struggle between the Swedish king and the Norwegian parliament over the constitution. Although the king had accepted the constitution, he tried to push through changes that would grant him more control. Starting in the early 1820s, there was a movement to begin celebrating May 17, the anniversary of the signing of the constitution. This was not popular with the king. The conflict came to a head in 1829, when one of Norway's two steamships, *The Constitution*, was in harbor. A large crowd gathered, and the Swedish authorities, led by the governor, tried to disperse it by force. This effort backfired, resulting in a political retreat by the king. From then on it became customary to celebrate May 17, and the king began appointing Norwegians to serve as governor. Eventually Norwegians were allowed to fly the red, white, and blue Norwegian flag, though with the Swedish colors in the corner, called by Norwegians "herring salad."

The 1800s was a time of nation building, both politically and culturally. Although the political and cultural leaders lived in the cities, they believed that true Norwegian character was found in the countryside. It was a time of great economic and population growth, which meant that an increasing number of people had to leave the rural areas and move to the cities. In 1875, only 25 percent of the population lived in cities, while by 1920 the percentage had increased to 45 percent. Younger children in families were especially likely to move because according to Norwegian allodial law, the oldest son had the right to take over the family farm undivided.

Many, particularly from the inland areas of south Norway, emigrated to America. From the 1830s on the largest settlements were in the American

Midwest; first Illinois, then Wisconsin, Iowa, Minnesota, and the Dakotas. The peak of emigration was between 1875 and 1930 when more than 800,000 Norwegians left for America.[1] The percentage of the population that emigrated was only exceeded by that of the Irish. At first those who left were primarily farmers. Among other reasons, they were attracted by the offer of free farmland promised by the United States Homestead Act of 1862. After a time, more urban people began emigrating as well as fishermen from north Norway who began settling farther west, creating a Norwegian-American community in Washington State.[2]

In 1820 Norway was one of world's poorer countries, on the periphery of Europe. Its peasantry depended on agriculture, and its small urban population on foreign trade. Industrialization arrived quite late to Norway. Indeed, it is said that Norway imported the industrial revolution, bringing the necessary equipment and expertise from England. Still, between the 1840s and World War I, modern Norway took shape, with increasing industrialization and urbanization. By 1875, only 54 percent of jobs were in the primary sector (agriculture, forestry, and fishing). The first wave of industrialization saw a growth in traditional industries like shipbuilding and sawmilling. The modern Norwegian textile industry and mechanical engineering workshops also begin to emerge. Industries like timber export, fishing, and shipping also continued to expand. By 1878, Norway was the third largest shipping nation in world, behind only the United States and Britain. When large trees for lumber began to run out, smaller trees were used to produce pulp for paper.

This century was also a time of populist movements led by such reformers as Hans Nielsen Hauge (1771–1824), a revivalist lay preacher who spoke out against the religious establishment. At that time it was against the law to hold a religious meeting without the supervision of an ordained minister, so Hauge spent many years in prison because of his defiance of that law. Søren Jaabæk (1814–1894), another activist, was a long-term member of *Stortinget* who organized farmers and helped found the Liberal Party. Jaabæk was an early proponent of women's right to vote as well as equal marriage rights for men and women. A third important figure is Marcus Thrane (1817–1890), who attempted unsuccessfully to organize the working class. In 1862, after spending several years in prison, he emigrated to the United States.

In the 1880s the first political parties were founded, beginning with the Liberal Party (*Venstre*) in 1883, then the Conservatives (*Høyre*) the next year, followed by Labor (*Det norske arbeiderpartiet*) in 1887. Increasing unhappiness with the union with Sweden led to disputes with the king about Norway's right to have its own foreign policy and diplomatic representation. In addition, Norwegian nationalism was on the rise, and other peoples, such as the Irish, the Finns, and the Poles, were also edging toward independence. Because more people could read now, newspapers brought news of current events and information about other independence movements more quickly than ever.

The political crisis came to a head in 1905 when the king vetoed parliament's bill establishing a Norwegian consular service. The Norwegian cabinet resigned over this veto. When the king was unable to persuade anyone else to form a government, on June 7 *Stortinget* declared that the king had failed to perform his constitutional duties as king of Norway, thereby bringing to an end the union between Norway and Sweden under a single monarch. The Swedish king was angered by this action and briefly considered military action. He consulted with his advisors and allies in Europe and decided against the use of force. He finally demanded a referendum on the matter, which took place in August 1905. Some 368,208 Norwegian men voted to end the union, while only 184 voted against. Women did not have the right to vote until 1913, but Fredrikke Marie Qvam, from the women's suffrage organization, organized a campaign that collected 279,878 signatures from women who supported the dissolution of the union. After further negotiations, Norway's independence was formally accepted by the Swedish Parliament on October 26, 1905, and King Oscar officially abdicated. The union between Sweden and Norway had been peacefully dissolved.

## AN INDEPENDENT NORWAY

While some radical Norwegians were in favor of creating a republic, in the end prime minister Christian Michelsen and his moderate allies prevailed. They favored adhering to the 1814 constitution, which had established a monarchy. In order to mollify the Swedish king, an offer was made to make one of his sons the new king of Norway. When he rejected this proposal, the politicians pursued negotiations, led by Fridtjof Nansen, with Prince Carl of Denmark. It was seen as an advantage that Carl was married to Maud, the daughter of King Edward VII of England, especially since they already had a son who would be heir to the throne. It was considered important to appease the great powers of Europe, and the king of England approved of his daughter becoming queen of Norway. Having heard rumors of the debate over whether Norway should be a republic or a monarchy, Prince Carl insisted upon a referendum. This referendum also passed with a nearly 80 percent majority in favor of a monarchy, and Carl was chosen King of Norway. Upon arrival in Norway, he took the name of Haakon VII and renamed his son Olav.

After 1905 Norway built up a system of foreign embassies and consulates, and adopted a policy of neutrality. It had already begun playing a role in promoting international arbitration agreements, which Norway has become known for. The period leading up to World War I was one of strong economic growth and expansion of industry. In the food industry, fish canning, which had begun in Drammen in 1841, became a big business. But the golden age for the industry was sardine canning in the first half of the 1900s, dominated by Christian Bjelland in Stavanger. By 1925, there were 198 canning factories in Norway, 59 in Stavanger.

The development of hydropower began between 1890 and 1920. Because it is difficult to transport electricity over long distances, factories and towns were built near the waterfalls. Norway became an exporter of electro-chemical and electro-metallurgical products like saltpeter, aluminum, and iron alloys. Initially foreign companies invested in waterfalls and hydroelectric power stations, as well as in forests and mines. By 1906, 75 percent of the water-power and 80 percent of the chemical industry were owned by foreign capital. Out of concern that too much of Norwegian industry was under foreign control, the first concession law was adopted in 1909. This law limited the right of foreigners to own waterfalls and mines in Norway. In addition to these restrictions, any foreign-owned waterfalls and power plants would revert to Norwegian state control after a number of years.

Norway remained neutral during World War I, although it lost a great number of ships and sailors due to submarines and mines. Enormous profits were made from shipping, however, enabling Norwegians to buy back control of various industries, including the coal mines on Svalbard.

The period between the wars, especially beginning in the 1920s, was a time of economic and social crises. Norway suffered along with the rest of the world during the Great Depression. Banks crashed, the Norwegian krone fell in value, businesses went bankrupt, and there was significant long-term unemployment. In 1932, nearly half of labor union members were unemployed. But 1932 also brought the beginning of a new economic upturn and a time of economic growth. New firms were established in rural areas, particularly furniture factories, and shipping expanded greatly. Because so many ships had been sunk during World War I, this was an opportunity to modernize the fleet. The mid-1930s brought a period of advancement for workers. The slogan in 1935 was "Work for All." Several benefit programs were introduced: 1936 brought the old-age pension, 1938 unemployment insurance, and health insurance was also expanded.

## WORLD WAR II

Although it had joined the League of Nations in 1920, when World War II broke out in 1939 Norway once again declared its neutrality. This declaration did not prevent Norwegian volunteers from joining Finnish and German forces against the Soviet Union, which had attacked Finland on November 30, 1939.

And it did not prevent Hitler from planning an invasion of Norway, later named Operation *Weserübung*. Vidkun Quisling, head of *Nasjonal Samling*, Norway's Nazi party, had already visited Berlin to discuss his own plans for a coup d'etat.

Norway appeared to have been caught by surprise when it was invaded on April 9, 1940, but in reality there were early warnings. Norwegians worried about both the British and the Germans, thinking that either side could attack. Both were interested in access to the iron mines in north Sweden, whose ore was exported through the ice-free port in Narvik, Norway. Indeed, a clash between Germany and Britain, the Altmark affair, took place in Jøssingfjord along the south coast on February 16, 1940. A British destroyer followed a German supply ship, the *Altmark*, into the Norwegian fjord in order to free the 299 British prisoners on board. It was a breach of Norwegian neutrality, but although the Norwegian authorities protested, they did not intervene. Later the term *Jøssing* was used to mean an anti-Nazi Norwegian. The Germans took the incident as an indication of Norwegian inability to maintain neutrality. The British were afraid of a German invasion, and indeed on April 7, 1940, British intelligence spotted German invasion forces on their way north and attacked the fleet with bomber planes. On April 8, 1940, Britain mined the Norwegian coast.

Early in the morning of April 9, German forces invaded both Norway and Denmark. In a well-coordinated invasion, German planes and ships attacked several cities simultaneously. They did not expect, however, that a tiny fort in the Oslo fjord, armed only with ancient canons, would be able to sink the German cruiser, the Blücher. This ship carried specially trained staff who planned to take over strategic positions in Oslo. The delay this caused provided time for the King, the royal family, the cabinet, and the *Storting* to escape by train north to the city of Elverum. Panicked Oslo citizens also attempted to flee, expecting a bomb attack by the Germans. In Elverum, King Haakon rejected the German demand to abdicate, and the *Storting* transferred all its authority to the cabinet and dissolved itself. As the King, Crown Prince, and cabinet fled north to Tromsø, confusion reigned in the Norwegian defense. Many cities, including Elverum, Molde, Bodø, and Narvik were destroyed by bombs.

The battle was soon over in the south, but in the north, military resistance lasted for two months, assisted by British and French troops. Once Germany attacked France, however, the allied troops were withdrawn to fight elsewhere, and Norway was forced to surrender. The King and his party were evacuated to London on June 7, 1940, where they remained during the war, running the government in exile. The government was able to use revenue earned by Norwegian merchant ships during the war to finance its activities. Most of the ships had been abroad at the time of the invasion and were organized into a shipping company called Nortraship.

## MILITARY RESISTANCE

Military resistance, referred to as *Milorg*, got off to a slow start but eventually became more organized and was brought under the control of London. By the end of the war, there were approximately 48,000 members of *Milorg*. Many were eventually sent to Britain for training in sabotage, espionage, transport of refugees, supply work, parachute drops, and communications. Before 1944, most sabotage was carried out by specially trained outsiders brought in for the purpose from Great Britain. Railroad sabotage was finally permitted in December 1944 by the allied leadership in an effort to prevent the Germans from moving troops from Norway to the continent, where they expected the Allies to invade. As many as 430,000 German troops were stationed in Norway, a number equal to 14 percent of the population. The actual effectiveness of *Milorg* has been debated in recent years. Arguably, their greatest contribution was in the area of intelligence.[3]

The civilian resistance, or *Sivorg*, shaped the lives of many more people than the military resistance. In November 1941 civilian radios were confiscated, although of course not all the radios were actually turned in. In order to provide accurate information on the progress of the war, people began sharing information received on their concealed radios through illegal newspapers. Women were heavily involved in this information service, working both to create the newspapers and to distribute them. More than one young mother carried a bundle of newspapers beneath her baby in its carriage. Women also helped to feed and shelter men involved in the military resistance as well as to smuggle Jewish children out of Norway.

*Holdningskampen*, literally the "attitude battle," or the battle for hearts and minds, was waged to keep people's spirits up and at the same time demoralize the enemy. Various symbols were used throughout the war to indicate loyalties. For example, people began wearing paper clips on their jackets, both because the paper clip was supposed to have been invented by a Norwegian and because the paper clip symbolized holding together. The royal monogram, H7, appeared painted on walls or carved into snow banks, people began wearing the traditional red wool Norwegian stocking cap, the *nisselue*, or simply red, white, and blue clothing, reflecting the colors of the Norwegian flag. There was strong resistance against the German attempts to Nazify the various labor unions and other professional organizations. Actors, writers, athletes, students, pastors, schoolteachers, and parents all participated in boycotts and organized resistance to Nazi demands.

Liberation day finally arrived on May 8, 1945. Although Norwegians were understandably a bit nervous over how the remaining armed German soldiers would respond, as it turned out, they surrendered peacefully. More than 10,000 Norwegians had died either in the fighting or in prison camps. On May 13, Crown Prince Olav arrived home, just in time to join in the first celebration of May 17 in five years. King Haakon returned on June 7, 1945, exactly five years after his evacuation from Tromsø. In 1945, 53,000 Norwegians were found guilty of treason. Twenty-five of these were executed, including archtraitor, Vidkun Quisling.

The five-year-long occupation served to unite the Norwegian people and define Norwegian national identity as never before. World War II for Norway has always just been called *Krigen*, "The War," and it still retains a fascination for Norwegians. In the years since 1945, countless novels, short stories, memoirs, histories, and movies have been produced, attempting to portray what really happened and to keep the experience alive for those too young to have lived through it. Where once books were written about the main players in the Resistance, particularly the men, more recently the stories of the women and children have been told.

In the first years after 1945, the members of the Resistance were often glorified, supporting the illusion that virtually all Norwegians were involved in fighting against the Nazis. In more recent years, historians have attempted to debunk the myths, and have even accused earlier historians of interpreting the past to suit their own ambitions. Nonetheless, it is true that the war represents a period of singular importance to Norwegian self-perception and to the identity of Norway as an independent nation. The period following the war marked a continuation of the solidarity and community forged during those five difficult years, and perhaps offers one explanation of why Norway has been hesitant to join the European Union.

## POSTWAR REBUILDING

Norway was a founding member of the United Nations in 1945, and Norwegian Trygve Lie served as its first Secretary General. Further rejecting its prewar neutrality policy, Norway also became a charter member of NATO in 1949. The years following liberation were politically stable. The Labor party took control and dominated politics for most of the postwar period. The main goals were to get everyone back to work, stabilize prices, repair transportation and communications systems, and provide housing. Beginning in 1948, Norway began participating in the Marshall Plan, eventually receiving three billion kroner for rebuilding. North Norway had been hit particularly hard during the war. Wishing to hinder the invading Russians, the Germans had burned and destroyed everything along their path as they retreated. They also attempted to evacuate the civilians, although many stayed behind, hiding in caves and mines. After the war, many people in North Norway lived in tents or barracks.

In fact, for several reasons there was a housing shortage in the entire country. Homes were not built during the war years. Peace meant new marriages and a resulting postwar baby boom. Many people migrated from rural areas to the cities, where they could find work. Increasing prosperity meant that people could afford better homes and were no longer satisfied with tiny apartments with no toilet or bath.

Responses to the housing shortage included both public and private initiatives. In 1946, the Norwegian State Housing Bank was founded, which made home ownership possible for more people and led to large-scale housing construction. The Oslo Housing and Savings Society (*Oslo Bolig og Sparelag*), which had existed since 1929, cooperated with the city of Oslo to start building the *drabantbyer*, or high-rise apartment complexes. The city provided vacant sites at a reasonable price, and in return bought one fourth of the completed housing projects for those in greatest need. Another innovation came about when builder Olav Selvaag started producing prefabricated houses in 1951.

The period between 1954 and 1973 in Norway is sometimes referred to as the golden years. Values of social justice were strong, and the system of social welfare, with a large public sector, was further developed. The government's goals were full employment, universal rights, and equalization of income through progressive taxation. Pensions, universal health insurance, poverty assistance, unemployment benefits, and free education were all achieved. It was believed that poverty could be eliminated.

The 1950s were a decade of change for consumers. The first self-service store came in 1947, although chain stores were not permitted until 1953 and goods could not be mixed under one roof. For example, meat and fish were sold in separate stores. Grain, coffee, butter, and sugar were rationed after the end of the war, with sugar and coffee rationing only ending in 1952. Cars, however, continued to be rationed until 1960.

These years represent the longest continuous period of strong and stable growth in modern Norwegian history. The GDP increased 5 percent a year, there was little unemployment, and the average pay more than doubled. New large-scale industries using cheap waterpower were created, and gradually a service society, or postindustrial society, began to develop. In addition to a marked improvement in material well-being, Norwegians enjoyed more vacation and free time. With more vacations came increased mobility. Norwegians began traveling to warmer locations, such as Spain and the Canary Islands. The movement from the country to the cities continued.

Some sectors that originally were nationalized were later privatized, including the aluminum, iron, steel and mining, rail, electricity, and telephone industries. Government policy permitted industry to purchase cheap electricity and encouraged centralization and growth of larger farms and fishing fleets. At the same time, efforts were made to enable people to continue living in the rural areas, especially in the west and north. Even today there are tax advantages to establishing businesses in the far north, and there has been a conscious effort to avoid concentrating state-owned institutions, such as the national library, in Oslo.

The 1960s brought increased internationalization, as well as increased prosperity, productivity, and cooperation among the Nordic countries. Norway became a founding member of the European Free Trade Association, and eventually dozens of other international organizations. Although Norway is known today for its oil wealth, it is important to note that it had become one of the richest countries in the world even before oil was discovered.

## THE OIL AGE

Serious exploration for oil on the continental shelf off the southwest coast of Norway began in the mid-1960s. The first discovery of commercially exploitable oil came in December 1969 in the field that would later be called Ekofisk. By 1971 Norwegian wells were producing oil, and by 1975 Norway was producing enough petroleum to satisfy all domestic needs and export large quantities to Europe. Environmental concerns surfaced early, and in 1972 the Ministry of Environment was formed. Heated political battles have been fought over how far north to allow drilling because of concerns over the fragile environment of the far north.

Today oil and gas make up one third of all exports, with the petroleum sector representing one eighth of the GDP. In 2008, Norway was the fifth largest exporter of oil and gas products in world, behind Saudi Arabia, Russia, the United Arab Emirates, and Iran. It is the third largest exporter of natural gas, behind Russia and Canada. Oil production reached its peak in 2000 and is declining, whereas natural gas production is still increasing.[4]

The Norwegian authorities made two astute observations about its oil wealth: first, the oil reserves were finite and would one day run dry, and second, if too much oil money was spent, it could overheat the economy. Therefore in 1990, *Stortinget* passed a law establishing the State Petroleum Fund. In 1996, the first deposit was made into the fund, and a few years later investments in stocks and bonds began. In 2004, ethical guidelines for the Petroleum Fund were established and an ethical advisory council named.

In 2006, the fund was renamed the State Pension Fund-Global, in order to underscore the purpose of setting aside the oil money.

Norway invests about 30 percent of its fund in the U.S. stock market, and about 50 percent in European stocks. In 2007, Norway gained international attention when it pulled investments from such American companies as Wal-Mart, Boeing, and Lockheed Martin for what it considered ethical violations.[5] Wal-Mart was accused of human rights violations, including the use of child labor and generally poor working conditions for its employees. Boeing and Lockheed Martin were singled out for their production of land mines and cluster bombs. Not only American companies were blacklisted. Norway also refuses to invest in companies in Myanmar, because of its continued house arrest of Nobel Peace Prize laureate Aung San Suu Kyi.

## NOTES

1. http://www.nb.no/emigrasjon/n_a&b.html. Accessed 1/18/10.

2. http://www.nb.no/emigrasjon/emigration/. Accessed 12/16/09.

3. http://www.regjeringen.no/nb/dep/hod/dok/nouer/1998/nou-1998-12/26/6/4.html?id=375564. Accessed 12/19/09.

4. Statistics Norway. http://www.ssb.no/english/subjects/10/06/olje_gass_en/. Accessed 12/29/09.

5. http://www.nytimes.com/2007/05/04/business/worldbusiness/04norway.html. Accessed 12/29/09.

# 3

# Religion and Thought

NORWAY has become increasingly secular as well as more religiously diverse in the post–World War II period. Although the Church of Norway is defined by the constitution as the established religion, or the state church, all registered religious and philosophical communities receive support from the state. Negotiations have been underway in the last several years to loosen the church's relationship with the state. As of 2009, approximately 81 percent of the population belonged to the Church of Norway.[1] An additional 4.5 percent were registered members of other Christian denominations, including Catholic, Pentecostal, Lutheran Free Church, United Methodist, Jehovah's Witness, and others.[2]

The remaining 14.5 percent are either members of non-Christian religions, which have increased in size with immigration from non-Christian countries, members of a philosophical community, or nonreligious. Islam is by far the largest non-Christian religious group, with 20 percent of non-Church of Norway members. Nineteen percent of non-Church members belong to a philosophical society, like the Humanists. The next largest group is the Buddhists, with only 2.7 percent of non-Church of Norway members. Since 1970 the membership in philosophical communities has tripled, while the membership in the state church has declined from 96 percent to 81 percent in the same period.[3] Because Norwegians automatically become members of the Church of Norway when they are baptized and must take action to be removed from the rolls, many can be characterized as passive members, who do not attend church regularly.

## EARLY PAGAN BELIEFS

Norway was a pagan country until approximately the eleventh century, when it was converted to Christianity. Before that time there is little direct information about actual belief systems because the pagan Norsemen did not leave written evidence. There are other types of evidence, however, including burial mounds, with their rich grave goods, and place names containing the names of gods. According to H. R. Ellis Davidson, there is evidence of religious practice dating back to the Bronze Age (1600–450 BCE).[4] Figures depicting a variety of gods in human form have been found in burial mounds, often carved into stone, metal, wood, or woven into tapestries. The various gods are recognized by specific attributes. Thor holds a hammer; Frey has a large phallus; one-eyed Odin is identified by his ravens, spear, and eight-legged horse; and Freyja wears the necklace made for her by the dwarves.

The few written sources that exist are written either by outsiders, after the conversion to Christianity, or both. The Arab writer and traveler Ibn Fadlan wrote one of the most famous accounts in the tenth century. Ibn Fadlan lived with Swedish Vikings in a camp on the Volga River. In his writings, he described the Vikings' physical appearance, their hygiene, and other customs. He recounted in detail the ship burial of a chieftain, which also included the sacrifice of a female slave. In the eleventh century, Adam of Bremen wrote *Descriptio insularum Aquilonis*, completed in 1075, about the people, geography, and customs of Scandinavia. He was interested in the missionary work being carried out by Christians in Scandinavia, particularly in what is now Uppsala, Sweden. In his work, he refers to the gods by name and describes cult activity, such as ritual sacrifices.

The Danish historian Saxo Grammaticus (1174–1241) wrote *Gesta Danorum*, the *History of the Danes*; much of what he wrote, however, differs significantly from the works of other scholars, most significantly Icelander Snorri Sturluson (1178–1241). Snorri as well as the anonymous writers of the *Elder Edda* recorded poems and legends of the gods of pre-Christian Norway and Iceland, written down approximately 200 years after the Christianization of the two countries. The *Elder Edda* is a collection of 35 pre-Christian poems, containing valuable information about the Norse gods, which Snorri apparently used as source material, as well as heroic poems. It begins with the *Prophecy of the Seeress*, or *Völuspá*, which summarizes the whole mythology from creation, to its destruction in Ragnarok, to its rebirth. This is one of the four poems attributed to Odin. The others contain the wisdom of Odin and stories explaining how he received his wisdom. An additional four poems recount the exploits of Thor. One of these, called *Thrymskviða*, or the *Lay of Thrym*, is quite entertaining. It features Thor dressing himself in women's clothing to retrieve his hammer, which had been stolen by a lovesick giant who wished to marry the goddess Freyja.

In addition to these works, there are also a number of poems attributed to specific poets, or skalds, who wrote poetry in such a complicated meter and structure that one can be confidant that they were passed down unchanged. This skaldic poetry not only contains information about the mythology, but also makes use of the myths as part of the poetic language. They make frequent use of kennings based on mythological narrative. For example the phrase "Siv's hair" means gold, referring to the time when Loki cut off the hair of Siv, Odin's wife. To compensate her for the loss of her hair, Odin commissions the dwarves to make hair for her out of gold.

Because a thorough knowledge of Norse mythology is required to interpret this Skaldic poetry, Snorri created a handbook for poets. His Prose Edda consists of three parts: *Gylfaginning* (*The Deluding of Gylfi*), about Norse mythology; *Skáldskaparmál*, a handbook for poets; and *Háttatal*, a list of verse forms. In all his writings Snorri made it clear that he was Christian, viewing the pagan beliefs through the eyes of a medieval scholar. Therefore, we cannot take everything he wrote as an accurate depiction of the pre-Christian beliefs. He did, however, quote extensively from earlier sources.

### Cosmology

The source materials describing Norse mythology are fragmentary and often contradictory, but the following provides a simplified overview. The Norse world features nine worlds divided into three realms. The three realms are connected by the tree of life, the ash tree, Yggdrasil, which has one root in each realm. An eagle with a hawk between its eyes lives in the top of Yggdrasil. By means of the squirrel Ratatosk, he hurls insults to the serpent Nidhogg, which lies gnawing on Yggdrasil's roots. In the top realm are Asgard, home of the Æsir gods; Vanaheim, home of the Vanir, or fertility gods; and Alfheim, home of the light elves. In the middle realm are Midgard, home of humans; Svartalfaheim, home of the black elves; and Jotunheim, home of the giants. The lowest level contains Niflheim, the element of ice; Muspelheim, the element of fire; and finally the realm of the dead, Hel. A flaming rainbow bridge called Bifrost connects Midgard and Asgard.

### Beginning, Middle, and End of the World

Three Eddic poems from the Poetic Edda describe the creation of the world. Snorri uses these, combined with some additions and changes, in his *Gylfaginning*. Here the world is formed without a creator. In the beginning was Niflheim, world of snow and ice, and in the south Muspelheim, world of fire.

Between the two realms was Ginungagap, the great emptiness. As these two worlds came together, the giant Ymir was formed from the melting ice. Ymir was the ancestor of all the giants and was nourished by the cow, Audhumla, who licked the salty ice blocks until another being appeared, Buri. A variety of traditions is described in the sources. According to one, man and woman were formed from the armpit of Ymir, and the frost giants came from his feet. In another version man and woman were called Ask and Embla. They were created by Odin, Vili, and Ve, who were sons of Bor, son of Buri, who killed Ymir. These gods then took Ymir's flesh to make soil, his bones to create mountains and rock, his hair for vegetation, and his blood for the sea. The sky was created from his skull, held aloft by four dwarves.

The fates of the gods culminate in the final battle between the gods and the giants called Ragnarok, which leads to the destruction of the world. Although the gods fight valiantly, they are defeated and Asgard is destroyed. Yggdrasil, The World Tree, is not destroyed, however, but rather shelters two beings who survive, Lif and Lifthrasir, and will repopulate the earth.

### Pantheon of Gods

In Norse mythology there are two kinds of gods, the Æsir and the Vanir, who warred with one another. The conditions of their truce involved exchanging of hostages. Hoenir and Mimir were sent to the Vanir, while Njord and his children, Frey and Freyja, fertility god and goddess, were sent to the Æsir. While the surviving sources are confusing, apparently the Vanir were not happy with the result of the transfer and ended up cutting off Mimir's head and returning it to the Æsir. Odin preserved the head of Mimir, and later consulted it as an oracle. Odin is the All-Father, god of battle, justice, death, wisdom, and poetry, and is married to Frigg. Odin is a complex figure. On the one hand he is wise and powerful, having sacrificed one of his eyes to obtain wisdom and poetry. Another source, the *Hávamál*, describes how he hanged himself on a tree, a self-sacrifice in order to acquire the magical arts.

On the other hand, Odin appears sneaky and sly, not to be trusted. He is often depicted in disguise, a hat pulled down to conceal his missing eye. He has a spear, Gungnir, and an eight-legged horse called Sleipnir, who is the offspring of Loki. He is also said to keep two wolves at his side during the feasting. Odin receives information from the two ravens he sends out: Hugin (Thought) and Munin (Memory). Odin's hall is called Valhalla, which appears to be a banquet hall with many doors. Maidens known as Valkyries have the job of bringing to Valhalla those warriors who fell bravely in battle. There they feast all night, after battling all day, in eternal preparation for Ragnarok.

Odin had several sons, the most powerful and popular, as well as the oldest being Thor, the thunder god. Judging by the number of place names containing Thor and the quantity of images, archeological evidence of hammer-shaped amulets, and literature, it is evident that Thor was widely worshipped among pagan Scandinavians. Often depicted as a large, powerful man with a red beard, he carried a hammer, Mjollnir. Mjollnir struck whatever he threw it at and always returned to his hand. Thor also had a belt of power, which doubled his strength, and iron gloves with which he grasped his hammer. The noise of Thor's cart, pulled by two goats, creates the sound of thunder as he drives it across the sky. He frequently battles giants, though his most difficult foe is the World Serpent, who lies coiled around the root of the World Tree. Thor's wife is Siv, whose hair is made of gold, as described above.

The twin fertility gods, Frey and Freyja, were also widely worshipped in Scandinavia. Frey was supposed to have possessed a golden boar Gullinbursti, made by dwarves. In addition to the boar, Frey was also connected with horses and with a special ship, Skiðblaðnir. This ship was large enough to hold all the gods, yet Frey could fold it up and put it in his pocket. Frey's twin sister, Freyja, also had a boar, Hildisvin. Her necklace, *Brisingamen*, was crafted by the dwarves. She drove a chariot pulled by cats, but she could also take on the shape of a bird or falcon for travel. The father of Frey and Freyja was Njord, god of the sea and ships, who was married to Skaði, actually a giant, associated with hunting, skiing, and mountains. She married him as compensation provided by the gods for killing her father, Thjazi. Because the two of them were so incompatible, they never found a place where they could settle down. Njord controlled winds and waves, and brought success to fishermen and sailors.

Heimdall is called the white god. He lived at the rainbow bridge, Bifrost, and served as the watchman for the gods. His senses are so acute that he can hear grass growing in the meadows and wool growing on sheep and can see to the end of the earth. His task was to blow his horn, Gjallarhorn, to warn of the beginning of Ragnarok, the final battle. Another son of Odin and Frigg was Balder, known to be good and pure. One day Frigg had a dream where Balder was killed. Determined to do what she could to guarantee his safety, she went around to all plants, trees, and metals and extracted a promise they would not harm Balder. But she overlooked the innocent mistletoe, never thinking it could harm anyone. As the gods amused themselves by throwing weapons at Balder, knowing nothing could injure him, Loki gave a spear made of mistletoe to the blind god, Hod, encouraging him to join in the fun. When Hod threw the spear, Balder was impaled and died. Loki not only caused Balder's death, but also later prevented Balder from returning from Hel. He took the shape of the old woman, Thokk, who refused to weep for Balder.

Loki is another quite complex and important figure in the mythology, although there is no evidence that he was ever worshipped. The son of a giant, he frequented Asgard and was a companion of Odin and Thor. But he also fought Heimdal and was responsible for Balder's death. Initially he is a trickster figure, but by the late Viking age, he becomes a darker and more evil figure. He gave birth to Odin's horse, Sleipnir, which was good and useful to the gods. But he also had several offspring who caused problems, including the Fenris wolf, the evil creature to which Bragi must sacrifice his hand to successfully bind, the World Serpent, and Hel, ruler of the world of the dead. Loki was involved in all manner of mischief, including stealing Siv's hair and the apples of eternal life. Sometimes, however, he assisted the gods. For example, he helped Thor retrieve his hammer from Thrym by dressing the two of them up as bride and bridesmaid. He was able to change his shape at will, sometimes appearing as a horse, other times as an old woman or a bird or a salmon.

### Norse Religious Practice and Belief

Little is known about actual religious belief or practice. The Norse apparently believed in some sort of afterlife, as evidenced by such practices as ship burials and myths about Valhalla and the realm of the dead, but they did not seem to believe in any form of redemption. They were especially concerned with the reputation that would live on after death. One stanza from *Hávamál* (Sayings of the High One) expresses this beautifully:

Cattle die, kinsmen die,
one day you die yourself;
I know one thing that never dies—
the dead man's reputation.

Old Norse religion had no central doctrine, and the Vikings were not interested in converting other peoples, the way Christians are. Through their travels, the Vikings became familiar with Christianity, and because they believed in a multiplicity of gods, they had no problem accepting the Christian God as one of many gods. In many cases they allowed themselves to be baptized to obtain trading privileges. Other Christian influences came from the missionaries who came from Christian countries to Scandinavia.

While some earlier kings had attempted to impose Christianity on Norway, the two kings who are most credited with accomplishing the conversion are both named Olav. Both Olav I Tryggvason and Olav II Haraldson, who became known as Saint Olav, the patron saint of Norway, had converted to Christianity in England. It must also be noted that the imposition of a single religion over Norway also made it more possible to join the country under the rule of one king. Thus, there were doubtless political as well as religious motivations behind the move to convert Norwegians. The methods these kings used were sometimes violent. It was Olav II's death, however, that became the most important event in the Christianizing of Norway. As described in Chapter 2, he was killed in the battle of Stiklestad in 1030. His burial site later became a pilgrimage destination for medieval Christians in Norway hoping for miracles.

### Folk Beliefs

It took several hundred years before people were willing to give up their beliefs in hidden spirits—both evil ones and ones that protected them. The fact that they hedged their bets is seen in the stave churches, which began to be constructed in the early years after the initial conversion. Some have both crosses and dragon heads on them. It is also common in Norwegian folklore for the sign of the cross to have protective power over the evil creatures that still existed. People feared the "underearthly" creatures such as *hulder, trolls*, and *oskorei* well into the eighteenth century, and relied on the power of Christianity to protect them. They believed these beings were particularly active on Thursday evenings and on Christmas Eve, so took special precautions to protect themselves. Women who had just given birth were especially vulnerable until they had been brought back to church. It is as if people still maintained the old beliefs, but trusted that the Christian God was more powerful.

Trolls are the large, ugly, stupid creatures that are believed to be found in the mountains and forests. They can usually be defeated by a clever opponent, and if they ever stay outside until the sun rises, they turn to rock. In addition to the trolls of folktale fame, they also figure in legends with St. Olav, who invariably outsmarts them. *Huldrefolk* are other land-based creatures. The *hulder* is usually viewed as a beautiful girl, who tries to seduce a young Christian boy. The only way she can be recognized as nonhuman is by her cow's tail. This tail drops off and she becomes ordinary in appearance once she marries.

The *nisse* was originally conceived of as the first farmer who cleared an area. He is also called the *haugbonde*, or farmer from the burial mound. His main duty is to watch over the farm and ascertain that the animals are well cared for. This was part of ancestor worship that continued even after the coming of Christianity to Norway, as one can see in some thirteenth-century laws forbidding the practice. Until the nineteenth century it was the custom in some places to leave the table covered with food all night long on Christmas Eve so that the spirits could come and eat. Although no one beyond childhood actually believes in the existence of *nisser* any more, even in 2009 some 350,000 Norwegians reported leaving porridge for the *nisse* every Christmas Eve, and another 75,000 do it every other year.[5]

There are also creatures of lakes, waterfalls, and the sea. The *nøkk* lives in a lake or pond and will try to drown a person who is not careful. Under the waterfall is the *fossegrim*, playing his fiddle. If an aspiring fiddler tosses in a juicy joint of meat, he will be taught to play. If, on the other hand, the pupil is stingy and throws in a tough piece, the *fossegrim* might only teach him to tune the fiddle. More dangerous is the *draug*, who sails in half a boat on the sea. If a sailor sees one of these when he is out fishing, he will die, unless he protects himself with the sign of the cross.

Most frightening are the spirits of the air, the *oskorei*, a host who fly around at night. These may have been restless spirits of the dead and are especially active around Christmas time as well as on Thursday nights.

## MEDIEVAL CHURCH HISTORY

The Roman Catholic Church grew in strength and influence during its first 500 years in Norway, until the Protestant Reformation in 1537. Thousands of churches were built, including the cathedral in Trondheim, as well as monasteries. Laws were changed and codified under the influence of Christianity. In 1152 Nidaros, now Trondheim, was declared an archbishopric, increasing the political and spiritual power of the Church. The king was now crowned by the archbishop and owed allegiance to the Pope in Rome. During the first appearance of the Black Death from 1349 to 1351, many priests, monks, and nuns died because they dedicated themselves to tending the sick. Impressed with their sacrifice, people gave gifts to the churches and monasteries, making the church the largest landowner in Norway by the end of the Middle Ages.

By the fifteenth century Norway was under the control of Denmark, and the Danish kings began making decisions on religious matters in Norway. Being so close to Germany, home of Martin Luther, the Danish kings quickly became familiar with the tenets of Protestantism. They found its emphasis on a national church, rather than one centered in Rome, particularly appealing and immediately saw the political benefits. In 1537, King Christian III declared Lutheranism the official religion of Denmark-Norway. The properties formerly owned by the Church, about half of the land in Norway, were now taken over by the crown. Roman Catholic worship was forbidden, and monasteries were emptied and in some cases destroyed. There was little public support in Norway for this change, so it is doubtful that it made much difference in ordinary people's lives for decades.

One result of the conversion to Lutheranism, with its emphasis on individual interpretation of the Bible, is that instruction in Bible verses and catechism was extended to all, not just the urban upper classes. Not all children went to school or actually learned to read, however, until 1739 when the first school law was passed. From this point, all children aged seven and above were required to attend school, where they received instruction in reading. Confirmation had been introduced a few years before. Everyone was required to be confirmed in order to marry or to hold certain jobs.

## Witch Trials[6]

As in the rest of seventeenth-century Europe and America, many were accused of witchcraft. At first the word "witch" (*heks*, in Norwegian) was not used in Norway. The accused were referred to as *trollkvinne* (troll woman) or *trollmann* (troll man); the word *heks* came into use only toward the end of the period. While mostly women were charged, men were also accused, and in some cases husbands and wives were put on trial together. Even young girls under the age of 12 were accused of witchcraft. In Norway more than 800 witch trials were held, and about 300 women and men were convicted of witchcraft and burned at the stake or beheaded between 1575 and 1704. About 40 percent of these executions occurred in the three sparsely populated northernmost counties of Norway, although many were also tried in Bergen. Many of the condemned were Sámi people.

## Pietism

Beginning in the early 1700s a more individualistic Lutheran movement reached Norway and was initially promoted by the King in Copenhagen. Stressing the sinfulness of human beings and the need for personal conversion and redemption, the pietistic movement also promoted education and introduced confirmation. Its popularity faded in the late 1700s as Enlightenment ideas took hold, only to be reawakened in the 1800s. One of the most important figures in this phase of Norwegian pietism was Hans Nielsen Hauge (1771–1824). Hauge, son of a pious farmer from southeastern Norway, had a personal conversion experience one April day in 1796 in a farm field. From that moment on he felt called to proclaim the word of the Lord, even though as a layperson it was illegal for him to do this. He eventually traveled all around Norway and Denmark leading revival meetings. He also wrote a number of books and started many businesses. His goal was to combine hard work with Christian morals. He was arrested several times for breaking the Conventicle Act, which forbade preaching not under the supervision of an ordained minister, and was imprisoned for nine years. Hauge is important in the renewal of the Lutheran church both in Norway and in the United States, where many of his followers emigrated. He never favored a separatist free church. He also promoted the position of women, allowing them to preach publicly and to be in charge of some of his friendship groups.

In the 1850s another pietistic movement began, the Johnsonian awakening, named after theology professor Gisle Johnson (1822–1894). It dominated the religious atmosphere of the second half of the 1800s, and preached a pietistic and somber Lutheranism, frowning on such things as dancing, card playing, the reading of fiction, and other cultural pleasures. Unlike Hauge's movement, it was led by trained clergy. An entire generation of theology students in Norway was influenced by this stern religiosity. A strict interpretation of the sacraments even led to a decline in participation in Holy Communion. While a few Johnsonian pastors left the state church, most remained, although they worked to loosen the ties between church and state.[7] The end of the nineteenth century was characterized by a conflict between liberal theologians at the University of Oslo and conservative ones, leading to the establishment in 1908 of a new, more conservative, private school of theology, the *Menighetsfakultet* (Congregation Faculty). This school still exists today, and trains most of the pastors in Norway.

Pietistic fervor led to the creation of a missionary movement. Beginning in the early 1700s, missionaries were sent to northern Norway by the king to convert the Sámi people from shamanism to Christianity. There they built churches and schools. While the early missionaries worked to improve the lives of the Sámi and also to preserve their cultural heritage, their work also led to integration and assimilation to Western culture and the loss of old religious customs. One of the most important missionaries to the Sámi was Lars Levi Læstadius (1800–1861), who was Swedish-Sámi. He founded a conservative Christian lay movement, which has approximately 20,000 members in northern Norway today. In the 1840s, Norwegians also began traveling to countries in Asia and Africa to do missionary work, and even today there are active missions in many different countries.

## LAY MOVEMENT

The nineteenth and twentieth centuries were characterized by the growth of the lay movement. What is unusual about Norway is that this movement is embraced by the church. The first *bedehus*, or prayer house, was built in 1853 in Skien. These houses were built by congregations of the state church for Bible classes and devotional meetings because this type of meeting was not allowed in the churches themselves until legal permission was granted in 1889. About 2,700 prayer houses have been built. Most people who attend prayer meetings today also attend services in the Church of Norway, although some prayer house meetings occur at the same time as these services. Ordained pastors of the Church of Norway participate in the prayer house movement, but some meetings are led by lay preachers and there is no connection with the leadership of the established church. These low-church prayer houses are most numerous in southwestern Norway, where Church of Norway membership also is higher.

Lay organizations have raised money for missionaries both to foreign countries and to places in Norway, the so-called inner mission. The Inner Mission

Association (*Indremisjonsforbundet*) is an umbrella association of 1,500 groups. These groups do their work in 600 prayer houses in southern and western Norway, as well as in Finnmark in the north.[8] Much of the inner mission work as well as the entire foreign ministry work of the Church of Norway is carried out by voluntary organizations not directly connected with the state church. Some of these groups include the Norwegian Missionary Society, the YMCA/YWCA, the Norwegian Church Ministry to Israel, and the Norwegian Lutheran Mission. They have their own school in Stavanger, The School of Mission and Theology. These organizations support approximately 800 missionaries and development aid workers in Asia, Africa, and Latin America. The foreign mission has founded independent national churches in the target countries for whom they now work, and many receive support from the Norwegian state.[9]

## THE CHURCH OF NORWAY DURING WORLD WAR II

The church played a central role during the German occupation of 1940–1945. Because Norway had a state church, the pastors and bishops were actually employees of the state. Despite their employment status, church officials felt duty-bound to protest against Nazi actions, such as the introduction of a service requirement for young people. As early as 1940, bishops of the state church began a cooperative effort with leaders of free churches and other Christian churches. The conflict reached a climax at Easter 1942 when the bishops, led by Bishop Eivind Berggrav, sent out a pastoral letter that was read from pulpits all over the country. The letter stated that they were resigning their positions as civil servants, but that they would continue as the spiritual leaders of their congregations. More than 90 percent of the pastors followed the lead of their bishops. The bishops were arrested and sent to concentration camps, along with some of the pastors. Bishop Berggrav sat in house arrest until the end of the war. Even after the formal resignation of the pastors, the church played an active role in the resistance and continued to protest Nazi actions, such as the arrest and deportation of the Jews. Most Norwegians boycotted the churches run by Nazi pastors, while church attendance increased in the other churches. After the war, the relationship between church and state was restored.

## RELIGION IN NORWAY TODAY

Freedom of religion in Norway has only been guaranteed by the constitution since 1964, although non-Lutheran Christians have been permitted to have churches since 1845 and Jews have been allowed in Norway since 1851. The Evangelical Lutheran Church is the official religion of Norway, but as mentioned previously, all registered religions and philosophical communities are supported by the state through general tax revenues, proportionate to their number of members. There is no specific church tax or membership fee paid by members. Changes are being considered in the relationship between the Church of Norway and the state. This may mean that, while the Church of Norway will continue to have a special position, it will no longer be the state church.

## STATE CHURCH[10]

What does it mean when Norway is said to have an established church or state church? Does the state control the church? Since the 1920s, the state has delegated more and more authority to church leaders, and in 1969 the term "state church" was officially dropped. In principle, the constitutional head of the church is the king (or regent), who by law must be a member of the Lutheran church, and those members of the council of state who are baptized members of the church. The king and council of state delegate authority to the Royal Ministry of Culture and Church Affairs. At least one half of the members of the council of state must be members of the Church of Norway. There is no such requirement for members of *Stortinget* (Parliament), although the vast majority belongs. The *Storting* passes laws regarding the financing of the church and other such issues, but all responsibility for liturgical and spiritual matters has been turned over to church leaders. Financial responsibility for salaries and church maintenance is shared by the state and the municipalities; benevolence, missions, and other such work are paid for by the congregations themselves. In addition to churches in Norway, there is also a system of churches for Norwegians living abroad, called *Sjømannskirker* (the Norwegian Mission to Seamen), located all over the world.

The Norwegian state church does not have an archbishop, but rather one bishop for each of its 11 dioceses. Until the constitutional changes expected in 2013, bishops are appointed by the Minister of Culture and Church Affairs from a list of candidates proposed by the council of bishops; pastors are appointed by the bishops. It has happened that the minister has used this authority to influence the church. In 1993, for example, Rosemarie Köhn, the first female bishop, was appointed bishop of Hamar over the protests of many of the sitting bishops, although women had been pastors in Norway since 1961. In 2009 the number-three candidate was selected to be the new bishop of Stavanger, perhaps because of his more liberal views on homosexuality. The parishes are divided up geographically, with membership being determined by what parish one resides in. Norwegians automatically become members of their local parish when they are baptized and must formally withdraw if they no longer wish to be a member.

Children in Norwegian schools are required to take courses in religion. This requirement has taken different forms over the years. Until 1997 the course was religious education, based in Lutheranism. It was not required for children who were not members of the Church of Norway. In 1997 the course was changed and called KRL (Christian Knowledge, Religious, and Ethical Education), and was now required of all school children with no exemptions. The main emphasis was on Christian education, but instruction was provided in other faiths. In 2004, the UN Human Rights Committee, and in 2007 the European Court of Human Rights in Strasbourg ruled that the compulsory nature of KRL violated freedom of religion. The course was therefore revised and renamed in 2007 as RLE (Religion, World Views, and Ethics).

## RELIGIOSITY

More than 80 percent of Norwegians are members of the Church of Norway, but few are active members. Approximately 3 percent of Norwegians attend church weekly, and 8 percent attend once a month. This varies geographically, with the greatest proportion of churchgoers in southern and western Norway. Despite low attendance at Sunday services, the majority of Norwegians still turn to the church for important rites of passage, although this practice is also on the decline. In 2008, 66 percent of 15-year-olds were confirmed in the church, and 70 percent of all children born in Norway were baptized. On the other end of the age spectrum, in 2008, 93 percent of all Norwegians received a church funeral.[11] Church weddings also remain popular, although the church does not conduct church weddings for same-sex couples. About 45 percent married in the church in 2008, while 33 percent had civil ceremonies, 5 percent married in other religious communities, and 17 percent married abroad.[12]

While traditional religious faith and practice have declined in the post–World War II era, there seems to be a growing spirituality and an increase in private and more individualistic religion. While 30 percent of Norwegians consider themselves to be nonreligious, 70 percent say they are either religious, spiritual but not religious, or both spiritual and religious.[13] While fewer people participate in such traditional religious practices as bedtime prayers with children or attending church, it has become more popular to light candles on graves, for example. While fewer believe in life after death, heaven, and hell, more believe in miracles. Many of the so-called spiritual people believe in contact with spirits, reincarnation, fortunetellers, and healing through prayer. Princess Märtha Louise sparked debate in 2007 when she opened an angel school, Astarte Education, and claimed to be psychic.[14] The motto of the school is "Use angels and your own power to create miracles in your life."[15]

Central Jamaat-e-Ahl-eSunnat Mosque. Located on the east side of Oslo on Urtegata. It serves the Pakistani Sunni Muslim community. (Courtesy of the author.)

The largest non-Christian religion in Norway is Islam, with nearly 93,000 members in 2009, mostly in Oslo, home of the largest immigrant population. Several mosques have been built in Oslo in recent years, with different ones established by different nationalities, but there are Islamic congregations all over Norway.

While there has been debate over the appropriateness of female police officers wearing a hijab, there are no laws against wearing religious symbols in public. Interestingly, studies have shown that ethnic Norwegian girls living in areas of Oslo dominated by Muslims appear to have been influenced by the more modest standards of dress common among Muslim girls.[16]

The next largest group is the Buddhists, with 12,000 members followed by Hindus, with 5,200. Of the nonreligious, philosophical societies, the

Humanist and Ethical Society (*Human-Etisk Forbund*) dominates, with more than 81,000 members. It was founded in 1956 and also arranges ceremonies that correspond to the rites of passage such as Christian baptism, confirmation, marriage, and funeral ceremonies.[17]

## NOTES

1. http://www.ssb.no/english/subjects/07/02/10/kirke_kostra_en/. Accessed 9/24/09.

2. http://www.ssb.no/trosamf_en/tab-2008-12-19-03-en.html. Accessed 9/24/09.

3. http://www.kirken.no/english/engelsk.cfm?artid=5276. Accessed 1/28/10.

4. H. R. Ellis Davidson, *Scandinavian Mythology* (New York: Hamlyn Publishing Group Limited, 1969).

5. http://www.aftenposten.no/nyheter/iriks/article3436503.ece. Accessed 1/10/10.

6. http://www.ub.uit.no/northernlights/eng/myths02.htm. Accessed 9/23/09.

7. Einar Molland, *Church Life in Norway 1800–1950*, trans. Harris Kaasa (Minneapolis: Augsburg Publishing House, 1957).

8. Inner Mission Association. http://bedehus.no. Accessed 1/20/10.

9. http://www.kirken.no/english/engelsk.cfm?artid=5277. Accessed 9/24/09.

10. http://www.kirken.no/english/news.cfm?artid=134384. Accessed 9/24/09.

11. http://www.ssb.no/english/subjects/07/02/10/kirke_kostra_en/. Accessed 9/24/09.

12. http://www.ssb.no/english/subjects/02/02/30/ekteskap_en/. Accessed 9/24/09.

13. Report by Pål Ketil Botvar. "Hva har skjedd siden 1991." KIFO, Centre for Church Research, based on a survey by ISSP (International Social Survey Programme), 2008. http://www.kifo.no/index.cfm?id=266947 Accessed 4/29/10.

14. http://www.nrk.no/nyheter/1.3024460. Accessed 9/24/09.

15. http://www.astarte-education.com/eng/. Accessed 9/24/09.

16. http://www.dagbladet.no/magasinet/2005/11/30/450847.html. Accessed 9/24/09.

17. http://www.ssb.no/english/subjects/07/02/10/trosamf_en/. Accessed 1/3/10.

# 4

# Marriage, Gender, Family, and Education

NORWAY and other Nordic countries are seen as leading the world in gender equality. Women have had the right to vote since 1913, and they are entitled to more than a year of paid maternity leave. According to the UN Human Development Report 2009,[1] Norway ranks second behind Sweden on the Gender Empowerment Measure, which includes such measures as number of female legislators, senior officials and managers, and female professional and technical workers, and the ratio of estimated female-to-male earned income. It also ranks second behind Australia on the Gender-Related Development Index,[2] which includes life expectancy, adult literacy rate, and estimated earned income for females and males. Norway appears at the top of Save the Children's 11th Annual Mothers' Index in 2010.[3]

Norwegian women have had equal status with men in divorce, child custody, and property rights since laws on these topics were passed in 1918 and 1927. Authors such as Henrik Ibsen have featured powerful women in plays and novels. Novelist Sigrid Undset won the Nobel Prize for Literature in 1928. Women hold and have held leadership positions in politics, including serving as prime minister, cabinet members, police commissioners, mayors, and leaders of political parties, including the far right party, the Progress Party. Although it cannot be said that Norway has achieved perfect equality between men and women, values of gender equality permeate society, both in terms of government policy and everyday life. There is a continuing debate on the topic, and numerous women- and family-friendly policies have been adopted into law.

## Marriage

Both popular practice and laws governing marriage and cohabitation have changed tremendously during the last 40 years. Until 1972, it was illegal for unmarried men and women to live together. Now it has become so usual and accepted for people to live together outside of marriage that there is a commonly used term for it: *samboerskap. Samboere,* or cohabitants, are defined as two people of any gender, over age 18, who live together in a condition resembling marriage. You can only be defined as a *samboer* with one person at a time. According to the Ministry of Children and Families, 70 percent of those who are living together in their 20s are *samboere* and only 30 percent are married. In fact, the age of first marriage has increased from 25.2 to 34.1 for men and 22.8 to 31.2 for women since the 1970s.[4] Four out of ten children are born to couples who are *samboere,* although it is common for couples to marry before they have a second or subsequent child.[5] Although some couples choose *samboerskap* because they believe it serves as a sort of practice marriage, in reality, the risk for breaking up among *samboere* with children is more than three times that of married couples with children.[6]

While the law does not treat married couples and cohabiting couples exactly the same, cohabiting couples have gained more rights in recent years. In 2009, the law was changed to allow *samboere* who have lived together for at least five years and who have children together the right of inheritance. If they do not have children together, the surviving partner has no right to inherit unless there is a will specifying the inheritance. Although it has been a topic of debate, *samboere* are not allowed to adopt children together.

A new, gender-neutral marriage law went into effect on January 1, 2009, making both *samboerskap* and marriage gender-neutral concepts. This means that gay or lesbian couples can get married and enjoy the same rights and privileges as heterosexual couples.[7] As of 2010, however, homosexual couples are still unable to marry in the Church of Norway, although the Church has received permission to develop a liturgy to permit such marriages. Other churches or philosophical societies have the right to marry same sex couples, if they so choose.

From 1993 until the new marriage law took effect, same sex couples could register a partnership. To enter into a registered partnership, at least one of the partners had to have Norwegian (or Danish, Swedish, or Icelandic) citizenship and had to be living in Norway. If neither partner was a Nordic citizen, a partnership still could be registered if one of the partners had lived in Norway the two previous years before the registration. Same sex couples were not allowed to adopt children together, although one partner could adopt the other partner's biological children. Registrations took place before a notary public, and not in the church and not outside Norway (in an embassy, for example). The minimum age was 18. With the exception of artificial insemination and adoption of children, all rights and privileges of marriage applied. Those who entered into a registered partnership before January 1, 2009, may either retain the partnership or have it converted to marriage.

## DIVORCE

The divorce rate in Norway is comparable to that in other Western countries. The government feels that it is in the best interest of the child to have a relationship with both parents, and the laws are designed to achieve that end. About 80 percent of the children of divorce end up living with their mother, with the father having visitation rights or partial custody. Many men find this arrangement unfair and are working toward more equitable standards. Custodial parents must negotiate with the noncustodial parents when they wish to relocate.

## GENDER

A 2003 report by the UN Committee on the Elimination of Discrimination described Norway as a "haven for gender equality" and said that the country's equality policy had provided positive examples for other countries.[8] Even though conditions are good for women and have improved markedly during the last 40 years, concerns were expressed in the report about continuing discrimination in certain areas, including inequalities in economic decision making, violence against women, prostitution, and the rights of immigrant women.

The 1970s was an important decade for women's rights. Laws were passed establishing preschools and guaranteeing the right to abortion, equal rights, and childbearing leave. The original Gender Equality Act was passed in 1978. It was based on The Convention on the Elimination of All Forms of Discrimination against Women adopted in 1979 by the UN General Assembly. This act required public authorities to promote gender equality in all sectors of life. In 2002, the Act was amended to apply to the private sector as well, requiring affirmative action to promote gender equality in the workplace. It also clarifies the concept of equal pay for work of equal value and grants additional protection during pregnancy and childbearing leave, as well as stronger rules against sexual harassment. The Act is enforced by the Equality and Anti-Discrimination Ombud,[9] an independent office, and the Equality and Anti-Discrimination Tribunal.[10] The Ministry of Children and Equality has overall responsibility for coordinating gender-related issues.

There is also a Center for Gender Equality, which is a publicly financed institution working to promote equal opportunity.[11]

Until the 1980s, Norwegian women were represented in the workforce at a lower rate than in the United States and elsewhere in Europe. The participation of women in the 15- to 64-year-old age group in the labor force has increased from 42 percent in 1972 to 70 percent in 2008, although a large number of women work part time. In 2008, the percentage of women working part time stood at 43 percent, which is significantly higher than the OECD average of 25 percent. Women are still overrepresented in fields such as health care and education, and underrepresented in business and industry.

Former Prime Minister Gro Harlem Brundtland put the issue of gender equality on the political agenda by naming women to 8 of the 18 ministerial positions in her second administration, which came into power in 1986. Her idea of having at least 40 percent and no more than 60 percent women representatives became known as the 60/40 rule and was quickly applied voluntarily to the election lists of most political parties. It then expanded to other areas of public life with the requirement that both genders be represented by at least 40 percent on all public committees, councils, and boards. The 60/40 rule was then extended to boards of state-owned and publicly traded companies in revisions to the Gender Equality Act in 2005. Although this new law triggered great debate and skepticism, it has been a success. While in 2002 only 6.6 percent of board members of publicly traded countries were female, by 2008 95 percent of all company executive boards had reached the required 40 percent.

The struggle for gender equality in Norway has long focused on increased rights and protections for women. In a Government White Paper released by the Ministry of Children and Equality in December 2008, however, it was pointed out that gender equality is about both men and women. Although conditions have changed and improved during the last 20 years, men still spend less time with their children and families than women, are overrepresented in crime statistics, are more likely to be perpetrators of domestic violence, and are more likely to drop out of school. On the other hand, they still make more money than women and hold more positions of power in society than women.

While women are entering previously male-dominated workplaces, men are still underrepresented in health care and lower level schools. Norway, along with the other Nordic countries, has the most gender-segregated labor market in the industrialized world.[12] The majority of people work with colleagues of the same gender. This is considered a problem because female-dominated jobs tend to be less well paid, which contributes to the pay gap that still exists between men and women in Norway. While precise comparisons are difficult to make, the median salaries of women are approximately 87 percent of those of men. Many explanations for the discrepancy have been offered. More women work part time than men, and men are more likely to receive larger bonuses and to work overtime. Women are overrepresented in lower-paying professions such as early childhood education and primary and secondary schools, and also in such professions as nursing, custodial services, and office work. More men are employed in higher education, construction, industry, and mining, and as craftsmen, engineers, and drivers. Genders are more balanced, however, in the postal service, marketing, and advertising. More women work in the public sector, where jobs tend to have lower salaries than comparable positions in private business. According to Statistics Norway, 47 percent of women and 19 percent of men work in the public sector, figures that have remained stable during recent years. Women are more commonly employed in local government, with a more equal representation in higher levels of government.[13] These figures have remained stable during the last few years.

Gender divisions are also seen in the educational choices of young people. More females tend to choose subjects such as humanities, arts, teacher training, and health and social services, whereas men choose sciences and technical fields to a greater degree. More women are, however, choosing such fields as medicine, finance, natural sciences, and engineering than previously. Men have not shown the same tendency to move into female-dominated fields. Although more women take lower university degrees, the gender balance shifts in favor of men at the doctoral level.

## FAMILY

The 2008 Government White Paper released by the Ministry of Children and Equality takes the position that positive steps are needed to ensure that men take an increasingly active role in childrearing, beginning at birth. Since the 1970s, fathers have been entitled to a portion of the childbearing leave. It was not until 1993, however, that a portion of the leave was reserved for the father's exclusive use. This paternal quota has contributed to a more active role on the part of fathers and revolutionized men's use of parental leave. Initially the leave was four weeks, but it has been gradually increased so that since July 2009 the paternity quota has been extended to a full 10 weeks of the total leave, which is 56 weeks with 80 percent pay or 46 weeks with 100 percent pay. (Adoptive parents are entitled to 53 weeks with 80% pay and 43 weeks at 100%.) The goal is for men to have 14 weeks. Twelve weeks of the total leave are reserved for the mother, three weeks before the birth and nine weeks post-partum. The rest can be divided between the parents. It is also possible to combine work and leave, with flexible parental leave until the child is three years old. This option is growing in popularity, especially among parents in the 30- to 34-year-old group.

But the right to the paternity quota must be earned by the mother, who must have been employed at least half-time for a minimum of six months prior to giving birth. The father does not have an independent right to the paternity quota, although since 2000 he has been able to earn the right to parental leave, if he has been employed prior to the birth, as long as the mother either goes out into paid employment or approved education. If the mother stays home after the birth, the father is not entitled to parental leave. Another recent change extends the right to parental leave to self-employed people. Most fathers do take advantage of the *pappapermisjon*, with about 90 percent of eligible fathers taking at least some of the time to which they are entitled, although this varies geographically. Few, however, take more than the minimum quota designated by law. The government has been discussing mandating that one third of the parental leave be designated for the father, but there is no consensus on this issue. Some point out that because the amount of money paid out during parental leave is determined by the mother's earnings, many families cannot afford to have the father take a leave from his job.

It is felt that establishing the father as an equal caregiver from birth ensures a greater participation later, for the role fathers play in the family once the parental leave period is over is equally important. It is common to see fathers out and about with their infants and small children. Statistics show that men contribute slightly more to housework and child care now than in 1971, about 30 minutes more. At the same time women's work in the home has declined by a greater amount, about two hours a day less since 1971. Both spend more time on leisure activities.

Families that do not send their young children (one to three years of age) to a state-subsidized day-care facility have the right to receive an extra monthly cash payment. The number of families taking advantage of this benefit has declined in recent years. There is some concern, however, that immigrant families, whose children would benefit from attending a Norwegian pre-school, are more likely to keep their children at home and receive the cash benefit. This cash benefit may be discontinued.

Another family-friendly law is the sick leave policy. Not only do Norwegians have sick leave available for themselves, as needed, but each parent also receives additional time off to care for sick children. If a family has one child, each parent may take 10 days a year if the child or the usual caregiver is ill. They may have 15 days a year if they have more than one child and 20 days if they are a single parent of one child or 30 days if they are a single parent of more than one child. Having a chronically ill or disabled child entitles parents to have an additional 10 days for each child, double that if they are a single parent. While this right ends the year a healthy child turns 12, it is extended to age 18 for chronically ill or disabled children.

Norwegians enjoy generous vacations, with all employees entitled to a minimum of four weeks a year. Those over 60 get an additional week. A minimum of three weeks of the vacation may be taken during the summer. Vacation pay is earned during the previous calendar year, which means that employees are entitled to a full vacation even if they switch jobs during the year.

## EDUCATION[14]

Today nearly all the schools in Norway are public. Only 2 percent of all pupils attend private schools—mostly Steiner (Waldorf) schools, Montessori schools, or religious schools. Norwegian children have 10 years of obligatory education beginning at age six, and the majority also complete some form of upper secondary education. The school year runs from mid-August through the third week in June. There are few after-school activities such as music, sports, or scouting. Volunteer organizations sponsor these activities outside the auspices of schools. Many younger children (grades 1–4) attend before- or after-school programs at their school. These programs are intended to provide care to young children whose parents are at work but are also supposed to have educational and socializing components. Children get snacks and help with their homework, and have time for free play.

Before the eighteenth century, educational opportunities for most children were limited. Since the Middle Ages cathedral schools had existed in the larger cities to educate the clergy. Wealthier children either had tutors at home or attended private schools. The earliest public school legislation, however, dates from 1739 when the right to a free education was extended to all children from the age of seven. Still, even with this law the level and content of education were determined by social class. The lowest classes received only the minimum basic reading knowledge necessary to read the Bible as well as Luther's catechism and Pontoppidan's explanation of the catechism. The first ABC books, designed to help in this process, were published in 1777. By 1783, the first school for boys and girls was established in Trondheim. Intended for middle-class children, it was the first such school in Scandinavia.

By the nineteenth century, school began to be viewed as a part of nation building, so children also required education to be effective citizens. This new philosophy was reflected in reforms of the 1840s and school laws of 1827 and 1848. These laws also aimed at improving both teacher training and the schools for the lower classes in the cities, which had lagged behind the rural schools. Although the schools in the rural areas were mostly *omgangsskoler*, or ambulatory schools, where the teachers traveled around from farm to farm, they were still better than the *fattigskoler*, or schools for the poor, available to the lower classes in the cities, where there might be 100 children in a single class. While only 5 percent of rural children did not receive any instruction, in the cities the percentage was as high as 18 percent. In 1860, a new law required a permanent school building in any area with more than 30 children and introduced the concept of education for good citizenship, instead of just religious training. In 1889, schools had to be divided into age groups and such subjects as history, geography, and science were added. That same year Nordahl Rohlfsen published his reader, a book that was used into the 1950s.

Further reforms have been undertaken with increasing frequency, and often reflected of a tug of war between local and central authorities. In 1974, for example, a national curriculum was created for all schools, but in 1986 local control was strengthened. In 1994 a reform of the upper secondary schools, reducing the number of vocational programs, was initiated. In 1997, there was again increased focus on knowledge and on common national content. That year the age children started school was lowered from seven to six.

The Quality Reform of university education was introduced in 2003. This reform changed the degree structure in Norwegian higher education to the common European one used in Bologna—with Bachelor's, Master's, and Doctorate degrees—and moved grading from a number system to letters—A, B, C, D, E, and F. In addition, students were to receive more feedback from professors and more contact outside of lectures.

The most recent reform of the 10-year compulsory and upper secondary education was the 2006 Knowledge Promotion, a comprehensive reform of curricula and school structure. It increased the focus on basic skills and improvement of education through outcome-based learning. Reading and writing are emphasized from first grade, new curricula have been created with clearly defined learning outcomes, the number of instructional hours for various subjects has been redistributed, and increased freedom has been given to local school districts with respect to teaching methods, materials, and organization of classroom instruction.

### Early Childhood Education

The government's goal of preschool access to all children has for the most part been achieved. Today about 87 percent of children between the ages of one and five attend preschool and day care. Fully 96 percent of children have attended before beginning first grade. Preschools (*barnehager*), called Kindergartens in Figure 4.1, are subsidized by the state, and a maximum cost has been established to make them affordable to all. Because preschool attendance is so ubiquitous, adjustment to school can be difficult for those few who do not attend. This adjustment can be particularly hard for minority children, who are less likely to go to preschool and often come from families where the

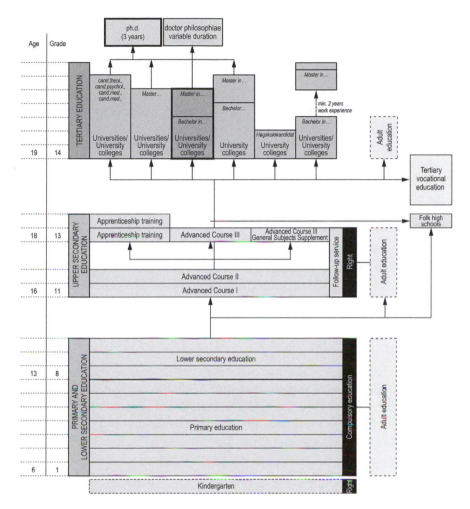

**Figure 4.1**
The Norwegian Education System 2010. (Statistics Norway.)

primary language spoken at home is not Norwegian. They are at risk of starting school at a disadvantage both linguistically and socially.

### Compulsory Education

Children start school the year they turn six. Normally they begin in the fall, but some schools have begun experimenting with allowing the children to begin in the spring of the year, if they have turned six. The first level of school is called *Barneskole*, which covers grades 1–7. The emphasis is more on socialization than academics, especially in the first few grades. The school day is relatively short, and students do not receive letter or number grades, just narrative evaluations shared during parent-teacher conferences. Schools do not serve hot lunches or have cafeterias. Instead students bring their lunch, called *matpakke*, from home. A proper *matpakke* consists of open-faced sandwiches with meat or cheese, and vegetables or fruit. Schools make milk and fresh fruit available for purchase.

Norwegian students start learning English as early as first grade. In grades 8–10, or *Ungdomsskole*, students begin receiving grades and base much of their work on projects and group work. The following subjects are covered in grades 1–10: Norwegian, math, social studies, arts and crafts, nature studies, English, second and third foreign languages, music, food and health, physical education, and religion, life view and ethics (RLE).

### Upper Secondary School

Upper secondary school, or *Videregående skole*, leads to university admissions certification, vocational competence, or competence at a lower level, and is not compulsory. Students normally apply for admission to educational programs at schools in the county in which they live. Students are admitted based on grades from lower secondary school, but have the right to be accepted to one of their three chosen programs. There are three university preparatory programs: music, dance and drama; sports and physical educational; or general studies. Students may choose a vocational program instead, selecting from nine different programs lasting three or four years, including apprenticeships. Some of these programs include building and construction, agriculture, fishing and forestry, and restaurant and food processing, among others.[15] While most students attend *Videregående skole* between the ages of 16 and 19, they have the right to attend upper secondary school until the age of 25. Unemployed adults or immigrants may also apply for special permission to attend after that age. Some 56 percent of the students complete their education in the standard period of time (three or four years, depending on the program), while 70 percent complete it within five years. In 2008, 78 percent of all Norwegians had completed upper secondary school. Students may also take supplementary courses to fulfill university admissions requirements or vocational competence at a later date. Teachers at the upper secondary level must hold a master's degree or similar advanced degree requiring at least five to six years of higher education.

The graduating seniors are called *russ*. Their parties and celebrations extend from May 1 to *Syttende mai* (May 17), Norway's national day, when they march both in the children's parade in the morning and a special *russetog* parade in the afternoon. They dress in colored overalls and caps corresponding to the program they have completed. The most common color is red, which indicates general university-preparatory studies. Blue is for economics, while the least common colors are black for vocational studies and green for agricultural. As described

Graduating upper secondary school seniors, "Russ," celebrating May 17 in the children's parade. (Courtesy of the author.)

in more detail in Chapter 5, *russ* spend their time leading up to *Syttende mai* in rather raucous celebration. What brings them down to earth are their final exams, which occur later in May and into June.

## POSTSECONDARY EDUCATION

The seven universities in Norway are located in Oslo, Bergen, Trondheim, Tromsø, Ås, Kristiansand, and Stavanger. The oldest and largest university is the University of Oslo, founded in 1811. Before that time students had to go abroad to study. In addition, there are several dozen university colleges offering a wide range of programs, and specialized universities and colleges for music, sports science, management, veterinary studies, theology, and architecture and design, among others. No tuition is charged for the vast majority of postsecondary institutions in Norway, although there are a number of private colleges as well. Norwegian parents are not expected to support their students financially once they have completed secondary school. Students are eligible for financial aid through the Norwegian State Educational Loan Fund, which grants both loans and stipends to pay for living expenses, travel, and books. Many of the loans are converted to stipends if students complete their degrees on schedule. As mentioned previously, Norway implemented the Bologna Accord, which stipulates a three-year Bachelor's Degree, two-year Master's Degree, and three-year doctorate, in 2002–2003. Exceptions to this degree structure are professional degrees in teaching, law, medicine, psychology, theology, veterinary science, and architecture.

### Folk High Schools[16]

Folk high schools are one-year boarding schools based on the ideal of lifelong learning and do not offer degrees. They were inspired by the educational ideas of N. S. F. Grundtvig, the nineteenth-century Danish philosopher who started the first one in Denmark in the 1840s. Students are usually between the ages of 18 and 25, although most are 19–20. Students often choose a year at a folk high school as a gap year before attending university. The schools also welcome international students and offer instruction in Norwegian as a foreign language. There are 77 folk high schools in Norway, offering a wide variety of academic and nonacademic programs. These range from arts and crafts, dance, theater, and music to organic farming, sports and outdoor life, and cooking and baking. Most schools have both required classes and activities as well as electives. They often take trips in Norway and abroad as part of the educational experience, and shared learning is emphasized. The schools are small, averaging 80–90 students each. About 6,000 students attended folk high schools in 2008–2009.

### Study Abroad

The number of students studying abroad has declined from its peak in 2002–2003, although the numbers increased slightly again in 2008–2009. According to statistics from the Norwegian State Educational Loan Fund, 21,629 students studied abroad in 2008–2009, with 11,994 working on a degree abroad and 7,129 participating in a short-term exchange program. About 58 percent of students studying abroad are women. While medicine and economics/administration were the most popular subjects for those students taking an entire degree abroad, social sciences and psychology were high on the list for exchange programs, along with economics and administration. The university educational reform of 2003 has made it easier for students to incorporate a study abroad program into their degree program in Norway, but the numbers have not increased as much as the government may have hoped, with only about 6.2 percent of all students studying abroad. Students cite various reasons for choosing not to study abroad, including difficulties with language, getting information, and with financing.

The most popular destinations have varied with changes in government policy. In 1998 the most popular study abroad site was the United Kingdom, followed by the United States and Denmark. Ten years later the UK is still number one, followed by Denmark and Australia, Poland, and the United States, which now hosts fewer than half the number of students it did in 1998. Australia had become a popular study location for many once the State Educational Loan Fund began financing study outside of Europe and North America. It appears, however, that the popularity of Australia is on the wane, and more students are selecting to study in various countries in Europe, perhaps as a result of exchange programs such as the ERASMUS Programme between Norway and EU countries, as well as the increase in English-language programs in Eastern Europe. On the rise are Poland, the Czech Republic, Slovakia, and Denmark, while Germany, Italy, Ireland, and Spain are declining. The most popular destinations for exchange studies are the United States, Australia, Great Britain, Tanzania, and China.[17]

Internationalization is a high priority for Norwegian universities, although much of the motivation comes from mandates by the Ministry of Education and Research. In addition to sending their own students abroad, Norwegian universities wish to attract more students from other countries. As a result, increasing numbers of programs are offered in English, particularly at the master's level. Nonetheless, only about 2 percent of students at Norwegian colleges and universities are international.

## GENDER DIFFERENCES IN SCHOOLS

Girls typically outperform boys in school. They earn higher grades, they read better, and they tend to go on to higher education at higher levels than boys. This phenomenon is particularly true among young people of immigrant background. Girls are also more likely than boys to study abroad.

### Issues and Challenges for Norwegian Schools

A major concern for Norwegian schools is poor student test results compared with other European countries, particularly in mathematics. Some have suggested that Norwegian schools lack discipline in the classroom and that the freedom Norwegian students enjoy affects learning negatively. Others say that Norwegian schools place greater emphasis on independent and critical thinking and less on rote learning than schools in other countries.

Another concern is the achievement gap between children coming from educated, wealthier families and those whose parents have lower education and income levels. Despite the fact that school is free in Norway, until fall 2009 students had to purchase their own books in upper secondary school. Since then, all schoolbooks and materials are free of charge at all levels (secondary and below).

Another issue is the academic achievement of children with immigrant backgrounds. An extensive debate over the issue of language and the best way to teach children from non-Norwegian backgrounds is ongoing. Children have the right to receive special instruction in Norwegian until they can function in a regular classroom, but the extent to which they should be taught their own native language in the Norwegian schools is controversial. The issue is complicated by the fact that hundreds of different languages are represented among the immigrant population. Another concern is the gender gap in educational achievement within the immigrant population. Although Norwegian-born girls from immigrant families complete secondary education at the same levels as ethnic Norwegian children, the same cannot be said for boys with immigrant backgrounds.

## Notes

1. http://hdr.undp.org/en/media/HDR_2009_EN_Complete.pdf. Accessed 10/1/09.
2. http://hdr.undp.org/en/statistics/indices/gdi_gem/. Accessed 12/28/09.
3. http://www.savethechildren.net/alliance/media/newsdesk/2010-05-04.html Accessed 5/7/10.
4. http://www.ssb.no/english/subjects/02/02/30/ekteskap_en/tab-2009-08-27-06-en.html. Accessed 9/3/09.
5. http://www.ssb.no/fodte_en/. Accessed 9/30/09.
6. http://www.regjeringen.no/upload/kilde/bfd/bro/2005/0004/ddd/pdfv/252014-samboere_2005.pdf. Accessed 9/30/09.
7. http://www.regjeringen.no/nb/dep/bld/tema/homofile-og-lesbiske/partnerskap.html?id=1067. Accessed 9/3/09.
8. http://www.un.org/News/Press/docs/2003/wom1377.doc.htm. Accessed 9/30/09.
9. http://www.ldo.no/en/. Accessed 9/30/09.
10. http://www.diskrimineringsnemnda.no/wips/1416077327/. Accessed 9/30/09.
11. http://www.gender.no/. Accessed 9/30/09.
12. http://www.regjeringen.no/en/dep/bld/Documents/Propositions-and-reports/stmeld/2008-2009/report-no-8-2008-2009-to-the-storting.html?id=556148. Accessed 9/30/09.
13. http://www.ssb.no/english/subjects/00/02/10/ola_kari_en/arbeid_en/. Accessed 10/2/09.
14. http://www.kildenett.no. Accessed 10/1/09.
15. http://vilbli.no/. Accessed 10/2/09.
16. http://www.folkehogskole.no. Accessed 10/2/09.
17. Information and statistics from the Norwegian State Educational Loan Fund. http://www.lanekassen.no. Accessed 1/23/10.

# 5

# Holidays and Leisure Activities

ONE OF THE HALLMARKS of post–World War II life in Norway has been the expansion of wealth and leisure time. Norwegians now spend significantly more time traveling, enjoying outdoor activity, watching television, and other such activities than as recently as 1970. At the same time as the workweek has shrunk to 37.5 hours, vacations have increased to a minimum of 4 weeks. Many workers have 5 or 6 weeks in addition to numerous other special holidays. In fact, Norwegians work an average of only 1,411 hours per year, which is among the lowest in the world.[1] Importance is placed on balancing work and leisure, and it is not considered inappropriate for either father or mother to leave the office promptly at 4 or 4:30 to pick up a child at daycare.

## HOLIDAYS

A look at a Norwegian calendar shows no fewer than 22 flag days and public holidays each year. Ten of these are official holidays from work, including religious observances, such as Christmas, Ascension Day, and the days surrounding Sunday religious holidays, such as Maundy Thursday, Good Friday, Easter Monday and Whit-Monday (the Monday after Pentecost), and the day after Christmas; and political or national days, such as Workers Day (May 1) and Constitution Day (May 17).

New Year's Eve is celebrated in Norway much like in the rest of the world. Fireworks are especially popular around midnight. Many Norwegians also gather around the television to listen to the King's New Year's speech earlier in the evening. On New Year's Day, the Prime Minister also holds a televised address to the nation.

Easter has lost much of its religious content in secularized Norway. School children have a long vacation lasting 10 days from the day before Palm Sunday through Easter Monday. Adults usually have several days off, from Holy Thursday through Easter Monday, although many people take extra vacation days. About one in eight Norwegians takes an Easter vacation, with higher income Norwegians dominating the vacationers. Traditionally the Norwegian Easter vacation was spent in the mountains, at a rustic cabin, skiing during the daytime and reading murder mysteries in the evenings around the woodstove. More recently, however, it has become popular to travel to someplace warm, such as Greece, Spain, or even Thailand, although Sweden and Denmark are also popular. About 20 percent of those taking an Easter vacation travel outside Norway.[2] Whether Norwegians choose to stay home or travel abroad, however, they will nonetheless claim that skiing in the mountains is the most typically Norwegian thing to do during Easter vacation. Nearly everything is closed on Good Friday and on Easter Sunday. Even newspapers shut down production for a few days during Easter. Because the stores in neighboring Sweden do not close, however, it is also quite popular to make a shopping run to the border towns to stock up on meat, sweets, and alcohol, all of which are considerably cheaper in Sweden.

May is a month of holidays in Norway, beginning with May 1, International Workers Day, which has been celebrated in Norway since 1890. This day has traditionally been dedicated to the struggle for workers' rights, both in Norway and internationally, and is marked by parades, speeches, and demonstrations. While in the early days the main issue was the eight-hour workday, today the concern is employment for all.

Norwegian Constitution Day is commonly referred to as *Syttende mai*, or the Seventeenth of May. While many Norwegian Americans incorrectly refer to this day as Norwegian Independence day, it is important to note that this day commemorates the signing of the Norwegian constitution, on May 17, 1814. Although Norway had a few months of independence that year, it did not finally become an independent nation until 1905. The celebration of the day actually began in the 1800s while Norway still shared a king with Sweden.

*Syttende mai* is a day dedicated to children. The children's parade, or *barnetog,* is the main event, arranged in every city and town in the country. The parade is organized by schools, with each school led by its banner and often its marching band. The children and their teachers either dress in their best clothes or in national costume (*bunad*). Nearly everyone wears a rosette with red, white, and blue ribbons. The graduating students from upper secondary school, called *Russ*, have a special status. As described in Chapter 4, they wear caps and overalls the color of their main course of study. In the period leading up to the big day, the graduating seniors celebrate in a variety of ways. They perform various stunts to earn trinkets or knots they tie into the tassels on their caps, ranging from the harmless—kissing a police officer or spending the night at a traffic roundabout—to risky behavior involving sex and alcohol. They also have parties, and sometimes even go a bit crazy and cause some damage in their local communities. They neither wash their overalls nor remove them, except when sleeping. They make calling cards with their names, photos, and funny slogans, which are both exchanged and eagerly collected by younger children. Spoof newspapers are published and sold. Many students join together to buy a car, bus, or truck painted the same color as their overalls, which they then equip with extravagant sound systems and use at the parties. The *Russ* participate in the children's parade in the morning, and then in some cities have their own parade in the afternoon. A more sedate *Syttende mai* tradition for adults involves the laying of wreathes, along with speeches and choir music at the graves and statues of famous Norwegian cultural figures such as Henrik Ibsen, Ivar Aasen, Bjørnstjerne Bjørnson, and Henrik Wergeland.

Other spring holidays include Ascension Day, which comes on the Thursday 39 days after Easter Sunday, and *Pinse*, known in English as Whitsunday or Pentecost. Pentecost comes 49 days after Easter, so it can fall as early as May 10 or as late as June 13. The first and second days of Pentecost (Sunday and Monday) are both holidays. Newspapers are not normally published on Pentecost Sunday, and television stations do not broadcast commercials. In the 1990s, the government proposed making these two days regular workdays, but the proposal failed in Parliament.

St. John's Eve (*Sankthansaften*), celebrated on June 23, is really more of a secular celebration than a religious one, but does have its roots in the commemoration of the birth of John the Baptist. Also called *Jonsok*, the day is celebrated in many parts of Norway with enormous bonfires. The evening is spent eating food grilled outdoors, plus *rømmegrøt* (sour cream porridge) and strawberries, listening to music, dancing, and going for boat rides.

*Olsok*, or Olav's Wake, commemorates the death of Olav II Haraldson, also known as St. Olav. He fell in battle on July 29, 1030, at Stiklestad, near Trondheim. While not as widely celebrated as *Sankthans*, it is celebrated in those areas of Norway where Olav traveled, especially in Trøndelag, in central Norway. The most extravagant events are those at Stiklestad itself, where the play *Spelet om Heilag Olav* has been performed on an outdoor stage every year since 1954. Olsok Days last a week, culminating on July 29, and feature concerts, exhibits, a medieval market, and workshops, as well as four performances of the play.

### Christmas (Jul)

The Christmas season begins in early December. Public Christmas trees and street decorations are usually put on display the first Sunday of Advent, when the first of four Advent candles is lit. Children often count down the days to Christmas with a *julekalender*, or advent calendar. Each morning they open a window of the calendar and usually receive a small gift, such as chocolate or a pencil eraser. In addition, the television stations broadcast Christmas calendar programs, featuring a new episode each evening from December 1 to December 24. While new programs are occasionally produced, old standbys such as *The Julekalender*, with the band The Traveling Strawberries, *Jul i Blåfjell* (Christmas in Blue Mountain), or *Jul i Skomakergata* (Christmas on Shoemaker Street) remain popular and are rebroadcast time and again. The Swedish tradition of celebrating Saint Lucia on December 11 has been imported to Norway and is particularly popular in elementary schools and day-care centers. One of the girls is chosen to wear a headpiece with candles (usually battery operated now) and a long, white robe, and boys dressed in white robes and carrying a stick with a star on it serve as the star boys. They process while singing *Santa Lucia*, which is usually quite a challenging song for small children.

The weeks leading up to Christmas are popular times for employees to enjoy the *julebord*, or company Christmas party, usually held at a restaurant. Restaurants also offer *lutefisk* dinners, at a premium price, which are then rated by the local newspapers. See Chapter 6 for more information on *lutefisk*. Many places offer *pepperkaker* (gingerbread cookies) and *gløgg* (spiced wine or juice) with almonds and raisins. Most Norwegians do not put up a Christmas tree until December 23, which is known as Little Christmas Eve, or even on Christmas Eve itself. The tree is decorated with white lights and other decorations, including strings of small Norwegian flags, heart-shaped baskets, and paper chains. The weeks before this date, however, are a time of preparation. The house must be cleaned thoroughly, and the traditional seven kinds of cookies must be baked—or purchased at the bakery. A bundle of grain is hung up for the birds—the *julenek*.

Christmas Eve is the main Christmas event in Norway. Many Norwegians who otherwise never attend church go to the afternoon Christmas Eve service. Christmas is welcomed at 5 PM with the ringing of church bells. Christmas Eve and Christmas Day are reserved for family celebrations. Most families have a dinner with foods traditional for their own family and region of Norway. Rice porridge is common on Christmas Eve, although in the olden days it was more common to eat sour cream porridge, or *rømmegrøt*. An almond is hidden in the porridge, and the lucky one who finds the almond wins a marzipan pig. For dinner on Christmas Eve, some people eat *lutefisk*,

*Julenek.* This bundle of grain is put out at Christmas to provide food for the birds. (Courtesy of the author.)

while others specialize in pork ribs or salted lamb ribs, called *pinnekjøtt.* Others eat fresh codfish or *medisterkaker,* meatballs made of a special mixture of ground pork and spices like ginger, nutmeg, cloves, allspice, salt, and pepper. After dinner on Christmas Eve, the gifts are opened, and families with children often receive a visit from the Christmas elf, or *julenisse.* Because the part of the *julenisse* is frequently played by a willing neighbor or uncle wearing a mask with a white beard and a red stocking cap and suit, his appearance is quite often identical to the American Santa Claus, although usually quite a bit slimmer. The *julenisse* brings a sack of gifts for the children, asking them first: "*Er det noen snille barn her?*" (Are there any nice children here?)

The days between Christmas and New Year's are called *romjul,* and are a time for celebrating with friends and people outside the immediate family. Children might be invited to a *juletrefest* (Christmas tree party) as late as mid-January. At these parties children walk around the Christmas tree while holding hands and singing Christmas carols.

Another tradition, performed by some between Christmas and New Year, is *julebukk.* Particular *julebukk* traditions have varied from place to place and generation to generation in Norway, and the tradition migrated to the United States and was common in Norwegian-American communities into the twentieth century. In Norway today it is mostly children dressed in costumes and masks who visit the neighbors and sing Christmas carols in exchange for cookies and candy. The word *julebukk* means Christmas goat, and refers to the Old Norse tradition of the straw goat, which probably represented goats belonging to Thor.

Celebrations continue throughout the Christmas season, which lasts until Epiphany (January 6, the thirteenth day of Christmas), or even until January 13, the twentieth day of Christmas.[3] That is a favorite time for a party to take down the Christmas tree and put away the decorations.

## Leisure Activities

Norwegian employees are legally entitled to a minimum of four weeks plus one day vacation, although many labor contracts stipulate five weeks. Employees over 60 years old get one additional week. Workers are entitled to take three weeks of this vacation between June 1 and September 30. Even new employees are entitled to vacation, although time is limited to one week if they began work after September 30. Vacation pay is earned the previous calendar year, with 10.2 percent of earnings paid the following year (12.5% for employees over 60). This means that if a person has just entered the labor market, having just completed an education program, for example, he or she will still have the right to take a vacation, but will not have accumulated vacation pay. An employee who becomes ill or injured during vacation and would have been on documented sick leave for at least a week is entitled to make up the lost vacation at another time.

About 85 percent of Norwegians travel away from home on vacation, averaging 1.5 trips a year.[4] This puts them at the top of European vacationers statistically, together with Germans. People with higher incomes are more likely to take a vacation, around 90 percent of them, although about half of lower-income Norwegians do so. Interestingly, these lower-income Norwegians tend to take longer vacations, perhaps because many of them are students or pensioners, who have more time than money. Many Norwegians vacation in Norway, either staying at a cabin in the mountains or at the seashore. Others visit friends and family or stay in hotels. Traveling abroad is also popular, particularly trips to warm and sunny destinations, if the summer is cool and rainy. According to Statistics Norway, nearly 60 percent of vacations lasting more than four nights are abroad. Spain is the most common destination for Norwegians, but Denmark, Sweden, and Greece are also popular.

According to a survey of OECD countries, Norwegians spend more time on leisure activities than people of any other country, around 27 percent of their time.[5] The amount of leisure Norwegians enjoy is increasing; since 1970 the average Norwegian has 75 minutes more per day for leisure activities, totaling about 6.5 hours a week. Because hours spent on work or education have remained stable since then, the difference seems to be due to the reduced amount of time spent on housework and personal needs.[6] Norwegians seem to agree that it is important to make a clear distinction between work and leisure.

Outdoor recreation is immensely popular among most Norwegians; 90 percent claim to engage in some kind of outdoor activities. Most are fond of saying that Norwegians are born "*med ski på beina*" (with skis on their feet). The Norwegian word for outdoor recreation is *Friluftsliv*, which translates as fresh air life. More than 70 percent of Norwegians exercise at least once a week, with fast walking, skiing, jogging or running, and bicycling the most popular. Eight out of ten Norwegians have taken a long hike in the woods or mountains in the last year. The popularity of a variety of sports and other activities is shown in Figure 5.1.

Hunting and fishing are also increasingly popular avocations. Norway ranks among the top four countries in Europe with respect to the percentage of the population who hunt, surpassed only by Ireland, Cyprus, and Finland. One of five men hunts, representing more than 90 percent of hunters. However, increasing numbers of women are added to the hunting registry each year. The number of women hunters increased by 50 percent between 2001 and 2009, while men's numbers only went up 12 percent. Red deer, roe deer, wild reindeer, moose, grouse, and other small animals, depending on location, are the most popular game.[7] Sports fishing in rivers and on the sea is also popular. There are approximately 600 salmon streams in Norway.

Norwegians are also avid readers. Seven of ten report reading the newspaper daily, although this number has declined in recent years. They also enjoy frequent visits to museums and libraries. On average, they borrow five books or other media from libraries annually and visit museums twice a year. On the other hand, few Norwegians attend opera, only about 8 percent. In fact, 64 percent of Norwegians have never been to the opera.[8] While men and women attend movies, museums, and concerts equally often, women tend to go to theater, opera, art exhibits, religious services, and community meetings more frequently than men do. Norwegians with higher incomes participate more frequently in cultural events than lower income people.

At the other end of the cultural spectrum, many Norwegians enjoy following sports teams, particularly the semi-pro soccer teams, and even engage in *tipping*, or betting, on both soccer and horse racing. The Norwegian national soccer team, while popular, has not enjoyed a high level of international success. Skiing and ski jumping are popular spectator events, both in person and on television. Norwegian athletes do better at winter sports, normally winning a

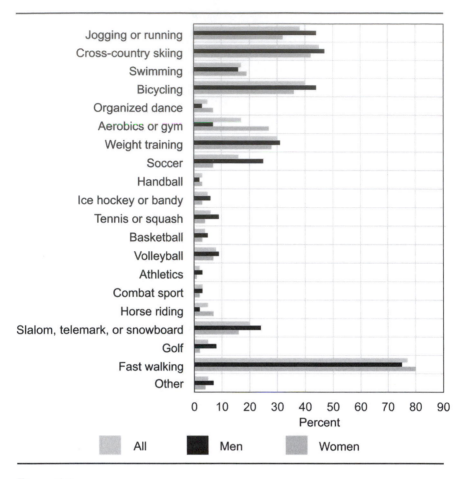

**Figure 5.1**
Percentage who are active in different sports in the last 12 months, all and by gender.
Ages 16+, 2007. (Statistics Norway.)

disproportionate number of medals in the Winter Olympics. Astoundingly, Norway ranks first in the overall number of medals won in Winter Olympics, well ahead of the runners-up: the United States, Austria, and Finland.[9]

### Organizations

Some 80 percent of Norwegians are members of one or more organizations, especially trade unions and sports clubs. Although the share of active members has declined in recent years, it still stands at a respectable 47 percent of the membership. As seen in Figure 5.2, in 2007 25 percent of Norwegians were members of a sports club, with most of those being active members.

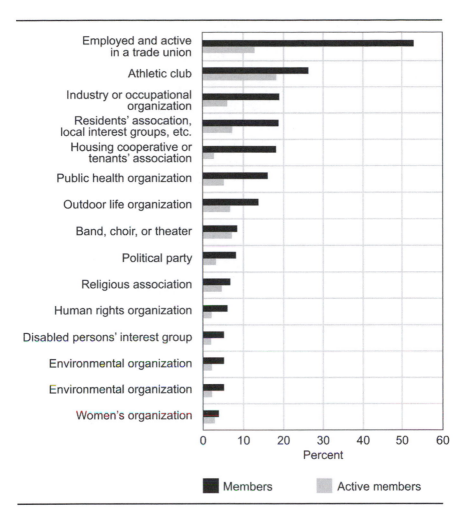

**Figure 5.2**
Membership and activity in organizations, 2007 (Statistics Norway.)

(Only 7% of members were not active.) Fewer Norwegians belong to cultural organizations such as bands, choirs, or theaters, but 85 percent of those who are members consider themselves to be active members.

Many people feel that it is difficult to make friends with Norwegians unless you already have connections. It is not common for Norwegians to invite someone they have just met to their home for dinner, for example, and it is unheard of to simply drop by without an invitation. Belonging to organizations seems to be a way for Norwegians to make social contact and to belong. In Oslo, for example, there are clubs for people coming from various rural areas. These clubs offer classes in local dance or music traditions, as well as social gatherings and children's activities. In addition to these regional clubs, there are dozens of organizations dedicated to folk music and dance.

It is said that there is an organization or club for everyone in Norway. And indeed in 1993 an organization for losers was founded, now called *Stiftelsen Rettferd for taperne* (Foundation: Justice for Losers). This is a voluntary organization dedicated to improving the lives of society's losers, including such people as victims of bullying, former residents of orphanages, those with learning disabilities, and children of German soldiers and Norwegian women from the German occupation during World War II. The foundation assists victims in receiving financial compensation for their suffering.

## NOTES

1. http://www.morgenbladet.no/apps/pbcs.dll/article?AID=/20081205/OAKTUELT/850203968. Accessed 4/30/10.

2. Statistics Norway. http://www.ssb.no. Accessed 6/4/09.

3. http://www.schulze.no/juletradisjoner/jul.html. Accessed 5/5/09.

4. http://www.ssb.no/vis/emner/00/norge/ferie/main.html. Accessed 6/4/09.

5. http://euobserver.com/?aid=28064#. Accessed 5/5/09.

6. Statistics Norway. http://www.ssb.no/english/subjects/10/04/10/jakt_fiske_en/. Accessed 4/30/10.

7. Statistics Norway. http://www.ssb.no/jeja_en/. Accessed 12/11/09.

8. http://www.ssb.no/english/subjects/07/media_en/. Accessed 6/10/09.

9. http://www.nationmaster.com/graph/spo_win_oly_med_all_tim-winter-olympic-medals-all-time. Accessed 1/18/10.

# 6

# Cuisine and Fashion

THERE ARE PROBABLY FEW THINGS that characterize a nation's culture more than its food and dress. Although Norway has never received international acclaim for either its cuisine or its fashion, there are elements of both that can be considered typically Norwegian. It is said that food is the one aspect of culture that immigrants maintain the longest, even after generations in another country. This is certainly the case among Norwegian Americans, many of whom still are fond of their annual helpings of Norwegian specialties.

## CUISINE

When many people think of Norwegian cuisine, they think of traditional Norwegian foods, such as *lutefisk* and *lefse*. While it is certainly true that Norwegians eat *lutefisk*, made of dried fish soaked in a lye solution, as we shall see, there's much more to Norwegian food than that! Young Norwegians today are just as likely to eat international fast food such as hamburgers, hotdogs, frozen pizza, or chicken tandoori. They are also maintaining tradition and working to find creative new ways of preparing food. Norwegians are rightfully proud of the wealth of quality raw materials they have access to: fresh fish and seafood, wild game, meats like lamb and pork, and berries such as strawberries, blueberries, currents, and cloudberries. One of the most famous television chefs today, Andreas Viestad, specializes in products from the wild. Norwegian chefs have also won international cooking contests. In January 2009 Stavanger chef Geir Skeie won the *Bocuse d'Or*, sometimes referred to as the Olympics of cooking, held every two years in Lyon, France, the fourth Norwegian to do so since the competition began in 1987.

### Traditional Food

Some traditional Norwegian foods go back hundreds of years. There is evidence of the use of grains such as barley and rye as far back as the Viking age, from 800 to 1300 CE. Flatbread dates back to the 1200s, when blacksmiths were able to fabricate iron griddles. Flatbread was made in large quantities by groups of women two or three times a year and stored for long periods of time—even years—in the *stabbur* or storehouse. In addition to flatbread, a staple of the diet in the medieval period was a porridge made of grain, called *graut*. *Rømmegrøt*, sour cream porridge, was often eaten on festive occasions such as childbirth, harvest time, or St. Olav's Day (*Olsok*—July 29) along with flatbread and *spekemat*, which is dried, cured meat, usually mutton, ham, or sausage.

These foods are popular today for festivities. For those who do not feel like cooking it themselves, fresh or frozen *rømmegrøt* can be purchased in the supermarket and dried, cured meat in vacuum packages. Rice porridge, or *risengrynsgrøt*, remains a part of the Christmas tradition for many. It is served with butter and cinnamon with an almond hidden in one of the bowls. The lucky person to find the almond might get a prize of a marzipan pig. And of course, one must not forget to leave a bowl of porridge for the *julenisse*, or Christmas elf. While most Norwegians might think that rice porridge is an ancient tradition, this type of porridge came into common use in Norway in the nineteenth century because rice only arrived in Norway in the 1700s and began being used in the Christmas porridge at the end of the 1800s.[1]

Another traditional Norwegian food that turns out to be a relatively recent addition, is the potato, which first arrived in Norway in the mid-1700s, but did not become widespread until the early 1800s, around the Napoleonic wars. Potatoes were eaten boiled and also used to make lefse. Unlike the traditional flatbread, though, this new, soft bread was made for festive occasions because it did not keep well. Other types of breads vary by region and have different names, such as *klappekake, nevebrød*, or *hellekake*. The same applies for a variety of pancake-type foods, such as *pannekaker, kvikaker*, and *sveler*.

A renaissance in *lutefisk* eating has occurred during the last 10 years, with lutefisk consumption increasing at a rate of 10 percent a year. While many urban Norwegians will claim that Norwegians never eat *lutefisk*, the statistics tell another story. According to surveys, in 2006 60 percent of women and nearly 70 percent of men eat *lutefisk* at least once a year, with the percentage increasing with age.[2] Men tend to eat it at restaurants, with beer, while women most often eat it at home, with a glass of wine. In 2008, more than 3,000 tons

Typical summer fare—*rømmegrøt* (sour cream porridge) and *spekemat* (cured meat). The *rømmegrøt* is served with cinnamon and sugar, and the *spekemat* is eaten with flatbread. (Courtesy of the author.)

of *lutefisk* were consumed in Norway during the *lutefisk* season, which runs from October through January. The majority of *lutefisk* sold in Norway is eaten in homes in Trøndelag and North Norway, but a sizeable quantity is served in restaurants in Oslo, where one must make reservations weeks in advance and might spend the equivalent of $50–$60 on a fine *lutefisk* dinner served with all the fixings. In 2008, 75 percent more *lutefisk* was consumed in restaurants than only two years earlier. In Norway, unlike in the Norwegian-American Midwest, where melted butter or white sauce are the norm, lutefisk is typically accompanied by bacon, goat cheese, mustard sauce, and syrup, with boiled potatoes, flatbread, and stewed, dried peas on the side. *Lutefisk* originates as dried codfish (*tørrfisk*), which later is soaked in water for a week or two, then in a lye solution made from ashes or caustic soda. Once the lye soaking is complete, after about two days, the fish must again be soaked in clear, cold water for another 10 days to make it safe to eat. Traditionally the fish was poached or cooked in a pressure cooker, but today it is just as common to bake it in the oven or even in a microwave.

Norwegians of previous centuries were masters at food preservation and developed a variety of methods of conserving fish and meat. Fish was dried, either on racks in the salt sea air, creating *tørrfisk*, or washed in salt water and then laid out on flat rocks to dry in the sun (*klippfisk*). This dried fish could be made into *lutefisk*, as described above, but other dishes were developed, including *bacalao*, which originated in Portugal. This stew is made of reconstituted dried salt cod, tomatoes, onions, potatoes, and sometimes garlic, green or red pepper, chilies and chili powder, green olives, and parsley. One of the first *bacalao* recipes in Norway was published in a cookbook from 1893.[3] Many

Norwegian coastal towns have *bacalao* festivals or cooking contests in the summer.

Yet another delicacy from eastern Norway is *rakfisk*, made of freshwater fish, such as trout, which is cured in brine for two or three months and then eaten raw. It is popular to wrap the *rakfisk* with potatoes, onions, and sour cream in a piece of *lefse*, as a sort of Norwegian burrito. The tradition goes back hundreds of years, and can be dated back at least to a written document from 1348.[4] Because of the risks involved in eating uncooked fish, it is not recommended that pregnant women or those with a lowered immune system eat *rakfisk*. As with *lutefisk* and *bacalao*, the eating of *rakfisk* is often in the context of a festival or celebration, with just a hint of initiation rite.

Other types of preserved fish include canned sardines and mackerel, and frozen fish. as well as pickled herring, *gravlaks* (sugar-cured salmon), and smoked salmon. Of course fresh fish, such as salmon (especially farmed salmon), *breiflabb* (monkfish), *sei* (pollock), and *torsk* (codfish), is also widely consumed, as is shellfish. The small, but flavorful Norwegian shrimp are particularly delicious, and are commonly served as an easy meal for company on summer evenings. The *rekeaften* fare usually consists of a large bowl of shrimp in the shell, sliced French bread, lemon slices or wedges, and mayonnaise. The guests peel their own shrimp and create open-faced sandwiches for themselves. Served with white wine, it makes for a festive evening.

In addition to eating fish, Norwegians are also great fans of a spoonful of cod liver oil every day. The oil sold today does not smell nearly as bad as the older generations remember, but still has an oily feel that can only be conquered by orange juice. Its healthful supply of vitamins A and D as well as Omega-3 fatty acids makes it worth the sacrifice.

### Dairy Products

In a country with a geography like Norway, it's not surprising that many farmers produce a lot of milk and dairy products from both cows and goats. Several cheeses are especially popular, including the Swiss-cheese-like Jarlsberg, soft, strong-tasting *ridderost* (knight's cheese), crumbly, smelly, yet mild-tasting *gamalost* (old cheese), *nøkkelost* (semi-hard yellow cheese flavored with cumin, caraway seeds, and cloves), and Norvegia, which is similar to Gouda. But the most Norwegian cheese of all is *geitost*, *brunost*, or *Gudbrandsdalsost*, a cheese made of a mixture of goat's milk and cow's milk. In fact, in a poll taken among Norwegians by the state-owned television station, brown Norwegian goat's cheese was chosen as most Norwegian. *Brunost* is actually not a cheese, because it is made from the whey remaining from cheese production, with additional milk and cream added. *Gudbrandsdalsost* contains at least 10 percent goat's milk. The whey mixture is cooked down until the milk sugar (lactose) becomes caramelized, giving it its characteristic brown color and sweet flavor. Seven liters of water is cooked away for each kilo of *brunost*. Because *brunost* is not aged, it can be consumed as soon as it is cool. About 30 percent of the cheese consumed in Norway is *brunost;* the average Norwegian eats 2.5 kilos of *brunost* a year, mostly thinly sliced on whole-grain bread or rye crisp, but sometimes also melted into gravy or eaten on a waffle for afternoon coffee.

### Meat

Pork and lamb are traditionally the most commonly eaten meats, although chicken and beef are also more common now. Some traditional dishes include *får-i-kål*, which is lamb and cabbage stew; pork or lamb ribs, which are traditionally eaten at Christmas; meatballs; and sausage, along with *surkål* and sweet and sour cabbage. Boiled potatoes accompany any traditional meal, although in many areas there is a variant of a potato dumpling called *klubb, raspeballer, kumler, kompe,* or *ball*. Reindeer meat and other game, such as moose, grouse, ptarmigan, and other birds are also popular. In western Norway a Christmas specialty is *smalahove*, or smoked sheep's head.

### Baked Goods and Sweets

The Christmas season brings out the creativity among bakers. Traditionally, any baker would feel morally obligated to have at least seven types of cookies on the plate to serve to guests. Popular Christmas baked goods include some made with irons, including *krumkake* and *goro*, and others that are deep fat fried, such as *fattigmann*, rosettes, and cake donuts. Others are cut into shapes and baked, such as *pepperkaker* and *sirupsnipper*, or formed in a mold or by hand, such as *sandkaker* and *Berlinerkranser*. *Mor Monsen* is more of a cake, with almonds and dried currents. *Julekake* is not a cake, but moderately sweet bread, with candied fruits and cardamom.

Other popular cakes and baked goods are *bløtkake*, which is the obligatory birthday cake for most adult Norwegians. It is a single layer sponge cake that has been sliced horizontally into three layers. The layers are then sprinkled with a liquid, such as fruit juice, milk, cream, or even liqueur, and filled with whipped cream and fruit. The cakes are beautifully decorated and sometimes covered with a thin layer of marzipan. The *kransekake* is another specialty cake, commonly used for weddings and other special occasions. The word *krans* means wreath, and the cake is made of ground almonds mixed with sugar and egg white, baked into concentric rings. These are stacked up from large to small in a tower of 18 or more rings held together with a white glaze. A bottle of wine fits nicely inside the tower. One wedding tradition is to have the bride and groom lift off the top ring. The number of rings that come off with the top ring provides a prediction of how many children the couple will have. *Eplekake,* or apple cake, is popular, especially the version served at the Frognerseteren restaurant in the hills overlooking the Oslo fjord.

Cakes are commonly served with strong Norwegian coffee. Norwegians consume about 160 liters of coffee per person a year, and 80 percent of the population drinks coffee. While coffee has long enjoyed great popularity, only recently have coffee bars with fancy espresso-based coffee drinks become common. They are found mostly in the larger cities.

Norwegians are also well known for their delicious bakery treats: Napoleon cakes, various types of Danish pastries, or *wienerbrød*, and *boller* (buns). The buns tend not to be as sweet as American sweet rolls, but are still prized by children as after-school treats.

One special treat for Norwegian children is the bag of sweets given to them on Saturdays, called *lørdagsgodt*. Traditionally, children would receive this to be consumed while they watched children's television on Saturday mornings or, before the advent of television, listened to children's programming on the radio. Norwegian children are fond of many of the same sweets that American children are: gummy bears, chocolates, caramels, peanuts, and gum balls. Norway makes delicious chocolate, and ranks fifth in the world in chocolate consumption. One type of candy that seems distinctive for Norway, though, is the salt licorice that is very popular there. Even salt licorice-flavored gum is available.

## MODERN FOOD

But what do Norwegians eat today, for everyday meals? Certainly their diet has become as international as anywhere in the world, with some people joking that Chicken tandoori is the new Norwegian national dish. Equally popular is frozen pizza (Grandiosa) and other easy-to-make frozen or packaged meals. American fast food restaurants, like McDonald's and Burger King, as well as TGI Fridays, are ubiquitous, and Coca Cola ads are found everywhere. In fact, Coca Cola is the most popular soda pop in Norway.

The first foreign foods to come to Oslo arrived through Chinese restaurants and pizza places, like Peppes Pizza. Later one could buy taco kits in the grocery stores. With the influx of Pakistani and Indian immigrants since the 1960s, Indian restaurants have become common. A favorite fast-food snack is the kebab, which is nearly as common as the hot dog in a bun or wrapped in *lompe* (potato lefse). Immigrants to Norway have also brought with them a wealth of formerly unfamiliar fruits and vegetables, and the east side of Oslo, with its immigrant markets, is a popular place to purchase fresh produce at a reasonable price.

Schoolchildren in Norway do not have a hot lunch available at school, but instead bring a *matpakke* with them from home. The tradition of *matpakke* dates back to the 1930s.[5] The ideal *matpakke* consists of two to four slices of bread, usually assembled at the same time as one eats breakfast. The sandwiches are open-faced with thin slices of meat or cheese garnished with vegetables like tomato or pepper. The slices are laid one on top of the other with specially cut pieces of paper between. The whole package is wrapped in waxed parchment paper. The addition of milk and a piece of fruit or vegetable makes a nutritious lunch. The *matpakke* tradition continues into the workplace, where it is much more common to bring your own lunch than to go out to a café.

### Smørbrød and Koldtbord

Norwegians are also well known for their tradition of *smørbrød*, or open-faced sandwiches. While any open-faced sandwich can be called a *smørbrød* and can be served for breakfast, luncheon, or a light evening meal, extra fancy ones, called *snitter*, are used for special occasions, such as weddings, confirmations, baptisms, funerals, or other receptions. Great emphasis is placed on beautiful appearance; the slices of cheese, meat, or fishes are carefully placed on the thin, diagonally cut slices of bread and garnished with vegetables or fruit. Popular combinations include shrimp and mayonnaise garnished with lemon slices and lettuce, smoked salmon with cold scrambled eggs and dill, roast beef with pickles, cheese with sliced bell peppers, and many others. *Koldtbord* is the name for the Norwegian buffet, which is known as *smörgåsbord* in Sweden. It is traditional on festive occasions, like weddings or funerals, as well as at fancy hotels. It is good manners to eat from one section of the *koldtbord* at a time, taking a clean plate each time. The *koldtbord* usually consists of a section of fish and seafood, perhaps even a whole salmon, smoked salmon, *gravlaks* (sugar-cured raw salmon) served with mustard sauce, and shrimp with mayonnaise and lemon. The meat and hot food section includes *spekeskinke* (dried ham) served with sour cream and potato salad, leg of lamb with boiled potatoes and vegetables, and pork roast with prunes. Desserts might include *karamellpudding* (custard with caramel sauce), ice cream, and cakes, as well as cheeses.

## ALCOHOL

Alcohol consumption in Norway has changed greatly during the last 100 years. In the 1800s, there were enormous problems with alcohol in Norway. Between 1830 and 1840, per capita consumption reached its peak at about 13 liters of pure alcohol (compared with 6.6 liters today). Finally, in 1919, a referendum was held to continue the prohibition that had been introduced three years earlier. Unlike in the United States there was never a complete ban of alcohol sales. But no strong alcoholic beverages were sold legally in Norway until 1922, when the *Vinmonopol,* or wine monopoly, was established. Pressure from France and other wine-producing countries induced the Norwegians to again permit the import and sale of strong wine and spirits. The wine monopoly was initially privately owned, but came under state ownership in 1939, where it remains to this day, although pressure from the European Union has forced the breaking up of the import monopoly, with a state-owned corporation called *Arcus* now in control of imports and wholesale sales, as well as production and bottling of spirits. *Vinmonopolet* retains control of retail sales. The age limits are 18 for beer and wine and 20 for stronger drinks. While there are still areas of the country where alcohol is frowned upon—especially on the west and southwest coast—alcohol consumption as a whole has increased greatly. In the past it was common for those Norwegians who drank alcohol to prefer beer or aquavit, a distilled product made from potatoes, or perhaps even a home-made product called *heimbrent* (home distilled), but as Norwegians have traveled more and had more contact with southern Europeans, the consumption of wine has increased greatly. The statistics show an interesting picture: from 1996 to 2007, per capita beer consumption increased by 3.7 percent; distilled liquor by 34 percent, wine by 86 percent, and most dramatically *rusbrus* (alcopop) by 500 percent, with much of the increase of this product due to easier access once sales in ordinary grocery stores were permitted in 2003. While strong beer is sold only at the wine monopoly, regular pilsner beer can be purchased in grocery stores. There is a long history of beer brewing, dating back to the Viking age. Today the best-known breweries are Ringnes, based in Oslo but owned by Danish Carlsberg Group, Hansa in Bergen, Mack in Tromsø, and Aass in Drammen. Every year at Christmas the breweries vie for the best *juleøl,* or Christmas beer. Breweries often bottle other soft drinks or alcopops as well.

## FASHION

The Norwegian sweater, with its multi-colored and intricate patterns, is probably the first thing that comes to mind when most people think of Norwegian fashion. As we shall see, however, there is much more to it both in terms of traditional clothing and modern high fashion.

### Traditional Dress

Although many people think a Norwegian folk costume consists of a red vest and black skirt with a white apron, originally folk costumes varied considerably from individual to individual and changed with fashions. The *bunads*—modern, agreed-upon version of a traditional folk costume—change very little once determined. While folk costumes were worn for everyday use, *bunads* are used on festive occasions. The *bunads* are actually a relatively new phenomenon. They began to come into use in the late 1800s, during the National Romantic period, as part of the desire to rediscover and preserve what remained of traditional Norwegian culture. By this time most of the traditional folk dress was no longer in use, and city people in particular were heavily influenced by fashions and trends from Europe. In some rural areas where traditional costumes were still in use, these were used to create the new *bunads*. In other areas the folk costume had gone out of fashion, but was still remembered. The *bunad* was created on the basis of remnants of these old costumes or even old paintings or illustrations.[6]

Two of the pioneers of the *bunad* movement were Hulda Garborg (1862–1934) and Klara Semb (1884–1970). Hulda Garborg's interest in creating a folk costume stemmed from her interest in folk dance. The folk dance group she formed in Oslo (then called Kristiania) performed for the first time in 1900, and eventually it toured both in Norway and abroad.

These *bunads* are from Setesdal and Telemark in southern Norway. They are worn for festive occasions such as the May 17, Norway's National Day. (Courtesy of the author.)

In the beginning the dancers wore a simplified Hardanger bunad, the so-called National Costume. This consisted of a red vest with beaded breast-plate; black skirt; white apron, often with Hardanger lace; and a long-sleeved, white shirt. This costume was often depicted on postcards, worn by women in unlikely situations such as milking goats or raking hay. While originally stress was placed on finding a national identity as expressed through a single national costume, by the twentieth century local and regional identities became more important, and people began to create and recreate local *bunads*. Hulda Garborg herself wore a version of the festive costume from Gol in Hallingdal. She felt it was important to simplify the costumes so that they would be more convenient to use. She wrote the first book on Norwegian *bunads*, published in 1903[7] and is credited with revitalizing both folk dance and folk costumes.

In contrast to Hulda Garborg, Klara Semb preferred copying old traditions as accurately as possible, rather than simplifying and modernizing. She was also a member of the original Bunad committee, *Landsnemda for Bunadspørsmål*, which was later replaced by the Bunad Advisory Board.[8] While Hulda Garborg believed in using only home-produced fabrics and designs, Klara Semb preferred to return to the old tradition of importing fine damask or brocade, and other fabric for this festival clothing.

There are hundreds of different local *bunads* for both men and women. Occasionally one *bunad* is used over an entire county (*fylke*), but other times an individual valley might have several different *bunads* in use. Today one usually chooses a *bunad* from an area that one has a personal connection to, although many people just pick one they think is beautiful. Advice is available from the Bunad and Folk Costume Advisory Board, located in Valdres, Norway.[9]

*Bunads* are worn for special occasions such as weddings, baptisms, confirmations, Christmas Eve, and most commonly, May 17, Norway's national day. Although *bunads* are more frequently worn by women, many of whom received their adult *bunad* as a confirmation gift, they have been growing in popularity among men, especially those interested in folk dancing. *Bunads* are considered the equivalent of formal apparel and are appropriate to wear at any such occasion, even a royal dinner.

While there is a great variety among *bunads*, many have common characteristics. They frequently consist of a sleeveless bodice with skirt (sometimes attached, but not always), worn over a long-sleeved, white shirt, which is often embroidered, either white-on-white, or colored. The bodice and skirt are often embroidered, but can also be made of a fancy fabric, such as damask or brocade, or even a plaid or striped material. Most festival *bunads* are made of dark wool fabric in black, blue, green, or turquoise, and the shirts of linen or cotton. Silver jewelry, brooches, called *søljer*, or sometimes chains or necklaces, are worn with the bunad, often to hold the neck of the shirt together. These *søljer* are also specific to the area, and have silver or gold dangles. Some *bunads* also have silver belts. *Bunads* are usually worn with black hose and black *bunad* shoes with a metal buckle. Wearing other jewelry or ordinary dress shoes or sheer hosiery is frowned upon. Some *bunads* have special headdresses for married women, while others use the same embroidered cap for both married and unmarried women. Extra fancy wedding *bunads*, sometimes even including a crown, are worn in some areas. Men's *bunads* often include knee breeches, although some have long trousers. They often include a vest and jacket, with buttons of silver or pewter. A variety of hats and caps is used in different areas of Norway.

### Norwegian Knitwear

Norwegians are known for their elaborate knitted cardigan and pullover sweaters, stockings, caps, mittens, gloves, and scarves, using the stranded color or Fair Isle style of knitting. The Norwegian sweater has become a concept, at least in the American Midwest, although the tradition does not really go back further than the 1700s. It was common for women to knit as they walked along, driving cattle up to the summer pasture, for example. The nineteenth-century lay preacher, Hans Nielsen Hauge is said to have knitted as he walked along on his mission journeys throughout Norway. By the 1800s knitting was a required subject in Norwegian schools, and even today, schoolchildren learn to knit in elementary school.

Most garments are knitted in the round, on circular needles or double-pointed needles, with two or more colors. This creates both an interesting pattern and a thicker, warmer fabric. Common patterns include the St. Andrew's cross and the eight-pointed star, or *Selbu-rosa*. The resulting knitted tube is then cut to create openings for sleeves and front plackets. Sweaters for both men and women often have a drop shoulder with set-in sleeves, whereas some women's sweaters have a circular yoke and raglan sleeves. The sweaters and cardigans were traditionally worn by men, sometimes as part of their *bunad*, for example in the Setesdal *bunad*, which dates back 150 years. This sweater, known as the *lusekofte*, has what has become known as the lice pattern, which consists of single stitches of one color (usually white) against a contrasting color (usually black). In the 1920s and 30s, as more women began to participate in outdoor sports and to wear clothing that previously had been reserved for men, such as trousers, women also began wearing the *lusekofte*.[10] Nowadays, many color combinations are seen and sometimes the *lusekofte* has no lice at all.

*Selbu* mittens, still the most common pattern found on Norwegian mittens in the handcrafts stores, can be traced back to one young woman, who invented the pattern in the 1850s. Her pattern soon became popular among the local people, and before long everyone was wearing black and white mittens in this pattern.

Knitting machines have been in use in Norway for more than 100 years, and no doubt contributed to the popularity of Norwegian sweaters by enabling the knitters to produce them much faster. Today hand-knitted sweaters have higher status, although some beautifully designed machine-knit ones, such as Oleana, are on the market. Genuine hand-knitted sweaters are actually difficult to find in stores today, due both to the high cost of labor in Norway as well as the shortage of people willing to knit by hand. Most commercially produced sweaters are knitted by machine, sometimes not even in Norway, but rather in Asia and Eastern Europe, where labor is cheaper. However, hand knitting as a hobby has enjoyed increased popularity in recent years, and yarn shops and local handcrafts societies offer classes and knitting groups.

The Norwegian sweater has an interesting symbolic value. While in the American Midwest people wear sweaters to church and on other dress-up occasions as a marker of ethnicity, in Norway it is mostly worn by tourists, members of the Norwegian national ski team, and high-profile defendants in court. The latter usage has been observed in more than one instance: Arfan Bhatti, Norway's first terrorism suspect to be put on trial, was accused of firing shots at the synagogue in Oslo. He wore a dark Norwegian pullover sweater to court; he was acquitted. David Toska, also clad in a Norwegian sweater, was accused of being the mastermind behind the infamous NOKAS

Norwegian sweaters knitted by author in traditional Norwegian style of two-stranded knitting. The sweater on the upper-left side was designed by fashion designer Per Spook (1939–). (Photo courtesy of David Gonnerman.)

bank robbery in Stavanger, which resulted in the killing of a police officer. In this case, however, the sweater did not work any magic, and he was convicted.

One of the best-known sweater producers in Norway is Dale of Norway, which created the sweater for the Winter Olympics, held in Lillehammer, Norway, in 1994 and also creates a new design each year for the National Ski Team. Some sweater producers also sell yarn and sweater patterns for hand knitters in order to increase their sales of yarn. Other companies, like Devold, Nordstrikk, and Volund, only produce machine-knitted, ready-made sweaters.

### Sweaters and Fashion

Per Spook (1939–) is a high-fashion designer who designed a traditional Norwegian sweater with a new look and shape. Born in 1939, Spook moved to Paris and apprenticed with the House of Dior before starting his own house. In Norway he is best known for the Norwegian sweater he designed in 1981 in honor of the ninetieth anniversary of *Den Norske Husflidsforening*, the Norwegian Handcrafts Association (top left sweater in the photo). A more recent designer who has taken the Norwegian sweater out of the realm of sports to fashion is Solveig Hisdal, who has designed Oleana sweaters since 1992. Founded by Hildegunn Møster, Kolbjørn Valstrand, and Signe Aarhus, Oleana uses natural fibers such as wool, merino wool, alpaca, and silk and produces all of its garments in Norway.[11] It employs about 60 people in its factory near Bergen, Norway, where it uses ultramodern knitting machines. Its philosophy is to prioritize job satisfaction and an egalitarian workplace. Each year it closes the factory for several days to take all the employees on a study tour, either in Norway or abroad. The sweaters are inspired by a variety of designs, including damask fabrics, flowers, and even an old sweater found in Vesterheim, the Norwegian-American museum in Decorah, Iowa. The sweaters are often paired with elegant silk skirts and shells.

### Fine Fashion

Norway does not have a tradition of fashion houses producing designer clothing for the wealthy. Even Sweden and Denmark have had more success in creating designs for export. In 2009, Norwegian Gunhild Nygaard was designated *Créateur de L'Année*, Designer of the Year, in Paris for a collection of women's clothing called *Gunhild*.[12] She does not live in Norway, however, but in Paris, where she began as a model. She later worked as a designer with Givenchy and Christian Dior, before launching her first solo collection in 2007.

In recent years, however, there has been a movement to encourage young designers and to create an infrastructure to help them to succeed in the international market. In 2008, a report published by the Oslo University College and Arts College in Oslo at the request of Norsk Form outlined measures the Norwegian fashion industry should take to increase exports in fashion design. These included better marketing abroad, a more professional and businesslike structure in the industry, the creation of a coordinating institution that could nurture the milieu, aid in establishing ties in the fashion capitals, advice and assistance with new projects, and improvements in communication with the press. In addition, such an institution could help create brand awareness for Norwegian fashion and lobby for a relaxation of various types of taxes and duties. The report points to recent international success enjoyed by Norwegian architects and recommends following their example by creating a recognizable Norwegian identity in fashion. This identity must be both distinctively Norwegian as well as internationally oriented.[13]

Innovation Norway has contributed 1.7 million Norwegian kroner (more than $2 million) to the establishment of NMI, the Norwegian Fashion Institute. Oslo Fashion Week has attracted increasing media attention for Norwegian designers. Both Queen Sonja and Crown Princess Mette-Marit have played an important role in promoting Norwegian fashion design. The Crown Princess is the high patron of the Norwegian Design Council. Some hot new designers include Fin Fashion and Moods of Norway, which opened a flagship store in Hollywood.[14] Excitement was high when Gwen Stefani was photographed by *People* magazine wearing one of its jackets.[15]

## NOTES

1. http://www.artoftaste.no/servlet/side?section=1000002&item=11517. Accessed 2/23/09.

2. http://www.seafood.no/page?id=207&key=28457. Accessed 2/23/09.

3. G. Haslund, *Min Medhjælp: Kogebog af Fru G. Haslund* (Kristiania: Huseby & Cos Forlag, 1893).

4. http://www.wangensten.no/historie.html. Accessed 2/25/09.

5. http://www.nrk.no/programmer/radio/p2_akademiet/3215600.html. Accessed 3/1/09.

6. Heidi Fossness, *Norges Bunader og samiske folkedrakter* (Oslo: Cappelen, 1993), p. 10.

7. Norsk klædebunad, Hulda Garborg, Oslo: Norigs Ungdomslag og Student-maallaget, 1903.

8. Heidi Fossness, *Norges Bunader og samiske folkedrakter*, p. 11.

9. http://www.bunadraadet.no/. Accessed 3/30/09.

10. http://www.kulturminneaaret2009.no/prosjekter/ukens-kulturminne/uke-12-lus. Accessed 4/20/09.

11. http://www.oleana.no/. Accessed 4/20/09.

12. http://www.norwegianfashion.no/nyheter/norske-gunhild-nygaard-er-arets-designer-i-paris. Accessed 4/20/09.

13. http://e24.no/naeringsliv/article2242758.ece. Accessed 4/29/09.

14. http://www.norwegianfashion.no/. Accessed 4/29/09.

15. http://www.people.com/people/gwen_stefani/photos/ 0,,20004350_20613652,00.html. Accessed 4/29/09.

# 7

# Language and Literature

THE OFFICIAL LANGUAGES IN NORWAY are Norwegian (in two written forms) and Sámi, the language of the indigenous Sámi people of Norway. Many countries have more than one official language, but Norway's language situation is unique because there are two official written standards of Norwegian but no standard spoken language. Norwegian is a north-Germanic language, part of the Indo-European language family. It is closely related to the other Scandinavian languages—Swedish, Danish, Icelandic, and Faeroese—and somewhat more distantly related to other Germanic languages like German, English, and Dutch. The alphabet contains the same 26 letters as the English alphabet, plus three additional vowels at the end: æ, ø, and å. Norwegian has imported many words from foreign languages, but there are also a few that have made their way from Norwegian into English: fjord, ski, and slalom.

## LANGUAGE HISTORY

During the 400 years Norway was under Danish rule, the Norwegian written language died out. Power was centered in Copenhagen, under the king. Once the Bible was translated into Danish after the Lutheran Reformation in 1537, Danish was the language taught in the schools and churches to Norwegian children. As mentioned elsewhere, because there was no university in Norway until 1811, students had to go to Copenhagen or elsewhere in Europe to study. As a result, the educated clergymen, teachers, doctors, civil servants, etc. all wrote in Danish, and no national literature developed in Norwegian until the nineteenth century. Although upper-class Norwegians spoke Danish on more formal occasions such as when conducting business or pastors spoke from the pulpit, Norwegians continued to use their spoken dialects despite the loss of Norwegian as a written language.

### Written Languages

The two written forms of Norwegian are *Bokmål* and *Nynorsk*, and they are mutually intelligible. Both forms were created during the 1800s as part of the creation of Norwegian national identity during the National Romantic period in Norway, and both were declared official languages in 1885. The two languages have equal legal status today, although *Bokmål* dominates by far, with more than 85 percent of schoolchildren choosing *Bokmål* as their main language. Each school district decides by referendum which language will be taught beginning in first grade. If, however, at least 10 students request the other language, the school must arrange for it to be taught. Beginning in eighth grade, all schoolchildren must learn to read and write both languages. This requirement is controversial, particularly in the strongly *Bokmål* areas in eastern Norway, where some schools have been requesting an exemption from this rule. Students who speak another language in the home are also exempted from the requirement to learn both *Bokmål* and *Nynorsk*. Table 7.1 shows how similar the two languages are.

### Danish→Dano-Norwegian→Rigsmaal→Riksmål→Bokmål

*Bokmål* is derived from Danish, the written language of Norway during the union between the two countries. Despite the dominance of Danish, some early writers, for example, Dorothe Engelbretsdotter and Petter Dass (eighteenth century), used a number of Norwegianisms in their written Danish. In the 1800s, after the end of the union with Denmark, many prominent Norwegian writers such as the poet Henrik Wergeland, lobbied for a gradual Norwegianizing of Danish by introducing Norwegian vocabulary,

**Table 7.1**
Comparison of *Bokmål* and *Nynorsk*

| English | Bokmål | Nynorsk |
|---|---|---|
| I don't know what her name is. | Jeg vet ikke hva hun heter. | Eg veit ikkje kva ho heiter. |
| They come from Norway. | De kommer fra Norge. | Dei kjem frå Noreg. |
| Let's see. | Skal vi se. | Skal me sjå. |
| I don't know the boys who live next to you (all). | Jeg kjenner ikke guttene som bor ved siden av dere. | Eg kjenner ikkje gutane som bur ved sida av dykk. |

syntax, and expressions. Wergeland maintained that an independent people should have its own language. He felt it would be easier for people to express themselves in a written form that was closer to their spoken language and that it would be better for democracy if more people learned to read and write. Peter Christen Asbjørnsen and Jørgen Moe, who collected and published Norwegian folktales, also played an important role in the development of *Bokmål*. They realized that they could not publish the tales in the original dialect if people were to understand them, nor could they maintain the integrity of the tales if they were to publish them in Danish. So they followed a middle road, using Danish orthography but Norwegian vocabulary and syntax. The teacher and linguist Knud Knudsen (1812–1895) is credited with introducing a written form of Norwegian that would be easier for children to learn to read and write. Beginning in 1845, he published a number of articles and books advocating a form of Norwegian that was closer to the language actually spoken by educated eastern Norwegians. He favored a more gradual approach than the one promoted by Ivar Aasen.

### Dialects→Landsmaal→Landsmål→Nynorsk

Self-taught linguist Ivar Aasen (1813–1896) took a more radical approach to creating a written form of Norwegian. Beginning in 1842 he traveled all over Norway, collecting samples of spoken dialects. He eventually visited every county in Norway, with the exception of the northernmost county of Finnmark. In 1848 he published his first book, *Det norske Folkesprogs Grammatik* (Grammar of the Norwegian People's Language). In 1850 he published a dictionary, *Ordbog over det norske Folkesprog* (Dictionary of the Norwegian People's Language), and in 1853 he published *Prøver of Landsmaalet i Norge* (Samples of the Language of the Country in Norway). His new language was based on rural dialects from western Norway and the mountainous regions. When he had to choose among possible forms, he preferred forms that were closer to Old Norse. Aasen also wrote poetry in his new language to demonstrate that it was suitable for artistic creations. Other writers, most notably A. O. Vinje and Arne Garborg also published in *Landsmål*. In 1929, the name of the language was changed from *Landsmål* to *Nynorsk* (New Norwegian).

Today about 25 percent of newspapers in Norway are published in *Nynorsk*, and about 10 percent are written in both *Bokmål* and *Nynorsk*. The rest are published in *Bokmål*, and these tend to be newspapers with larger circulations. About 7 percent of all books published are in *Nynorsk*. Poetry and song lyrics are the most common *Nynorsk* literary form. About one third of church parishes, serving about 1.3 million Norwegians, use the *Nynorsk* liturgy. A number of *Nynorsk* hymns are used in both *Nynorsk* and *Bokmål* congregations. It is logical that the percentage of *Nynorsk* churches is greater

than that of *Nynorsk* schools because people living in the *Nynorsk* areas of
Norway (the south and southwest) tend to be more active churchgoers.

### Bokmål and Nynorsk—Where?

Of the 19 counties, or *fylker*, four, representing about 12 percent of the
population, use *Nynorsk* as administrative language in the majority of their
municipalities, nine use mainly *Bokmål*, and six, including Oslo, are neutral.[1]
The *Nynorsk* areas are concentrated in the southwest, and the *Bokmål*
counties are in the east, surrounding Oslo, and north. Of the 430 municipalities, 160 have designated *Bokmål* as the administrative language, 114
*Nynorsk*, and 156 are neutral. Kven (related to Finnish) and Sámi are used
in a few northern municipalities.

### Language of the Sámi People

Sámi is a Finno-Ugric language, distantly related to Finnish, Estonian, and
Hungarian. It is used by Sámi people living in Norway, Sweden, Finland, and
Russia. Sámi has several different dialects in Norway, including North Sámi,
South Sámi, and Luleo-Sámi. These different dialects of Sámi are not mutually
understandable. North Sámi has the largest number of adherents, and is the
dialect used most in literature and education.

Sámi did not have its current written form until the 1800s, when the Bible
was first translated into Sámi. For generations the Sámi language was repressed
by the authorities, and Sámi children were punished if they spoke Sámi at
school. Since 1992, however, Sámi has had equal status with Norwegian and
is designated as the administrative language in some municipalities in the
northernmost counties of Finnmark and Troms. There are Sámi-language
newspapers, radio, and television, and Sámi-language literature and films
are produced. Sámi children in the Sámi districts have the right to language
instruction in Sámi. Outside these areas, Sámi instruction must be provided
if at least three children request it.

### Spoken Language

Norwegian spoken dialects are generally divided into four groups, Eastern
Norwegian, Western Norwegian, *Trøndsk* or *Trøndersk* (in central Norway),
and Northern Norwegian. Within each dialect area there are dozens of slight
variants, but each area has certain major features in common. One important
difference between dialects of south and southwestern Norway and the rest of
the country is the pronunciation of the letter *r*. In most of Norway, the *r* is
rolled with the tip of the tongue. In the south and west, the uvular *r* (like
French) is most common. Interestingly, the uvular *r* is actually spreading to
other areas of the country. Other differences include vocabulary, intonation

patterns, stress, palatalization, pronunciation of the letter l, and apocope, or the dropping of vowels on the ends of words. Dialects in Norway have high status, and it is acceptable and even encouraged to speak dialect anywhere, whether in school, on television or radio, or in politics. While 30 or 40 years ago it was common for people to try to lose their dialect when they moved to Oslo, now they are proud of their dialects.

### Laws Regulating Language Use

Since 1885 a number of reforms have affected both *Bokmål* and *Nynorsk*. Frequently, the goals of the reforms have been contradictory. One goal of reform has been to bring the written forms as close as possible to spoken forms. A second has been to bring the two languages together as much as possible, and a third to allow individual choice in language usage at the same time as greater standardization. In the 1950s, textbook standards were created for both languages, with much stricter rules than those in effect for private individuals. Even the counting system was standardized in 1952, with the new norm being the English form "twenty-one" rather than the German form "one and twenty." Despite the fact that generations of Norwegians have been taught this "new" counting system in school, many Norwegians still use the "old" system, or even a combination of both. Until the 1980s, some people even lobbied for a single version of Norwegian, called *Samnorsk* (Common Norwegian), but that goal was officially abandoned in 2002.

Because *Bokmål* and *Nynorsk* are legally equivalent, schoolchildren must learn both, designating one as their primary language and the other as their secondary language. Since 1969 all school textbooks must be published in parallel editions, although there has been some experimenting with creating a single edition with alternating *Bokmål* and *Nynorsk* chapters in order to save money. Language laws regulate official use of language. All official government forms must be published in both languages. In 2007, for example, about 11 percent of the population requested the *Nynorsk* version of the tax form. Government employees must respond to correspondence in the same form used in the initial query. Other laws regulate the use in the media. Since 1970 the state-owned television station NRK has been required to use *Nynorsk* 25 percent of the time. Despite efforts at enforcement, it has recently been noted that *Nynorsk* is rarely used for subtitles in feature films shown on television, for example.

### Linguistic Challenges in Norway

It can be challenging to maintain two separate yet similar written languages in a country with fewer than 5 million people. In such a small market, it is extremely expensive to publish in both languages. Television stations are required to use *Nynorsk* in subtitles of foreign language programs, yet must deal with complaints from urban viewers who do not like to have to read *Nynorsk* subtitles.

The requirement that all schoolchildren learn *Nynorsk* as well as *Bokmål* is a frequent source of complaints. Some claim that Norwegian children would be better served if they were to spend more time mastering *Bokmål*. There have been proposals to drop or modify the requirement. Others have suggested that schoolchildren not be required to learn to write *Nynorsk* but only to read it, so that they still are exposed to the richness of the literature.

A recent controversy involves the use of spoken dialect on television. It is well accepted that private individuals may speak their own dialect in any setting. The question has been raised, however, about the use of local dialect on news programs on the state-owned network, NRK. Sylfest Lomheim, a proponent of *Nynorsk* and director of the Norwegian Language Council, and Finn-Erik Vinje, a linguistics professor and linguistically conservative *Bokmål* supporter, both agree that news readers should use a standard version of spoken *Nynorsk* or spoken *Bokmål* on television and radio, in order to maintain a neutral posture.

### Will Norwegian Survive?

There is a great deal of concern in Norway today about the effect of English and other foreign languages on Norwegian. While Norwegian has always been influenced and enriched by loan words from other languages, in recent years English has played an increasingly dominant role in language use, particularly in business, advertising, higher education, and research. Some have expressed concern about whether Norwegian is in danger of disappearing as an academic language because scholars must publish in English if they want their research to be disseminated internationally.

Are Norwegians more obsessed with language than other people? Quite possibly! There is a weekly radio program about language, *Språkteigen* (About Language), and a popular television show *Typisk norsk* (Typically Norwegian) that took up language questions in a humorous way every week for three seasons. Another game show featured contestants who competed on their ability to identify and localize dialects.

*Språkrådet* (The Language Council) advises the *Storting* on language issues. The Language Council's recommendation that the year 2010 be pronounced "two thousand and ten," rather than "twenty ten" has caused much debate. The state-run Norwegian Broadcasting Company is required to follow this recommendation, while the privately owned TV2 station has announced that it will not. Research has also been conducted on the influence of immigrant languages like Urdu and Arabic on youth language in Oslo and other use of slang among the young.

In 2009, the *Stortinget* adopted a White Paper on language policy in Norway: *Mål og meining: Ein heilskapleg norsk språkpolitikk* (Language and Meaning: A Holistic Norwegian Language Policy). The main points of this document were recommendations to bolster the position and importance of the Norwegian language—both *Bokmål* and *Nynorsk*—in every sector of society and specific suggestions to strengthen its status, quality, and range, including increasing the role of the Language Council. Measures were also proposed to benefit Sámi, Kven, and other minority languages in Norway. The government claims that this is the first time the language situation has been so systematically and comprehensively discussed in a White Paper. The document sparked a wide-ranging debate in *Storting*.

## COMPARISON OF SCANDINAVIAN LANGUAGES

Danish, Swedish, Bokmål, and Nynorsk are all mutually intelligible, with a modest amount of goodwill and effort. Some examples of similarities are given in Table 7.2.

**Table 7.2**
Comparison of Scandinavian Languages

| English | Danish | Swedish | Bokmål/Nynorsk |
|---|---|---|---|
| to write | at skrive | att skriva | å skrive |
| Read! | Læs! | Läs! | Les! |
| like | kan lige | tycker om | liker |
| I don't know. | Jeg vet ikke. | Jag vet inte. | Jeg vet ikke / Eg veit ikkje. |
| Language name | dansk | svenska | norsk |
| Name of country | Danmark | Sverige | Norge/Noreg |

Scandinavians have an easier time understanding each other's written language than the spoken forms. It is also generally easier for Norwegians to understand other Scandinavian languages (both oral and written forms), and it is easier for Swedes and Danes to understand Norwegians than for them to understand each other's languages. Scandinavian literature is, however, frequently translated into the other languages, and interviews with people speaking other Scandinavian languages are often supplied with subtitles on television programs. Television programs in Swedish, Danish, and Norwegian are often subtitled when broadcast in one of the other Scandinavian countries.

## LITERATURE

The earliest literature in Norway, broadly defined, can be said to date from approximately 3000 BCE and consisted of rock carvings. In the earliest part of this period, Scandinavians had no written language, but carved pictograms on rocks, many of which survive today. One of the largest and best-known fields is in Alta, in North Norway. Once Scandinavians were introduced to literacy, around the year 150 CE, they did not use the Latin alphabet, but rather created a native system of runes. The runic alphabet is called the *futhark* (which stands for the first six individual runes), which came in two versions. The older *futhark* had 24 letters, and the younger version, which appeared just before the year 800 CE, had 16. Runes resemble upper-case letters from the Latin alphabet, but are simplified, made with straight lines, suitable for carving into hard surfaces, like rock, metal, or wood. In Norway there are about 200 inscriptions that survive in the older *futhark*. Most of these are short, often simply identifying the carver of a rune stone (Figures 7.1 and 7.2).

| f | uth | a | r | k | g | w | h | n | i | j | p | æ | R | s | t | b | e | m | l | rg | d | o |

**Figure 7.1**
Older Futhark

| f | u | th | a | r | k | h | n | i | a | s | t | b | m | l | R |

**Figure 7.2**
Younger Futhark

### Viking Age (750–1050)

Hundreds of rune stones have been found in southern Sweden and Denmark, but only about 65 in Norway. They tend to be formulaic, often commemorating someone who has died. They normally contain a description of the deceased and name the person who commissioned the stone and how they are related. Some of the stones also contain illustrations and even lines of poetry, though runes did not seem to be used for longer literary works. In addition to runic inscriptions on stones, they were also carved into wood and metal.

Most Norwegian poetry from this period was actually preserved in oral tradition in Iceland, which was mainly settled by Norwegians beginning around 870 CE. The language at the time is referred to as Old Norse, and was virtually the same in Iceland and Norway. Old Norse verse consisted of two types, Eddic poetry and Skaldic poetry. Eddic poems are usually anonymous and can be grouped into three categories: poems about heroes, gods, or wisdom. Skaldic poems, on the other hand, are composed by named poets in honor of the king or chieftain who employed them. They are much more complex in rhyme and meter. None of this poetry was actually written down until the 1200s, after the arrival of Christianity in Scandinavia.

### Middle Ages: Literary Old Norse (1050–1370)

When Scandinavians were introduced to Christianity, they also learned the Latin alphabet and language. The literate wrote on calfskin vellum, using quill and ink. The earliest literature was religious texts used in worship. Religious verse, stories of saints' lives, and sermons were all recorded. Initially the learned ones wrote in Latin, but around the end of the eleventh century, they began writing texts, particularly laws and religious texts, in Old Norse. But in the 1200s they began writing secular texts, such as Eddic and Skaldic poetry, as well as prose texts, the sagas. Sagas can be divided into various genres, including kings' sagas, family sagas, and legendary sagas. Most of the sagas were actually written in Iceland but dealt with Norwegian kings and heroes. The most famous kings' saga is *Heimskringla*, by thirteenth-century Icelandic historian Snorri Sturluson. More about Snorri's writings is included in Chapter 3. The most famous work of Norwegian literature from the 1200s is *Konungs skuggsjá* (The King's Mirror). Consisting of a series of questions and answers, it provides guidance on good manners and proper conduct for royals.

### Medieval Oral Literature

Because such a large proportion of educated people perished in the Black Death, there was little written literary activity for the next 200 years or so. Oral tradition did continue, however, and many medieval ballads and other songs, as well as legends and folktales survived at least in part until they could be written down in the nineteenth century. The ballads are described in more detail in the chapter on performing arts.

### Reformation/Humanism (1500s)

The 1500s marked a low point for Norway's culture, economy, and sovereignty. Norway had been in a union with Denmark for more than 100 years, but in 1536 the Danish king declared Norway to be a Danish province, and a year later established Lutheranism as the official religion of the Kingdom of Denmark-Norway. The church was now under the sovereignty of the King rather than the Pope. Lacking universities or an educated middle class, Norwegians were ill prepared for the change from Catholicism. The translation of the Bible into Danish helped solidify the position of Danish language in Norway. Because religious services were now conducted in Dano-Norwegian, rather than Latin, sermons and hymns were written and published in the vernacular.

Toward the end of the century, there was an upsurge in scholarly activity and an exploration of the humanism that had arisen elsewhere in Europe 100 years earlier. It was a period of historical and topographical writing.

### Baroque (1600s)

The 1600s brought increasing prosperity and education to Norway. The first printing press came in 1643, and writings on history and topography continued to dominate, in addition to hymns, devotionals, collections of sermons, and occasional poetry. Toward the end of the 1600s, two poets stand out: Dorothe Engelbretsdotter (1634–1716) and Petter Dass (1647–1707). Engelbretsdotter wrote hymns in a Baroque style and was very popular in her time. Dass, a clergyman from North Norway, remains an important literary figure today. He wrote hymns and secular as well as religious songs and occasional poetry, but his masterpiece is *Nordlands Trompet* (*Trumpet of Nordland*). In this work, which has been translated into German and English, he combines lessons on Christianity with a lively description of life and geography of the coast of northern Norway. Almost none of his work was published during his lifetime, but distributed as handmade copies. Once they were printed, however, they became exceedingly popular and were reprinted again and again. He wrote in Danish, but introduced the use of Norwegian words for geographical terms that could not be expressed in Danish. A Petter Dass museum was established in his home community of Alstahaug in 1966 in the old parsonage. In 2007 a modern museum building was opened, designed by the architectural firm Snøhetta.

### Enlightenment (1700s)

The eighteenth century was characterized by a belief in reason, science, and progress and was a reaction to the religiosity of the baroque period. The foremost poet of this century, for both Norway and Denmark, was Ludvig Holberg (1684–1754). Born in Bergen, Norway, he moved to Copenhagen as a student and remained there for the rest of his life. He is therefore claimed as the father of both Norwegian and Danish literature and theater. He was a poet, novelist, and moral philosopher and wrote satirical poetry, history, essays, and letters. His most widely read book was a travel novel called *The Journey of Nils Klim to the World Underground* (1742), written in Latin and translated into several languages. Often called the Molière of the North, Holberg was most successful as a playwright. He wrote 26 comedies, some of which are still produced. Two of his most popular plays are *Jeppe på Bjerget* (Jeppe of the Hill) and *Erasmus Montanus*, both from 1722.

In 1772, a group of Norwegian students in Copenhagen founded a literary society called *Det norske Selskab* (The Norwegian Society) that lasted until 1813. They expressed a dawning Norwegian nationalism, and poets like

Johan Nordahl Bruun, Claus and Peter Frimann, Thomas Stockfleth, Claus Fasting, and Jens Zetlitz produced a number of works ranging from drinking songs to hymns and tragedies. Johan Herman Wessel was the most successful with his parody of classical tragedy, *Kierlighed uden Strømper* (Love Without Stockings) from 1772.

### Romanticism (1830s–1870s)

Romanticism represented a reaction to the intellectualism of the Enlightenment period. While Romanticism appeared in Europe in the late 1700s with the writings of Rousseau, Goethe, William Blake, and others, it arrived several decades later in Norway. Romanticism is characterized by idealism, love of nature, and a yearning for the idealized past. Civilization and culture are viewed as destructive of human nobility, and the artist is seen as genius. Norway's growing nationalism, combined with Romanticism, became National Romanticism. Henrik Wergeland (1808–1845) is a true representative of Romanticism in Norway, rejecting the ideals of classicism and developing a deeply personal style of poetry. He was also a strong nationalist as well as an idealist and political activist. He wrote songs for oppressed peoples, including American blacks as well as the people of Spain, Russia, and Poland. He spoke out in favor of reforming the Danish written language then used in Norway and making it more Norwegian. He also worked for improved educational opportunities for farmers and working-class people and for a change in the Norwegian constitution of 1814, which contained an article prohibiting Jews from living in Norway. This article was finally dropped six years after his death. In 1829, Wergeland organized the first celebration of the Seventeenth of May, the date Norway's constitution was signed in 1814. This was unpopular with the Swedish king, who did not want any reminders of Norway's brief independence.

Wergeland's main literary rival was Johan Sebastian Welhaven (1807–1873), who leaned more toward the Danish cultural heritage and emphasized clarity and harmony in his poetry. He also became one of Norway's leading National Romantic poets, combining his desire for harmony and order with his love of Norwegian nature. Welhaven was for a time romantically involved with Wergeland's younger sister, Camilla. Their relationship was doomed, however, because of Welhaven's strained relationship with both her father and her brother, Henrik. Camilla, though she still loved Welhaven, married Peter Jonas Collett, a member of Welhaven's pro-Danish Intelligence Party. Collett strongly encouraged her to write, and Camilla Collett (1813–1895), widowed after only 10 years, wrote the first Norwegian novel *Amtmandens døtre* (The District Governor's Daughters, 1854–1855) after her husband's death. This novel dealt with the subjugation of women in patriarchal Norwegian society, and is said to be the inspiration for later writers, such as Henrik Ibsen and Jonas

Lie, who also wrote about women's issues. She also inspired later female authors, such as Amalie Skram and Sigrid Undset.

### National Breakthrough

The years 1840–1880 are considered the time of Norway's national breakthrough, a time filled with enthusiasm for all that was Norwegian and the search for Norway's national identity. Two especially important figures were the folktale collectors Peter Christen Asbjørnsen (1812–1885) and Jørgen Moe (1813–1882). Inspired by the Grimm brothers in Germany, they traveled around rural settlements in Norway, collecting and recording the folktales and legends in the oral tradition. They later published several collections of tales and legends, which helped establish Norwegian cultural identity as well as begin to develop a Norwegianized form of the Danish written language. Asbjørnsen and Moe did more than simply publish the tales as they were told. They combined different variants of tales, adjusted the language to make it intelligible to the reading audience, and frequently used a frame story to create a context for their tales. While others have published collections of tales, for ordinary Norwegians it is Asbjørnsen and Moe's tales that have retained their significance to this day.

Many of the characters and stories in Asbjørnsen and Moe's collections have become an important part of Norwegian literature, language, and culture. The main character of many of the tales is Askeladden, the Ash lad. The youngest of three brothers, Askeladden is ignored by his family and thought of as unimportant, a bit slow, and lacking in initiative as he sits by the fire, stirring the ashes. A typical storyline involves a scenario where the two older brothers go out on a quest, attempting to defeat a troll or solve a riddle in order to win a reward, such as a princess or pots of gold. Each of the two older brothers is defeated, one after the other, until only Askeladden remains. Although his family thinks it ridiculous that he should even try where his brothers have failed, he insists on having his chance. At first it appears that he, too, will be defeated, as he wastes time collecting useless objects or behaving in a kindly fashion toward random people he meets along the way, perhaps sharing the little food he possesses. In the end, however, he is rewarded for his kind nature, curiosity, and inventiveness. The people he has treated well turn out to be magical helpers and assist him in defeating the trolls or solving the riddle. Although he begins as the underdog, he ends up winning the princess. Even today, someone who has risen from rags to riches in Norway is compared to Askeladden, and it is considered more legitimate for an underdog to achieve wealth and success than to be born with it.

Another prominent folktale character is the troll, who is large, ugly, stupid, and evil, but easily defeated by a clever opponent like Askeladden. Trolls often have more than one head, perhaps three or a multiple of three. They turn to stone if they are exposed to sunshine and cannot stand the sound of church bells. Multiples of three or seven are common in the tales because these numbers have magical significance.

Many of the tales illuminate human behavior and Norwegian values. While kings, queens, and princesses are common, the royalty depicted are quite down to earth. It is usual, for example, for the king to answer the door himself, perhaps dressed in a bathrobe. One tale, called *Kjerringa mot strømmen* (The Old Woman Against the Current), tells of an old man and woman who are fighting about how to cut the hay—with a scissors or with a knife—as they cross a bridge over a river. The woman's insistence on using a scissors infuriates her husband to such a degree that he finally pushes her under the water. Even as he holds her head under, she does not capitulate, but sticks her hand out of the water snipping, as if she were holding a scissors. Suddenly he loses his grasp on her, and she floats away. Later, filled with regret, the man searches downstream. Unable to find her, he finally he calls in the neighbors to help in the search. Instead of finding her in the logical downstream location, however, they locate her upstream, above the waterfalls. Although one might raise the issue of spousal abuse with this tale, those who admire her courage to go against the patriarchy have actually viewed the character's stubbornness with pride.

### 1850–1875: Transition from Romanticism to Realism

The 1850s marked the debut of a new generation of authors. The most significant were Henrik Ibsen (1828–1906) and Bjørnstjerne Bjørnson (1832–1910). These two writers would dominate the Norwegian literary scene for the next 50 years. Along with Alexander Kielland and Jonas Lie, Bjørnson and Ibsen were celebrated by Gyldendal, their publisher, as "The Four Greats" of Norwegian literature.

#### Henrik Ibsen

Henrik Ibsen was born in 1828 in Skien, in southern Norway. When Ibsen was only seven years old, his father declared bankruptcy. He was forced to give up his business, and his properties were auctioned off. At the age of 15 Ibsen left home to start an apprenticeship in an apothecary in Grimstad. There he fathered an illegitimate child by Else Sophie Jensdatter, one of the servants. At this time he also studied and wrote his first play, *Catiline*. In 1850, he relocated to Christiania to study for the university entrance examination, and he was able to publish *Catiline* under the pseudonym of Brynjolf Bjarme. Ibsen never did study at the university, but rather accepted an offer from Ole Bull to be the director and in-house playwright of the Norwegian Theater in Bergen. He later made the first of many study tours abroad but returned to Norway to become the artistic director of the Christiania

Norwegian Theater. After his marriage to Suzannah Thoresen and the birth of their son, Sigurd, he took his family and left for Italy in 1864. He lived abroad, mostly in Rome, Munich, and Dresden, for the next 27 years.

While Henrik Ibsen began his career writing historical drama, he made his breakthrough with two plays that broke with National Romanticism. His two dramas *Brand* (1866) and *Peer Gynt* (1867) were immediate successes and resulted in Ibsen being granted a state stipend. *Brand's* rigidly idealistic central character demonstrates the folly of his willingness to sacrifice all to achieve his lofty goal, whereas Peer Gynt was Brand's antithesis—a man who had no core values but lived according to his own whims. While Brand's motto was "All or nothing," Peer Gynt's was "To thine own self—be enough."

In the 1870s, Ibsen came to know Georg Brandes, the Danish intellectual who ushered in The Modern Breakthrough. In a famous lecture, Brandes asserted that the role of literature should be to subject problems to debate. Ibsen took up the call and began writing dramas that identified and criticized the corrupt practices and hypocrisy of modern society. His first such play was *Pillars of Society* in 1877, a criticism of the immoral and corrupt practices of modern society. In 1879 he published *A Doll's House*, whose main character, Nora, ends up rejecting her childlike life as Helmer's wife, leaving her husband and—more outrageously—her children. This play was almost immediately translated into German and English, and set off a firestorm of debate over its treatment of the role of women in marriage and society. Ibsen was even pressured to create an alternate ending in German, in which Nora has second thoughts about abandoning her children and reconciles with her husband. Ibsen continued writing problem plays, producing *Ghosts* in 1881, which sparked moral outrage over its themes of venereal disease, incest, and euthanasia. *An Enemy of the People* followed in 1882, about a man who reveals the truth about the polluted waters in the health spa of his city. His next two plays, *The Wild Duck* in 1884 and *Rosmersholm* in 1886, both deal with the consequences of telling the truth without attention to its cost. These plays, and *Lady from the Sea* (1888) and *Hedda Gabler* (1890), can be considered transitions from realism to his more psychological and symbolic plays.

In 1891, Ibsen returned to Norway, where he wrote his last four plays: *The Master Builder* (1892), *Little Eyolf* (1894), *John Gabriel Borkman* (1896), and his final work, *When We Dead Awaken* (1899). Ibsen suffered his first stroke in 1900 and died in 1906. The apartment on Arbiensgate in Oslo where he lived for his last 11 years has been restored and is an Ibsen museum.

### Bjørnstjerne Bjørnson

A theater director and editor at various stages of his life, Bjørnstjerne Bjørnson was a prolific author, publishing numerous plays, novels, short stories, and lyric poems. Among his poems is Norway's national song, *Ja, vi elsker dette landet* (Yes, We Love This Country). Bjørnson was politically active and a nationalist, working for the causes of peace and international understanding. Although he had previously considered himself a republican, he spoke out in favor of a monarchy in 1905, when Norway finally achieved independence from Sweden.

Bjørnson is credited with being the creator of Norwegian historical drama harking back to the saga period. He also was the first Norwegian to write realistic contemporary problem plays, although they have not had the lasting success of Ibsen's works. Bjørnson is, however, best known for his peasant tales, including *Synnøve Solbakken*, published in 1857. In 1903, Bjørnson was awarded the Nobel Prize for Literature, an honor shared by only two other Norwegians, Knut Hamsun in 1920 and Sigrid Undset in 1928.

### Lie and Kielland

Jonas Lie (1833–1908) and Alexander Kielland (1849–1906) were the other two members of The Four Greats. Lie, from northern Norway, was a prolific writer, producing more than 30 books about the seafaring communities of the north. Like many Norwegian writers and artists at the time, he ended up living abroad for a lengthy period of his life. His masterpiece is *Familien paa Gilje* (The Family at Gilje, 1883), which criticizes the inferior position of women in marriage and society, though some, including the Danish critic Georg Brandes, thought he was too detached in his critique.[2]

Kielland, from the west-coast city of Stavanger, marks the transition of Norwegian literature from realism to naturalism. His central work is *Garman & Worse* (1880), a novel about a shipping dynasty. Encouraged by Georg Brandes, he writes sharp societal commentary rather than the objective description of the realistic tradition. Influenced by such thinkers as Darwin, John Stuart Mill, and Charles Dickens, he wrote out of a sense of guilt at his own unearned material well-being.[3]

### The 1880s and Naturalism

Amalie Skram (1846–1905) was the foremost representative of the naturalism that dominated the 1880s with its emphasis on the influence of heredity and environment and its focus on the tragic lives of the lower classes. Skram's first major work was a novel about marriage and the subservient position of women, *Constance Ring* (1885), which caused a scandal over its explicit sexuality. She also wrote of the cruel treatment of the mentally ill in *Professor Hieronimus* and *At St. Jørgen* (both from 1895; English translation *Under Observation*, 1992), which was based on her personal experience as a mental patient. Her greatest work is the four-volume, multigenerational saga, *The People of Hellemyr* (1887–1898).

Arne Garborg (1852–1928) approved of Skram's radical writing. He became heavily involved with the morality debate of the time as well as the controversy between religious conservatives and radicals. The theme of one of his major works, *Bondestudentar* (Peasant Students, 1883), is the tension between the traditional rural way of life and the growing urbanization of Norway. Written in *Landsmål* (*Nynorsk*), the book deals with the psychological difficulties of a farm boy who moves to Christiania to attend the university. What lives on in an international context, however, is his lyric poem cycle *Haugtussa* (1895), inspired by folktales and song. It was set to music by Edvard Grieg and is part of soprano repertory today.

### Knut Hamsun

Knut Hamsun (1859–1952) is one of the most prominent figures in modern literature, although his position in Norwegian literature today is clouded by his loyalty to Hitler and Nazism during World War II. The year 2009 marked the 150th anniversary of his birth, and despite the controversy over his life versus his art, Norwegians seem to have come to terms with the reality that he was a complex man who both created great art and held abhorrent views.

In his youth Hamsun gave a series of lectures criticizing his predecessors, The Four Greats, including Ibsen, for creating social types, rather than complex characters. He laid out his own program, stating that literature should be art, not educational or political, and expressed his interest in delving into the depths of the souls of his characters. Hamsun is known for his many novels, including *Sult* (Hunger, 1890), which was his breakthrough success; *Mysterier* (Mysteries, 1892); *Pan* (1894); and *Markens grøde* (Growth of the Soil, 1917), for which he won the Nobel Prize for Literature in 1920. He did not enjoy immediate success, however, having struggled unsuccessfully to publish novels since the 1870s. He traveled widely, including two stays in the American Midwest, where he grew to despise what he considered American materialism and hypocrisy. Later he published a book titled *Fra det moderne Amerikas aandsliv* (The Cultural Life of Modern America, 1889) detailing his criticism of American culture, politics, and art.

Hamsun felt a great attraction toward German culture and philosophy, and was an admirer of Nietzsche. In the 1930s, he expressed support for ideals of the Nazi movement in Germany and his opposition to Communism. After Norway was occupied by Germany in 1940, he maintained his sympathy toward the Nazis. He wrote a series of articles in support of Hitler, traveled to Germany to meet Hitler in 1943, and even wrote a glowing obituary after Hitler's death in 1945. Some have argued that Hamsun was old, deaf, and out of touch, and manipulated by his German-speaking wife. The authorities even tried to prove that he was mentally ill. After the war he was detained in an old people's home, where a psychiatric examination declared him to have permanently impaired mental faculties. He himself was offended by this suggestion, and at the age of 90 he published a memoir reflecting on this period of his life, *På gjengrodde stier* (On Overgrown Paths, 1949), demonstrating his undiminished mental acuity.

### The Twentieth Century

The twentieth century also marked a continuation of the realistic tradition in Norwegian literature. Sometimes called neo-realism, the period is also characterized by an increased attention to the interaction between social setting and human psychology and by a greater emphasis on moral and religious values. Many authors write from a local setting, and a number of epic, multivolume historical novels were published. One of these was by Sigrid Undset (1882–1949), who in 1928 won the Nobel Prize for Literature for *Kristin Lavransdatter* (1920–1922). This three-volume work is set in the 1300s and deals with the themes of love, passion, and selfishness versus duty to God and family.

Other women who began writing in the 1920s and 1930s were Cora Sandel (Sara Fabricius, 1880–1974); poet, translator, and children's book author Halldis Moren Vesaas (1907–1995); and poet Inger Hagerup (1905–1985). Cora Sandel wrote a trilogy about the struggle of a young woman from northern Norway finding herself as an artist: *Alberte og Jacob* (1929; Alberta and Jacob, 1962), *Alberte og friheten* (1931; Alberta and Freedom, 1963), and *Bare Alberte* (1939; Alberta Alone, 1965). Halldis Moren Vesaas's beautiful and elegant poetry, which she wrote in *Nynorsk*, was often about human relationships.

Olav Duun (1876–1939) also wrote multivolume epic novels, including the six-volume *Juvikfolket* (The People of Juvik, 1918–1923). He often focused on the fate of the individual who struggles against the forces of nature or society. Duun came from the North-Trøndelag area of Namdal, and wrote in Namdal dialect.

Kristoffer Uppdal (1878–1961) and Johan Falkberget (1879–1967) are two great proletarian writers. Uppdal wrote about the new working class that was emerging after the industrialization of Norway, building railroad lines and working in factories. Falkberget wrote about the mining community in Røros and the challenges posed by the advent of capitalism.

### 1920–1960s: Political Radicalism and Psychological Realism

Influenced by Freudianism and Marxism, the period from 1920 to 1940 is marked by political radicalism and psychological realism. With an interruption during the last part of the German occupation of 1940–1945, when most authors boycotted the Nazified publishing houses, the psychological realistic tradition continued after the war into the 1960s. Sigurd Hoel (1890–1960), who had been an important literary and cultural figure since the 1920s, became interested in Freud in his youth. In his novel *Møte ved milepelen* (Meeting at the Milestone, 1947), Hoel attempted to understand why some people became Nazi traitors whereas others risked their lives fighting in the resistance. In psychoanalytical fashion, he found the answers by looking back at events in their childhood and youth. Others who wrote about the war include Kåre Holt, Sigurd Evensmo, Odd Bang-Hansen, and Johan Borgen among others. Most of these novels dealt with male resistance fighters, either recording events in a documentary fashion or dealing with the psychological and moral struggles of the heroes.

Taking a different approach was Torborg Nedreaas (1906–1987). She debuted in 1945 with a short story collection about everyday life of women and children during the occupation, *Bak skapet står øksen* (The Axe is Behind the Cupboard). Here she presents a sympathetic portrait of the young women who had love relationships with German soldiers. Her best-known work is the Herdis trilogy: *Trylleglasset* (The Magic Prism, 1950), *Musikk fra en blå brønn* (1960; Music from a Blue Well, 1988), and *Ved neste nymåne* (By the Next New Moon, 1971), portraying Herdis from her childhood to adulthood through a socialist and feminist perspective.

Ebba Haslund (1907–2009) was a prominent feminist and peace activist who also wrote about everyday life during the occupation as well as the lives of middle-class women. A prolific writer, she published her last book the year she died, at age 92. An active participant in societal debate until her death, she spoke out in favor of gay marriage before it became legal in Norway.

### Modernism

Although the realistic tradition remained dominant in prose writing, one author stands out for his symbolic and allegorical novels. Tarjei Vesaas (1897–1970) wrote several novels in *Nynorsk* that have entered the canon, including *Fuglane* (The Birds, 1957) and *Isslottet* (The Ice Palace, 1963), which are a blend of symbolism and realism. He also wrote short stories and poetry. Other modernist poets include Rolf Jacobsen (1907–1994) whose poetry focuses on the conflict between nature and technology, and Olav H. Hauge (1908–1994), *Nynorsk* poet whose works were firmly rooted in his home region of Hardanger. He was also internationally oriented and translated poetry by many writers including Yeats, Browning, and Brecht, and was inspired by Chinese poetry.

### 1970s: Social Realism and Social Modernism

By the late 1960s, the political winds began to change and a new, idealistic, extreme leftist generation of young writers emerged in the literary journal

*Profil* (Profile). These authors would later be referred to as the *Profil* group, and included Dag Solstad (1941–) and Tor Obrestad (1938–), who were members of the Maoist AKP m/l (Workers Communist Party Marxist/Leninist), which had little or nothing to do with the real working class. Initially, these writers were rebelling against the dominant psychological realism in prose literature and were skeptical of what they considered was the overuse of metaphors and symbolism in postwar modernism in poetry. They called for more concrete depictions of everyday life.

The 1970s brought the revitalization and politicization of social realism, which took up such social problems as gender and class struggles. Other important authors who debuted during this decade include Knut Faldbakken (1941–) and Edvard Hoem (1949–). Modernistic prose also developed into social modernism, with such authors as Kjartan Fløgstad (1944–), who writes in *Nynorsk* and Øystein Lønn (1936–). Both of these authors have written novels combining modernistic prose with social criticism. The 1970s was also an important period for the new feminist movement, and women's literature began receiving more attention. Significant women writers include Bjørg Vik (1935–), Herbjørg Wassmo (1942–), Gerd Brantenberg (1941–), and Tove Nilsen (1952–), although many of these women resist being categorized primarily as women writers.

### The 1980s and Beyond

The 1980s and 1990s mark a move away from social realism and toward fantasy, science fiction, diversity, and simply telling a good story, with less overt ideology. Significant authors were Jan Kjærstad (1953–), Lars Saabye Christensen (1953–), and Roy Jacobsen (1954–). Some, such as Kjærstad and Hoem, have been influenced by Latin American magical realism and experimented with surrealistic fantasy or post-modernist metafiction. Ingvar Ambjørnsen (1956–) and Erlend Loe (1969–) are popular both among adults and young people, and have been translated into English and other languages. Several of their books have been made into films. Dramatists Jon Fosse (1959–) and Cecilie Løveid (1951–) have also gained some attention abroad.

Per Petterson (1952–) is the most internationally successful Norwegian writer in the first decade of the twenty-first century, though others, such as Linn Ullmann (1966–), daughter of Liv Ullmann and Ingmar Bergman; Lars Saabye Christensen (1953–); and journalist Åsne Seierstad (1970–) have also enjoyed success abroad. The *Times-online* has selected Petterson's *Ut å stjæle hester* (2003; Out Stealing Horses, trans. Anne Born, 2005) as one of the 100 best books of the decade and one of the 50 outstanding literary translations of the last 50 years.[4] Since then three more of Petterson's novels have appeared in English, *To Siberia* (1998), *In the Wake* (2002), and *I Curse the River of Time* (2010).

## LITERATURE FOR CHILDREN AND YOUNG PEOPLE

Norwegian children's literature lagged behind that of other European countries until the late 1800s. Before then little was produced specifically for children, who were viewed as small adults. In the late 1700s, creation of a literature for children became part of the movement to create a Norwegian identity. The works themselves were intended to teach children proper behavior as well as religion. By the end of the nineteenth century the authority of religion had declined, and literature began being produced for its entertainment value.

### The Golden Age

The period from 1890 to 1914 is usually referred to as the golden age of Norwegian children's literature. As more children learned to read, there was a greater demand for books to teach reading as well as books for children to read on their own. Nordahl Rolfsen (1848–1928) published the magazine *Illustreret tidende for børn* (Illustrated Journal for Children, 1885–1892), where many well-known writers published stories before they appeared in book form. Rolfsen also produced a five-volume series of readers for the public schools containing works by such famous authors as Jørgen Moe, Henrik Wergeland, and Bjørnstjerne Bjørnson. He is also credited with establishing the centralized system of school libraries. Dikken Zwilgmeyer (1853–1913) is known for her Inger Johanne books, which have been translated into English. These feature something new for Norwegian children's literature, a girl who is free of rigid gender roles and is unafraid to do anything the boys do. Barbra Ring (1870–1955) also rejected the traditional female role, placing her young female protagonists outside being physically active rather than indoors helping with the housework. Collections of songs and nursery rhymes were also important, especially *Kom, skal vi synge* (Come. Let's Sing, 1905) by Margrethe Munthe (1850–1931), which is still in print.

### Before and during World War II

The period between the wars represented a time of rapid change in Norwegian society, with increased industrialization and urbanization, as well as greater political awareness. In Norwegian books, there continued to be a systematic distinction between books for boys and books for girls. Not much of lasting quality was produced, and the earlier books remained popular. During the German occupation, Thorbjørn Egner was the only important author who debuted. Most books that were published were classics, like folktales, though some had hidden anti-German messages, most notably *Snorre Sel* (Snorri the Seal, 1941).

### After World War II

In the immediate postwar period the state began showing an interest in children's literature, offering a literary prize for best children's book beginning in 1948 and also supporting authors through the Norwegian Cultural Council. Because children in the immediate postwar period had experienced the insecurity of war and occupation, the books tended to be lighthearted and friendly, rather than deal with the events of the occupation. Many books emphasized international understanding and responsibility. Translations of series like *Nancy Drew* (beginning in 1941) and the *Hardy* Boys (from 1950) were especially widely read.

Children's radio programs became popular, and some authors became beloved radio hosts as well. Two of the most well liked were Thorbjørn Egner (1912–1990), who also published a series of early readers for the schools, and Alf Prøysen (1914–1970), who wrote children's songs, poems, and stories. His series about *Teskjekjerringa* (Mrs. Pepperpot) has been translated into many languages.

Anne-Cath. Vestly (1920–2008) is another writer who was active in children's radio. She was significant in Norwegian children's literature because she was the first to write about urban children solving problems themselves, alternative families, and where babies come from. Her books depicted life in the postwar high-rise complexes called *drabantbyer* (satellite towns). She created a scandal in 1954 when she told children on the radio about a mother with a baby in her tummy. This was the first pregnant woman in Norwegian children's literature! Vestly remained active until her death, and even acted in movies based on her books.

The 1960s brought a greater willingness to depict the problems of children. Interest grew in the lives of outsider children who had handicaps or who were lonely, sometimes involving sad or scary stories. The 1970s was characterized by great variety in form and type. By now the categories of boys' books and girls' books has been dropped in the book catalogs, and writers are much more likely to take up problems like divorce, drugs, or mental illness.

By the 1980s, writers moved away from the stark reality of the 1970s and began writing more playfully in fantasy and science fiction genres, but the 1990s marked a return to more serious topics. Children's books dealing with issues such as ethical dilemmas, life and death, and the meaning of new technology were common. A prime example of this new tendency can be found in the books of Jostein Gaarder (1952–), who in 1991 published the international best seller *Sophie's World: A Novel about the History of Philosophy.*

It was translated into 53 languages and sold more 30 million copies. In 1995, *Sophie's World* was the most-sold novel in the world. It has since been made into a film (1999), a computer game, and recently launched its own Facebook page with over 50,000 fans and growing. Gaarder's other books have not enjoyed the same success, although many have been translated to English, including *The Solitaire Mystery: A Novel about Family and Destiny, Through a Glass, Darkly, Vita Brevis: A Letter to St. Augustine, The Ringmaster's Daughter, The Orange Girl, Maya,* and *The Christmas Mystery.*

Norwegian children have always read translated literature from abroad. Books ranging from *Winnie the Pooh, Alice in Wonderland,* and *Nancy Drew* to *Harry Potter* are immensely popular. Recently, Norwegian picture books have been receiving international attention, particularly in Europe. It is more difficult to break into the American market, although a few books have been published, including one by Princess Märtha Louise, illustrated by Svein Nyhus, called *Why Kings and Queens Don't Wear Crowns* (Skandisk, 2005). The princess, who is the great-granddaughter of Norway's first king after independence in 1905, writes a fairytale-like story of the desire of little Crown Prince Olav to be like other Norwegian children. He finds it too difficult to play properly with a crown on his head, so the family finally decides to put the crowns away. This book illustrates the desire of the royal family to be viewed as regular Norwegians.

The position of Norwegian children's literature was strengthened beginning in the 1970s when children's literature was included in the Norwegian Arts Council purchasing program (see below). Between 160 and 170 books are published each year for children and young adults.

## CRIME FICTION

While Norwegian crime fiction has yet to achieve the same international stature as Swedish, it has nonetheless grown tremendously in popularity and status in recent years. Like Swedish crime fiction, Norwegian writers have tended to focus on societal failure as a root cause for criminal behavior, rather than following the American/British tradition of looking at individual psychology. Some current writers whose books are available in English are Gunnar Staalesen (1947–), Jo Nesbø (1960–), Anne Holt (1958–), Karin Fossum (1954–), Kjersti Scheen (1943–), and Kjell Ola Dahl (1958–).

## LITERARY BIOGRAPHY

In addition to crime fiction, literary biography is the other genre that has enjoyed tremendous popularity in the last two decades. Biographies of famous authors, such as Knut Hamsun, Sigrid Undset, Amalie Skram, Arne and Hulda Garborg, and political figures such as Gro Harlem Brundtland have been immensely popular.

## LITERATURE BY NORWEGIANS WITH IMMIGRANT BACKGROUND

Immigration to Norway is nothing new, but it is only since the late 1960s that a significant number of people from non-Western cultures have settled in Norway. In recent years, these new Norwegians have begun creating their own literature, some written in their native languages but most in Norwegian. Their short stories, poetry, and novels provide a different perspective on modern Norwegian experience and reflect a new, multicultural Norway. One of the first immigrant novels was *Pakkis* (1986), written by Khalid Hussain, a 16-year-old immigrant from Pakistan. Other authors include Czech writer Michael Konupek (1948–) and Roda Ahmed (1975–) from Somalia, who now lives in New York.

## SÁMI LITERATURE[5]

The oldest Sámi-language texts date back to the 1600s, consisting mostly of beginning readers and religious literature written with Norwegian or Swedish orthography. The oral tradition has a longer history, going back generations, and continues today. Until the 1960s, few Sámi were literate in their own language. Before then most had been forced to learn Norwegian in school. Modern Sámi literature began in the 1900s, but relatively little was published before 1970. At that time the first Sámi publishing companies were established and the Arts Council of Norway began providing financial support. Now all support is administered through the Sámi Parliament.

Sámi literature is thriving today, with approximately 10–20 titles published each year in all genres. Some of these have also been translated into Norwegian in recent years. Some central figures are Nils-Aslak Valkeapää (1943–2001), who won the Nordic Council Literary prize in 1991; Kirsti Paltto (1947–); Rauni Magga Lukkari (1943–); Jovnna-Ánde Vest (1948–); Synnøve Persen (1950–); and Inger-Mari Aikio (1961–). *In the Shadow of the Midnight Sun: Contemporary Sámi Prose and Poetry* (1996) is a collection of Sámi poetry and prose by 21 Sámi writers from all four Nordic countries translated into English.

## PUBLIC POLICY IN SUPPORT OF LITERATURE

Since 1965 Norway has had a program providing public support of contemporary literature. Through this program publishers are guaranteed minimum sales of 1,000 copies of literature, both fiction and nonfiction, prose and poetry; 1,550 copies of new children's books; and 500 copies of translated children's literature. About 500 titles in all benefit from this program each year. These books are purchased by the Arts Council of Norway and distributed to public libraries and school libraries. The Arts Council is an independent agency funded by the Ministry of Culture. In addition to benefiting authors and publishers, this program also ensures that all public libraries, no matter how small, have a complete collection of contemporary Norwegian literature.

## NOTES

1. http://www.lovdata.no/for/sf/ku/tu-20070401-0378-020.html. Accessed 1/25/10.

2. James McFarlane, "Norwegian Literature 1860–1910," in Harald Næss, ed., *A History of Norwegian Literature* (Lincoln: University of Nebraska Press, 1993), p. 142.

3. McFarlane, p. 150.

4. http://entertainment.timesonline.co.uk/tol/arts_and_entertainment/books/book_reviews/article6914181.ece. Accessed 11/25/09.

5. http://www.utexas.edu/courses/sami/diehtu/giella/lit/sami-lit.htm. Accessed 11/24/09.

# 8

# Media and Cinema

## MASS MEDIA[1]

Norway's media have undergone rapid change in recent years, as shown in Figure 8.1. In one generation, Norway has gone from being one of the most backward countries in the developed world to one of the leaders. In 1970, for example, a new subscriber might have to wait months to get a landline telephone installed. Today there are more mobile phone subscriptions than there are people in Norway; 90 percent of 10-year-olds have a cell phone. In 1970, there was one television station and one radio station. Today there are dozens. Internet use has grown dramatically, increasing from 10 percent daily users to 71 percent in 10 years. Norway remains at top of newspaper readership statistics in the world. Although the percentage of Norwegians reading the newspaper on a daily basis has declined, nearly 70 percent of Norwegians still read at least one newspaper a day.

### Newspapers[2]

Nearly 220 newspapers are published in Norway, with the largest papers located in the capital city, Oslo, but sold over the entire country. Yet newspapers are struggling for survival despite government subsidies and high readership numbers compared to other countries. Approximately 68 percent of Norwegians over age nine read a paper daily in 2008. The number is higher among women, those over 45, and those with higher education. Norwegians commonly subscribe to one newspaper and purchase additional ones from the newsstands. Some 72 percent of Norwegians subscribed to at least one

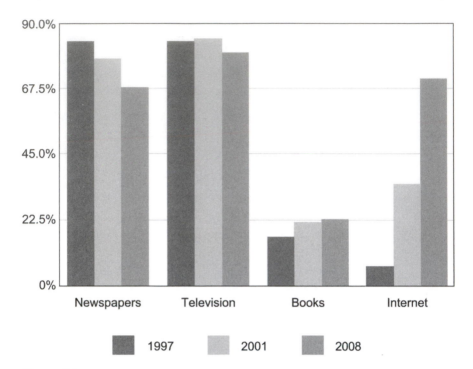

**Figure 8.1**
Norwegians using various mass media on an average day. (Statistics Norway.)

paper at home in 2008, and 11 percent of Norwegians ages 9–79 read three or more papers daily.[3] While these numbers are impressive, they show a marked decline since 1997. At that time 84 percent of Norwegians read the paper every day.

Circulation figures reflect the decline in readership. The largest paper is Oslo-based Aftenposten, with a daily circulation of more than 242,000 for its national morning edition, although it showed a decline of 2 percent since 2009. Previous leader, *VG* (*Verdens gang*), had held the top spot for 29 years, but its circulation has dropped 7.6 percent in the past year and nearly 40 percent since its high point in 2002. The only newspaper with increasing circulation figures is the financial paper, *Dagens Næringsliv*, with 83,000.

### Historical Background

Freedom of expression is guaranteed by the Norwegian constitution adopted in 1814. Norway's first daily newspaper was *Morgenbladet*, first published in 1819, although weekly papers were published in Norway as early as 1763. *Morgenbladet* is still in existence today, but as a weekly.

When political parties first came into existence in 1884, they began using newspapers to spread information and opinion. The Labor Party, founded in 1887, had its own organ, *Arbeiderbladet*. This paper, now called *Dagsavisen*, has been fully independent since 1999. While no newspapers have direct political ties now, political leaning can be observed in editorials and coverage.

The period 1850–1915 was one of great expansion, with the number of newspapers increasing from 40 to 250. From 1915 to the beginning of World War II, the number of papers remained constant. Under the German occupation, from 1940 to 1945, however, newspapers were either Nazified or shut down. For example, the newspapers of the Labor Party and Communist Party were stopped. Other newspapers were merged, sometimes even with papers having different political leanings. In addition to the Nazified papers with prewar roots, the Nazi party had its own organ, *Fritt Folk* (A Free People). By 1943, only 118 newspapers remained in Norway.

A desire for information unfiltered by the Nazis led to the establishment of the illegal press. As many as 300 illegal newspapers were published at one time or another in various parts of Norway. These papers were often simple mimeographed sheets based on information received through radio broadcasts from London. They were produced and distributed by volunteers at great personal risk.

The postwar years were a period of rapid growth for the industry until economic difficulties forced newspaper closings in the 1960s. A free press, with a variety of viewpoints represented, was considered so important for democracy and an informed citizenry in Norway that in 1969 the state began providing financial support to smaller papers and to minority-language newspapers. More than $38 million in subsidies was paid in 2009. In addition, all newspapers are exempt from the value added tax, an arrangement that also benefits the largest papers.

Rapid change has characterized the newspaper industry since 1945. Sunday newspapers began being published in 1991. Technological advances, including electronic typesetting and color have transformed the product. The old broadsheet papers have converted to a tabloid format, and there is more emphasis on personality-oriented journalism. In total 181 of the 220 newspapers have a web presence, though *Aftenposten* was recently forced to drop its English-language Web site due to financial considerations.[4] Although many small independent newspapers still exist, more than half of all newspapers in Norway are owned by one of three companies: Schibsted (with 47 newspapers, including *VG* and *Aftenposten*), A-pressen (62 papers, including *Bergensavisen*), and Edda Media (27 papers).

In 2007, a newspaper code of ethics was adopted by the Norwegian Press Association. The Ethical Code of Practice for the Press establishes the responsibility of the press with respect to the freedom of expression guaranteed by the constitution. This code, which applies to printed press, radio, television, and net publications, addresses the role of the press in society, integrity and responsibility, journalistic conduct and relations with the sources, and publication rules.[5]

## Computers and the Internet[6]

Norway is one of the most wired countries in the world: 90 percent of households have access to a PC, and 85 percent have internet access. While 73 percent of households already have broadband internet, nearly 100 percent of Norwegians potentially have access to it in their homes. In 2008, 71 percent reported using the internet every day, an increase from 66 percent the year before. Only 11 percent did not use the internet at all during the previous three months. The most common use of the internet is e-mail, although many also use it to obtain news and for banking services, shopping, and ordering tickets. Social media are especially popular in Norway, with approximately 1.5 million Norwegians on Facebook. In fact, almost half of Norwegians with web access are on Facebook once a week.[7] According to Statistics Norway, the number of users of social networking sites such as Facebook and MySpace doubled from 2007 to 2008. The strongest growth in Facebook usage is in the age groups 0–17 and over 36. Increased use of Facebook is especially seen among those over 60. As of 2009, Twitter was not as popular in Norway as other social media.

## Radio[8] and Television[9]

The first radio broadcasts in Norway were in 1925, near the cities of Oslo, Bergen, Ålesund, and Tromsø. Radio service was expanded to additional cities in the 1920s, and by 1930, Norway had a commercial, nationwide radio network. By 1925, a license was required to own a radio. In 1933, the state took control over radio in hopes of making better quality programming available and providing more coverage to rural areas. That year, NRK (Norwegian State Broadcasting Corporation) was established by the parliament with a monopoly over all broadcasting. During World War II radio was used as a tool for information and propaganda. The most popular programs were the broadcasts from London, which provided a corrective to the misinformation provided by the Nazified radio stations in Norway. These broadcasts were so successful that the Germans decided to confiscate all radios in November 1941. While most radios were indeed surrendered, a number of illegal radios were concealed in lofts and barns. Information gleaned from these was disseminated by means of illegal newspapers, as described previously.

The golden age of radio in Norway extended from 1945 to 1960, when television was introduced. Only one Norwegian radio station existed at that time.

Because people listened to the same news broadcasts, music, radio plays, entertainment, and children's radio programs, there was a feeling of solidarity and shared culture throughout the entire country. Things started changing in the 1970s, when NRK began to establish regional radio broadcasts. By 1975, NRK's radio monopoly had ended as other operators were finally permitted to have radio stations, beginning with school and student radio stations.

In 1988, after a period of experimental commercial radio, a law was passed permitting local radio stations. In 1982 NRK established a second channel, P2. After a good deal of debate over the format, it ended up as a music station, whereas P1, the original radio station, retained a mixed format. Since then NRK has established P3 (*Petre*), aimed at a younger audience. P4 was started as a privately owned, commercial station. Since the 1990s, the commercial Radio 1 network, owned by Norsk Aller and the American company Clear Channel Communications, has established itself as an urban radio station.

Digital radio arrived in Norway in 1999, enabling NRK to establish niche stations NRK *Alltid Klassisk* (Always Classical) and NRK *Alltid Nyheter*, its first all-digital channels. Also available now are such specialized channels as NRK Jazz, NRK Folk Music, as well as Sámi radio. In additional to being broadcast, these channels are also available on the internet streamed live and as podcasts.[10] Today, in addition to the state-owned/public-funded NRK, there are two national commercial radio stations and 248 licensed local radio stations, both commercial and noncommercial.[11]

Television arrived late to Norway. It was one of the last countries in Western Europe to launch television. The first official broadcasts came in 1960; in 1969 the landing of Apollo 11 on the moon was carried. In 1975 color television was introduced, and in 1985 private satellite antennae began to appear. Today about 35 percent of Norwegians use satellite television and 48 percent have cable, although in the Oslo area, 73 percent have cable television. An additional 28 percent viewed broadcast television through the air. In 2007, digital television was introduced, and by 2009 the analog broadcast system was discontinued.

NRK maintained its television monopoly until 1990, when TVNorge and TV3 began commercial cable service. Finally, in 1992, TV2 started the first nationwide commercial television station. NRK (including NRK1, NRK2, and NRK3) remains the largest television station, operating independently, although fully owned by the State. Anyone owning a television in Norway must pay a license fee to NRK (Norwegian State Broadcasting). In 2010, the $300 license fee paid by each household provided 94 percent of NRK's income. In the 2009 election campaign, the right wing Progress Party proposed eliminating the license fee and making NRK dependent on government support and advertising income. The idea caused great concern among NRK executives. Some Norwegians object to paying this fee, but it is not a huge issue for the majority.

While many television channels are available to Norwegian viewers today, both domestic and international, the two most popular channels remain NRK 1 and TV2, which each have about 44 percent of the viewers on an average day. This does, however, represent a decline. News programs remain the most popular programs on both channels. The most viewed programs on television otherwise are series, entertainment shows, feature films, and sports programs.[12] Reality TV is popular. In 2010, a popular series ran called *Alt for Norge* (All for Norway). It featured 10 Norwegian-Americans who competed to prove who was the most authentic Norwegian. The episodes required the participants to complete such stereotypically Norwegian tasks as eating *smalahove* (smoked sheep's head) or herding cows. The winner would win $50,000 and meet his or her Norwegian family. Many programs on Norwegian channels are purchased from abroad, including sitcoms and other series, movies, and talk programs from the United States such as *CSI, Oprah, Lost*, and *Grey's Anatomy*. Programs in foreign languages are not dubbed into Norwegian, but rather supplied with subtitles, meaning that Norwegians are exposed to other languages on a daily basis.

NRK, TV2, and TVNorge are available on the internet, NRK (http://www.nrk.no) free of charge, and TV2 (http://www.tv2.no) and TVNorge (http://www.tvnorge.no) by subscription. Here the majority of television programs produced in Norway are available, in addition to live streaming of radio. A number of NRK's offerings, both radio and television, can be downloaded as podcasts.

### Books and Libraries

Reading books for leisure has actually grown slightly in popularity during the last few years. About one in four Norwegians reads a book on an average day, although women and people with higher education are more likely to do so.[13] It is also common to go to the library; almost half of all Norwegians have visited library in the last year. Youth aged 16–24 as well as women of all ages use the library more frequently. Each Norwegian borrows on average five books or other media from libraries each year.

### Recorded Music

About 42 percent of Norwegians listen to music every day, although the percentage increases to 75 percent among young people between 16 and 19 years of age. Use of CDs is declining, particularly among the young, and MP3 players and digital files on computers, either copied from other media or downloaded from the internet, are increasing in popularity. See Chapter 9 for more on what kinds of music are popular.

## CINEMA

Norwegian filmmaking, along with film production in the other Nordic countries, has long been viewed as offering an alternative to the dominant Hollywood films.[14] While films have been made in Norway since the early twentieth century, unlike Sweden and Denmark, Norway has not had a long and distinguished history in filmmaking or internationally known directors. In fact there was not even a school of filmmaking in Norway until 1997, when a national film school was established in Lillehammer. In 2001, a national film fund was created to help provide financing for film projects.[15]

### Early History

Movies arrived in Norway in 1896, only three months after the first public film screening in Paris in 1897. By 1904, a Swedish company had established the first movie theater, and soon cinemas appeared all over the country and became quite profitable. At this time, however, filmmaking was not considered a legitimate artistic endeavor and suffered under both state censorship and, with the movie theater law of 1913, municipal control. This meant that each municipality could control who would be allowed to show movies within its boundaries. Most municipalities elected to run their own cinemas, with only about 10 percent of theaters being privately owned.

The first film success came in 1905, with a film documenting the arrival of the newly elected King Haakon VII and his family in Oslo. Continued fascination with the new royal family made it natural that a very popular film was made of the king and queen's tour to Trondheim for the coronation. This success encouraged the increased use of film as media. The production of shorts and newsreels continued in the 1910s, including films of celebrity funerals, such as that of Bjørnstjerne Bjørnson, as well as sports events. Advertising films, like the promotion of Bjelland sardines by celebrities of the day, were also popular. Silent films were produced, normally accompanied by piano, accordion, or violin, but sometimes by orchestras in larger theaters. Few feature films were made, and these were not on a par with international films. They were very popular, however, especially among the working class. At the time there were few censorship or age restrictions. Moviegoing was quite controversial, however, because some believed that films promoted questionable morals and were especially dangerous for children. In addition to the morals issues, some thought they might cause damage to eyesight. Finally in 1913 *Kinoloven*, the movie theater law, was passed. Censorship was introduced, and *Statens filmkontroll* (the state censorship authority) evaluated each film before it could be shown in Norway.[16]

Unlike in other countries, where the film producers owned the theaters and profits went toward production of new films, Norway followed a different path. From 1913 to 1923 the municipalities took over the running of cinemas, and private owners were pushed out. It remained a profitable business for the municipalities.

The first feature film was made in 1907 or 1908, shortly after Norway became an independent country: *Fiskerlivets farer—Et Drama paa havet* (Dangers of a Fisherman's Life—An Ocean Drama). A single-reel silent film about a fisherman whose son falls overboard and is lost, witnessed by the mother on shore, it disappeared (although it was reconstructed in 1954). Little information is available about its reception. Seventeen films were made during this early pioneer period, but the quality of the films was not much to brag about. They were mostly melodramas based on serials because there was little money or involvement from the theater community.

A breakthrough came when Swedish films were made of the Norwegian classics, *Terje Vigen* (Victor Sjöström, 1917) and *Synnøve Solbakken* (John Brunius, 1919). Many people felt these movies should have been made in Norway.

### Early Norwegian Films

The first important Norwegian film was Rasmus Breistein's *Fante-Anne* (Gypsy Anne) from 1920. Breistein, the most important director of the 1920s, not only directed the film but also wrote the script and played the violin during screenings both in Norway and in Norwegian communities in America.[17] This success marked the beginning of a period of growth for Norwegian film, although 70 percent of the movies shown at the cinema at that time were Hollywood films. In fact, Mary Pickford and Douglas Fairbanks even visited Oslo in 1924 while on a European tour. Although it remained difficult to find the capital to produce film, *Fante-Anne* marks the first movie production partially financed by the owners of the movie theaters and *Kommunernes Filmcentral* A/S.

In the 1920s, most Norwegian films emphasized the romantic innocence and beautiful nature of rural Norway. The city was a decadent place filled with drugs, cigarettes, and booze, while the countryside was idyllic. Nature films and travelogues were also popular, and several were made documenting Roald Amundsen's various expeditions, beginning with his journey to the South Pole in 1911.

During 1920s and 1930s, filmmakers began using literature as a basis for their films. Several films were based on works of well-known authors such as Mikkjel Fønhus and Kristofer Janson, and marked the beginning of a new National Romantic period of filmmaking. In 1921 came *Markens grøde* (Danish director Gunnar Sommerfeldt), based on the novel *Growth of the Soil*, for which author Knut Hamsun had won the Nobel Prize in literature the year before. This movie was tinted and had special music written to be played by orchestras in the theaters. The score has been reconstructed, and the music recorded for a newly restored version of the film created for the International Hamsun Festival in 2009. In 1922 *Pan*, another Hamsun novel, was filmed, this time directed by Norwegian actor-director, Harald Schwenzen. In 1934 Tancred Ibsen, grandson of literary greats Henrik Ibsen and Bjørnstjerne Bjørnson, remade *Synnøve Solbakken*. (Another version was made in 1957.) In 1929 came *Laila* (Danish director, George Schnéevoigt), about a Norwegian girl who was lost as an infant and raised as a Sámi. Love and conflict between people of different classes and races was a common theme of films from this period. The last silent film was *Kristine Valdresdatter*, from 1930, also directed by Rasmus Breistein.

The first sound film was *Den store barnedåpen* (The Great Christening, 1931), directed by Tancred Ibsen and based on a play by Oscar Braaten. Tancred Ibsen would become one of the biggest names in Norwegian film, working as writer, director, editor, production manager, and producer until the 1960s. His wife was the famous actress, Lillebil Ibsen, whom he followed to New York in the 1920s. From there he went to Hollywood, where he spent two years working for MGM and learning about filmmaking. He later worked in Sweden. His films marked a move away from the rural romanticism toward more urban themes, particularly the struggle of the working class. Other Tancred Ibsen films include *To levende og en død* (Two Living and One Dead, 1937), a psychological thriller, and *Fant* (Tramp), also from 1937. This latter film is based on a novel by Gabriel Scott and made a film star of the famous stage actor, Alfred Maurstad. Maurstad starred in several additional Ibsen films, including *Gjest Baardsen* (1939) and *Tørres Snørtevold* (1940), as well as films directed by Leif Sinding (1895–1985). Sinding and Olav Dalgard (1898–1980) were two other important directors of the 1930s. For the first time Norwegian films were able to compete successfully with American ones, and the late 1930s are sometimes referred to as the golden age of Norwegian cinema.

The municipalities eventually came to understand the necessity of their participation in the financing of film projects. They formed a distribution company, Municipalities Film Central A/S, which in 1932 became Norsk Film A/S. For the first time a fixed percentage of film income was to go to film production. In 1934 a studio was built at Jar near Oslo, and the first film from that studio was Tancred Ibsen's *To levende og en død* (Two Living and One Dead, 1937).

## Wartime Film

During World War II when Norway was occupied by German forces, the resistance movement encouraged the public to boycott films as they had done with sporting events and the theater. But while fewer people went to movies during the first couple of years of occupation, after that attendance rose to prewar levels and above. In addition to the feature films, German newsreels were shown as propaganda. The Germans quickly Nazified the film industry, imposing strict censorship and replacing the cinema directors with Germans or Norwegian Nazis. No American or English movies were permitted, and German ones were encouraged. Leif Sinding was appointed director of the film directorate, which controlled Norsk Film A/S and the film studio at Jar. Sinding was one of the most prominent directors after Tancred Ibsen and Rasmus Breistein, and was involved in all aspects of movie making, including screenwriting, production, and editing nearly 20 films, including *Fantegutten* (The Gypsy Boy, 1932) and *De vergeløse* (The Defenseless, 1939), which had the theme of outsiders in Norwegian society. After the war he was convicted of treason. Although he made a few films in the early 1950s, his career was ruined because of his collaboration with the Nazis.

Comedies and thrillers were the two most popular genres produced during the war. One of the most popular ones is considered a classic today, *Den forsvundne pølsemaker* (The Lost Sausage Maker, Toralf Sandø, 1941). Only one feature film produced during this period can be said to be slanted toward Nazi ideals, *Unge Viljer* (Youthful Will, Walter Fyrst, 1943). Professional actors refused to participate, necessitating the use of amateurs who were Nazi party members. Not even Sinding liked the result, and it was a flop among the public. In addition to the feature films, newsreels became popular and remained so until the early 1960s, when they declined in popularity with the advent of television.

## Postwar Film

After World War II, movie attendance figures skyrocketed, partly because of a hunger for news fed by the newsreels. The budding film industry was able to take advantage of an endowment of 10 million *kroner* left behind by the Nazified Quisling administration, money that had been collected through an entertainment tax on each ticket sold. This was the beginning of the state subsidy for film production that continues to this day. This money was to go not only to production of new films but also toward the development of a program to bring movies out to the rural areas where there were no movie theaters. This program became known as *Norsk Bygdekino*.[18] The initial motivation for the establishment of the program came from the Labor Party, which desired to spread culture all over Norway in an egalitarian fashion. While there was some discussion of whether or not movies constituted culture, the plan was passed by the *Stortinget* nearly unanimously and with little debate in 1948.

The program got off to a rocky start in 1950. Distances between communities were great, and the roads were bad. In northern Norway, most buildings and many roads had been destroyed by the Germans toward the end of the war. In many places there were *samfunnshus* (community meeting halls) or *ungdomshus* (youth meeting halls), but in others they had to use old barracks remaining from the war or even prayer houses. The program was introduced somewhat later to south Norway, where the little yellow trucks were on a three-week schedule. In the west it was often necessary to transport equipment and operators by boat. The typical evening's entertainment consisted of a children's film, followed by short films and a film for the adults. Some of the most popular films in the 1950s dealt with World War II, including the partially documentary *Shetlandsgjengen* (The Shetland Gang, 1954). In some areas hundreds of people would show up, dressed in their finest. While *Norsk bygdekino* was not alone in bringing movies to rural areas—there were nearly 30 other operators—it was the only nonprivate option.

The program was not, however, immune to criticism. Some of the films, such as those by Swedish director, Ingmar Bergmann, were criticized for being immoral. Many of the actors were declared to be bad role models for young people.

The popularity of *Bygdekino* began to decline in the 1960s with the arrival of television. In addition it is thought that with increased financial well-being, people had more things with which to fill their leisure time. Ironically, routes were first dropped from the most outlying areas because they were the most expensive to service. These were, however, also the areas that needed it the most because they were the last to receive television. It was only in 1967 that television reached the northernmost areas of the country.

The coming of television meant a decline in movie attendance in all forms, including the traveling movie service. Although the service continued for a number of years, by 1970 the name *Norsk Bygdekino* had disappeared, as it had merged with *Statens filmsentral* (State Film Central). The name did, however, return in 1987 with a merger with the KKL (the National Association of Municipal Cinematographers). In 1971 the last boat route was discontinued, and the viewership continued to decline in the 1970s and 1980s from its peak in 1961. The most popular ambulatory film ever was the Norwegian animated *Flåklypa Grand Prix*, although other popular films included James Bond, the Rocky movies, and the Rambo films of Sylvester Stallone, along with other Hollywood productions. The *Bygdekino* still exists today in a modern form[19] although because of the concessions law, the local municipality must give permission for them to visit. By 2010 the service will be fully digital, and creative options such as outdoor screenings have already become popular.

Films about the occupation were immensely popular in the late 1940s and 1950s because they usually offered a heroic portrayal of the resistance. Immediately after the war several of these included actual participants in the resistance in leading roles. Examples of such films include *Vi vil leve* (We Want to Live, Dalgard/Randall) and *Englandsfarere* (We Leave for England, Sandø), which both came out in 1946. Undoubtedly the most famous film was *Kampen om tungtvannet* (The Battle for Heavy Water, Vibe-Müller, 1948), depicting the sabotage carried out against the heavy water production facility in Rjukan, Telemark. This movie was later remade in a Hollywood version, called *The Heroes of Telemark* (Anthony Mann, 1965) starring Kirk Douglas, which, while popular, took considerable liberties with the facts.

The most significant director/writer of the postwar period was Arne Skouen (1913–2003), who made 17 films between 1949 and 1969, including *Gategutter* (Street Boys, 1949) and *An-Magritt* (1969), starring Liv Ullmann in the title role. He also made several films about the German occupation of World War II, often calling into question the hero worship of the Resistance fighters. One such film was *Ni liv* (Nine Lives, 1957), which was nominated for an Oscar. The popularity of the war film genre remains high. In 2008, a film depicting the work of resistance hero Max Manus came out and was the most viewed Norwegian film in 20 years.

### 1950s and 1960s

In the immediate postwar period, the mood was optimistic, and romantic comedy was popular. *Vi gifter oss* (We're Getting Married, Nils R. Müller, 1951), *Fjols til fjells* (Fools in the Mountains, Edith Carlmar, 1957), and *Støv på hjernen* (Dust on the Brain, Øyvind Vennerød, 1959) are three typical films, dealing with gender roles within marriage, housing shortages, and the relocation of new young families into the *drabantbyer*, the high-rise apartment complexes on the outskirts of Oslo. The first female director was Edith Carlmar (1911–2003), who made 10 feature films between 1949 and 1959. Her last film, *Ung flukt* (*The Wayward Girl*, 1959) marked Liv Ullmann's acting debut. (Ullmann, who later worked with and married Ingmar Bergmann, is probably Norway's most internationally famous actor.)

State support of film production increased, particularly for children's movies, which became very popular. Norsk Film A/S became a joint state and municipal venture with certain requirements for artistic quality to get support. Later, after 1955, the level of support was made dependent on the popularity of the film. Documentaries, such as Thor Heyerdahl's *Kon-Tiki* (1950) were also popular.

*Kon-Tiki* is the only Norwegian feature film ever to have won an Academy Award. The mid-1950s marked the high point for movie attendance. The introduction of television in 1960 meant a drastic decline in attendance figures, and the end of both the feature-length documentary film and the weekly newsreels. Also in the 1950s there was more openness to sex, as youth became the most important audience. *Line* (Nils Reinhardt Christensen, 1961), based on Axel Jensen's novel of the same name, competed in the Cannes film festival in 1961, although it did not win any awards.

### 1960s and 1970s

A few modernist films were made in the 1960s, inspired by the French new wave films. Most notable were those by Pål Løkkeberg, who made *Liv* in 1967 and *Exit* in 1970. Another experimental film director was Lasse Henriksen, who only made one feature film, *Love Is War* (1970). This film won a Silver Bear award at the Berlin Festival in 1971. A successful pan-Scandinavian cooperative effort was Knut Hamsun's *Sult* (Hunger, 1966) with Danish director Henning Carlsen and Swedish star, Per Oscarsson. It was shot on location in Oslo. These more experimental films were rare because by the 1970s most films were characterized by social realism. Just like the literary writers of the time, filmmakers attempted to create works for and about the working class, illuminating the social and political issues of the day. The titles of some of the films indicate the tone: *Streik* (*Strike!*, 1974) and *Det tause flertall* (The Silent Majority, 1977).

In contrast to the serious tone of some films, probably the most popular films during this decade were the 13 comedy crime films about *Olsenbanden* (The Olsen Gang, 1969–1999) and *Flåklypa Grand Prix* (Ivo Caprino, 1975), a children's film using a puppet animation with stop-motion technique. *Flåklypa* is the most popular film ever made in Norway, and is still loved today. It is shown regularly on television and is available on DVD and as a video game. Despite the popularity of these films, movie attendance continued to drop, and the popularity of Norwegian-made films declined further relative to Hollywood movies. The success of Hollywood-type films did not escape the attention of Norwegian film producers, who began to emulate the Hollywood genre films in an effort to gain popularity at home.[20]

Not until the 1970s did more female directors emerge, including Vibeke Løkkeberg, who made eight films between 1971 and 1993, Anja Breien (14 films between 1969 and 2005), Nicole Macé, and Laila Mikkelsen who worked extensively in the 1970s and 1980s. More recent women directors include Eva Isaksen, Unni Straume, and Liv Ullmann, who in addition to acting in many films, has also directed several, including *Kristin Lavransdatter*, in 1995.

### 1980s and 1990s

In the 1980s, for the first time foreign companies were invited to help finance more ambitious film projects, which tended to contain more action and be internationally oriented. Action films from this period included *Orions belte* (Orion's Belt, Ola Solum, 1985), *Etter Rubicon* (Rubicon, Leidulf Visan, 1987), *Blücher* (Oddvar Bull Tuhus, 1988), and *Dykket* (The Dive, Tristan de vere Cole, 1989). The 1980s were also a productive period for Norwegian children's films. The most successful film of the 1980s, however, was *Veiviseren* (The Pathfinder, Nils Gaup, 1987). It was the first ever to be shot in the Sámi language and be directed by a Sámi. It was even nominated for the Academy Award for Best Foreign Film in 1988, only the third Norwegian film ever, after *Ni liv* from 1959 and *Kon-Tiki* from 1950.[21] Since then only two other feature films have been nominated, *Søndagsengler* (Sunday Angels, Berit Nesheim, 1997) and *Elling* (Petter Næss, 2001), although a joint Norwegian-Canadian animated short film, *Den danske dikteren* (The Danish Poet, Torill Kove, 2006) won in 2007.

### 2000s

The late 1990s and the first decade of the twenty-first century have been a period of success for the Norwegian film industry. Several popular films were *Elling* (Petter Næss, 2001) and two prequel/sequel films based on the novels of Ingvar Ambjørnsen, and other films, such as *Buddy* (Morten Tyldum, 2003), *Hawaii, Oslo* (Erik Poppe, 2004), *Himmelfall* (Falling Sky, Gunnar Vikene, 2002), and *Reprise* (Joachim Trier, 2006), which all feature mentally disturbed outsiders as protagonists. All of these films won awards both in Norway and abroad. After his success with *Veiviseren* (The Pathfinder), Nils Gaup has directed several more feature films, including one for Disney in Hollywood. His most recent film, *Kautokeinoopprøret* (The Kautokeino Rebellion, 2008) broke attendance records for its first weekend and won a record five Amanda prizes, including for Best Actress, Cinematography, and Score.

The Amanda Prizes are the Norwegian equivalent of Hollywood's Academy Awards. First awarded in 1985, they are given out annually at the Norwegian International Film Festival held in Haugesund, Norway, each August. At first these prizes went to both movie and television productions, but since 2005, they have been reserved for film. *The Kautokeino Rebellion* has also won audience awards at film festivals in Rouen, France, and Minneapolis/St. Paul, Minnesota.

The year before, the film *O' Horten* (Bent Hamer, 2007) was nominated for seven Amandas and won in two categories. *O' Horten* also did well in the European Film Awards and the Flanders International Film Festival, where it won for Best Director. *O'Horten* has also been released in the United States and was Norway's submission for the foreign language Oscar. Bent Hamer has also directed several other critically acclaimed films, including *Eggs* (1995), *Salmer fra kjøkkenet* (Kitchen Stories, 2004) and *Faktotum* (2005), and has won numerous awards. Even more popular than any of these films was the latest World War II movie, *Max Manus* (Espen Sandberg/Joachim Rønning, 2008). Recounting the true story of Norway's most celebrated resistance fighter and his comrades, *Max Manus* won seven Amanda Prizes in 2009, breaking the record set only a year earlier for *Kautokeinoopprøret*, including awards for best film, actor, and actress, as well as the people's choice award.[22] *Max Manus* had its North American debut at the Toronto Film Festival in September 2009 where it was the first Norwegian film ever to be invited for a gala screening. It was Norway's entry for the 2010 Oscar, but did not make the Hollywood short list.

These successful films can be viewed as part of a relatively recent phenomenon referred to as Norwave. Norwave represents the efforts of the Norwegian film industry to realign itself so as to appeal both to a domestic audience and the international market.[23] The term was first used in 1997 to describe two films that were introduced at the Cannes Film Festival: *Budbringeren* (Junk Mail, Pål Sletaune, 1997) and *Insomnia* (Erik Skjoldbjærg, 1997). *Insomnia* was later remade in Hollywood (Christopher Nolan, 2002).

Another popular genre among Norwave directors is the date movie, romantic comedies told "from the perspective of young, misfit male characters struggling against adult responsibility and expectations."[24] In her article about Norwave, Ellen Rees traces the beginning of Norwave to *Detektor* (Detector, Pål Jackman, 2000), and also includes *Buddy, Jonny Vang* (Jens Lien), *United* (Magnus Martens), and *Kvinnen i mitt liv* (The Woman in My Life, Alexander Eik), all from 2003. All make an effort to appeal to men as well as to women.

Several Norwegian directors have been successful internationally. Erik Skjoldbjærg, Hans Petter Moland, Petter Næss, and Bent Hamer have all made films in the United States, with films such as *Prozac Nation* (Skjoldbjærg, 2001), *The Beautiful Country* (Moland, 2004), *Mozart and the Whale* (Næss, 2004), and *Factotum* (Hamer, 2005). Whether or not Norwave is an actual movement with lasting success remains to be seen.

The Norwegian government has recently decided to increase its investment in and support of Norwegian film production. This policy is important, given the small size of the Norwegian linguistic and cultural community. In 2005 The Norwegian Media Authority was established, bringing together the former offices of the Norwegian Film Authority and other official media-related offices. This agency, which is under the government's Ministry of Culture and Church Affairs, regulates all media, including radio, television, film, DVDs, computer games, and print media. The Norwegian Media Authority has more than 100 employees and a budget of $13 million and distributes NOK $38 million in film subsidies annually. It has achieved the government's stated goal of supporting 25 Norwegian feature films annually, although some film-makers are opting to make films without state support in order to avoid what they see as interference with their artistic freedom.

## Notes

1. Culture and Media Theme page, Statistics Norway. http://www.ssb.no/media_en/. Accessed 8/31/09.

2. 2008 figures from MediaNorge. http://medienorge.uib.no/english/. Accessed 8/31/08.

3. http://medienorge.uib.no/english/?cat=statistikk&medium=avis&aspekt=&queryID=238. Accessed 9/1/09.

4. List of online newspapers. http://www.houses-europe.com/norske-aviser/. Accessed 9/1/09.

5. http://presse.no/Spesial/Skjulte_artikler/?module=Articles;action=Article.publicShow;ID=250;. Accessed 8/31/09.

6. Statistics from http://www.ssb.no.

7. Statistics from TNS Gallup quoted in *Aftenposten*. http://www.aftenposten.no/kul_und/article3160777.ece. Accessed 1/28. 10.

8. Much information in this section comes from http://www.engberg.com/historiestart.htm. Accessed 9/1/09.

9. http://www.nrk.no/informasjon/about_the_nrk/1.3698330. Accessed 9/1/09.

10. Norwegian State Broadcasting Network. http://www.nrk.no/informasjon/about_the_nrk/1.3698330. Accessed 4/29/10.

11. www.medietilsynet.no/en-gb/The-Norwegian-Media-Authority/English-Menu/The-Media/. Accessed 9/1/09.

12. http://www.ssb.no/emner/07/02/30/medie/sa106/sa_106.pdf. Accessed 9/1/09.

13. http://www.ssb.no/emner/07/02/30/medie/sa106/sa_106.pdf. Accessed 9/1/09.

14. Tytti Soila et al., eds., *Nordic National Cinemas* (New York: Routledge, 1998).

15. Information in this section comes from "Norsk films historie—i kort versjon," by Jan Erik Holst, Norsk filminstitutt http://www.cinemateket-usf.no/Arkiv/LENGRE_ARTIKLER11.august2005/HOSTEN_2005/NORSK_FILMS_HISTORIE.html. Accessed 4/29/10.

16. Information in this section comes from Gunnar Iversen, "Norway," in *Nordic National Cinemas*.

17. Iversen, "Norway," pp. 108–109.

18. Mona Vaagan et al., *Film på vei. Bygdekinoen gjennom femti år* (Oslo: Norsk Filminstitutt, 2000).

19. http://www.filmweb.no/bygdekinoen/. Accessed 9/1/09.

20. Gunnar Iversen, "Norway," p. 136.

21. "Norsk films historie—i kort versjon," by Jan Erik Holst, Norsk filminstitutt http://www.cinemateket-usf.no/Arkiv/LENGRE_ARTIKLER11.august2005/ HOSTEN_2005/NORSK_FILMS_HISTORIE.html. Accessed 4/29/10.

22. http://www.variety.com/article/VR1118007624.html?categoryid=13&cs =1&query=norway. Accessed 8/31/09.

23. Ellen Rees, "Norwave: Norwegian Cinema 1997–2006," *Scandinavian-Canadian Studies: Journal of the Association for the Advancement of Scandinavian Studies in Canada*, Fall 2009.

24. Ibid.

# 9

# Performing Arts

IN THE SPRING OF 2009, Norway roared to Europe's attention when Alexander Rybak won the Eurovision Song Contest 2009 with a record-breaking number of votes.[1] This annual contest, which features pop groups competing from all across Europe, has been Europe's most popular television show for more than 50 years. In his unlikely and thrilling victory, Rybak, a 23-year-old who immigrated to Norway from Belarus at age four, encapsulates both the past and present identity of Norway. At the same time as he himself represents the modern face of the new, multicultural Norway, his song, which he also composed, is a fusion of Norwegian folk music and dance with modern pop music. Playing his violin in the manner of the traditional Hardanger Fiddle, he was backed up by two beautiful women, resembling *huldrer*, or troll maidens, and three members of the dance company Frikar, who performed a modern version of the traditional Halling dance. This athletic dance, designed to show off the physical prowess of male dancers, culminates in the kicking of a hat from a stick held high. Some of the moves bear such a strong resemblance to the Russian Cossack dance, that a few commentators incorrectly assumed it was a nod to the venue for the Eurovision 2009 final, Moscow.

One analysis that followed the competition observed that Rybak himself resembles the beloved underdog hero of Norwegian folklore, Askeladden, or the Ash lad, the somewhat mischievous, likeable, clever, creative young fellow who wins the princess and half the kingdom.[2] Because Norway has won the Eurovision contest only three times since its start in 1960, and in fact has the distinction of earning zero points in four separate competitions,

Norwegians consider themselves to be the underdog. Ironically Rybak and his troupe were hardly underdogs, coming into the competition as the favorite. Rybak himself has years of classical music training under his belt, and was pursuing a bachelors degree in violin performance before his win. The Frikar dancers are part of a professional dance company that has performed with the Oslo Philharmonic Orchestra and the National Ballets of Norway and Zimbabwe, produced five full-length dance productions, and is the company behind the moves of the computer game, *Age of Conan*.[3]

## TRADITIONAL MUSIC

Norway has a long and rich tradition of folk music and performance, including instrumental, vocal, and dance, that continues to this day. Folk music is usually characterized by being passed along from one performer to another, with no documented composer. This definition is not entirely accurate, however, because many fiddle tunes in particular are known to have been composed by specific fiddlers.

Folk music in Norway was first studied, collected, and written down during the National Romantic period of the 1800s. This music was considered part of the Norwegian cultural heritage and thus could contribute to the nation-building project of that time. It was something that set Norwegian culture apart from other Nordic or European cultures because it originated in the "authentic" rural culture, rather than the more international urban culture. Beginning in the 1840s, scholars such as L. M. Lindeman (1812–1887) as well as composers such as Edvard Grieg and Ole Bull traveled around the countryside systematically collecting tunes. Grieg frequently took inspiration from the folk tunes when he composed. M. B. Landstad (1802–1880) and Jørgen Moe (1813–1882) published collections of folk songs and song texts in the 1840s and 1850s. Much of Landstad's and Lindeman's work was based on early collecting of both music and text by Olea Crøger (1801–1855). In 1842, she submitted a manuscript for publication. Unable to get it published in the male-dominated world, she began a collaboration with M. B. Landstad. Despite the fact that she was barely mentioned in the foreword of Landstad's *Norske folkeviser* (Norwegian Folk Songs, 1853), Professor Moltke Moe (1859–1913), son of Jørgen Moe, declared that one third to one half of Landstad's collection was her work. While her letters have survived, only two of her manuscripts exist, but her valuable contribution has been recognized and celebrated in recent years.[4]

## VOCAL MUSIC

One of the oldest types of music is the unaccompanied human voice. Traditionally songs were used along with work and celebration, and often were accompanied by dances. They were used to accompany repetitive work of women such as weaving, spinning, milking, and making butter and cheese. Men sang along with work in fields or forest, or while fishing. This category of songs is called *arbeidsviser*, or work songs, and has many subcategories. One type was used by the herd girls at the mountain summer farm to entertain themselves, to communicate with or signal to others, to call to animals such as cows (*kulokk*) or goats (*geitelokk*), or to calm them during milking. Because Norwegian cows and goats have individual names, the songs might consist of a list of their names, interspersed with nonsense syllables. *Hjaling*, also known as *huv* or *laling*, carried over a great distance because of the use of both head tones and chest notes, somewhat similar to yodeling in other mountain cultures. These were used to communicate over long distances, to make contact between friends and lovers, or perhaps also to exchange information about something as prosaic as the time of day.

Shanties were popular on the many sailing vessels of this seafaring nation. Strongly influenced by shanties from England, many have refrains in English or words that are easily identified with English, such as *Rullan gå*, which means "Roll and go" in English. Nineteenth-century poet Henrik Wergeland (1808–1845) tried to write lyrics that were less obscene than the traditional sailors' songs, but with mixed success.[5] One of his shanties was used by Eivind Alnæs (1872–1932) in his motet *Sidste Reis* (The Last Journey, Op. 17, number 2).

Other common types of vocal folk music include the *bånsull*, or lullaby, and the *stev*. The *stev* is very short, consisting of only four lines, and is an example of a type of singing that was used to entertain. The oldest *stev*, or *gammelstev*, consisted of four lines, with the second and fourth lines rhyming—xaya. They often were haiku-type depictions of nature, and date back as far as the 1200s. As seen in Table 9.1, several *gammelstev* would sometimes be strung together to make a longer song, but without any narrative connection.

The new *stev*, or *nystev*, had a specific rhyme scheme—Aabb—and stricter rhythm, and probably dates back to about 1700. These were frequently created

**Table 9.1**
Examples of *gammelstev*

| | |
|---|---|
| *Hanen stend på stabburshella* | The rooster stands on the storehouse step |
| *Bonden gjeve honom konn.* | The farmer gives him grain. |
| *Rakkin skvakkar i bergjet nord,* | The fox barks in the mountains north, |
| *og hjuringen blæs i honn.* | and the shepherd blows his horn. |
| | |
| *Sutine og sorgjene* | Troubles and sorrows |
| *dei trør eg under fot.* | I crush them under my foot. |
| *Då er eg aller gladaste* | I am happiest of all |
| *når det gjeng meg mest i mot* | when things go most against me |

spontaneously. Often two singers would engage in a competition, each singing *stev* back and forth, responding with amusing or even insulting verses.

*Og vil du hava meg te å kvea*
*så skal eg kvea av største glea.*
*Og eg vil kvea så vent før deg,*
*at du gløymer gud og du gløymer meg.*

And if you want me to sing
I will sing with greatest pleasure.
And I will sing so beautifully for you
that you forget God and you forget me.

The word *stev* was also used to designate a refrain from a medieval ballad. Ballads were narrative songs, often containing many stanzas with either a four-line refrain (like a *stev*) or two-line refrains in the middle and the end of each stanza. Ballads were often used for dancing, and the refrains often make reference to dance. The tradition of dancing to ballads was lost in Norway, but maintained in living tradition on the Faeroe islands. Hulda Garborg, who traveled to the Faeroes in 1902, brought the tradition back to Norway and expanded upon it as part of her effort to revive interest in folk dancing. Ballads were not as common in Norway as in Denmark and Sweden, where the aristocratic tradition inspired chivalric ballads involving knights and princesses, but particular types of ballads were sung in Norway. Most common were the *kjempevise*, or heroic ballad, as well as the supernatural ballads or *trollviser*, which featured trolls and giants.

The most famous Norwegian medieval ballad is *Draumkvedet*, or the Dream Ballad. It is said to date back to the 1200s or even earlier, but its age is uncertain. Considered a national treasure, and not found in the other Scandinavian countries, it has inspired modern artists and been recorded numerous times. The best-known versions were collected in the 1840s in Telemark in southern Norway. The narrative is about Olav Aasteson, who falls asleep on Christmas Eve and sleeps through the 12 days of Christmas. When he awakens on Epiphany, he rides to church to tell about his visionary dream, which is a mix of pagan and pre-Reformation Christian images. He has made a pilgrimage over *Gjallarbrua*, the bridge that leads him to the Kingdom of the Dead. On the other side of the bridge, he sees Purgatory, Hell, and the joyful souls in Paradise. He also watches the battle between Christ, St. Michael and the angels, and the Devil and his army. The Devil's name is *Grutte Gråskjegg* (Grutte Greybeard), which was one of many names used for the Norse god, Odin. Finally, Olav witnesses the Day of Judgment, when each soul is weighed on a pair of scales by St. Michael. Most singers only knew fragments of the ballad.

The longest single version was collected by M. B. Landstad, and consisted of 30 stanzas. Landstad reconstructed a version with 60 stanzas by joining together variants from many different informants. Fairytale collector Jørgen Moe had his own reconstruction with 52 stanzas.[6]

Hymns were also important for Norwegians. Petter Dass (1647–1707), the North-Norwegian poet, wrote many hymns that were later transformed into folk songs. M. B. Landstad's hymnal, originally from 1853, was used well into the twentieth century. Sometimes hymns were reworked and sung as folk songs by people without access to organs or other musical accompaniment. This traditional style of folksinging is called *kveding*. It contains much ornamentation as well as half tones, where some notes of the scale sound slightly out of tune to modern ears.

While the old folk songs are maintained and performed by people in the old style, many have come into use as children's songs or have been modernized and performed and recorded either with modern instruments in a rock or jazz style, or with medieval instruments. They are even available through iTunes, by simply searching for *norsk folkemusikk* in general, or a specific artist, such as Agnes Buen Garnås, Tone Hulbækmo, Sinikka Langeland, Arve Moen Bergset, and Annbjørg Lien, among others.

## INSTRUMENTAL MUSIC

Some of the earliest musical instruments were used by the mountain herders and were sometimes made out of natural materials. The *bukkehorn* was made from the horn of a ram. The *seljefløyte* was made from a willow branch and could only be played for a few weeks in the spring. This flute has no finger holes and is played by blowing across a wooden pin pushed into one end. The pitch is regulated by overblowing and by using the index finger to open, half close, or close the hole at the far end. The natural scale is formed by the overtones. Today *seljefløyter* made of a plastic tube covered with birch bark are sold in stores, making it possible to play the instrument year-round, but instructions are available for making one from a willow branch. Another flute, which resembles a European recorder, is the *tussefløyte*. It is usually decorated and lacks the double holes of the recorder. The *munnharpe*, or jaw harp, is yet another small instrument that could have been used to entertain the young people as they watched the animals.

The *lur* is a long, narrow horn with a flared end, which may even date back to Viking times, and is similar to the alpen horn, though smaller, being 60 to 80 inches long. Wooden *lurs* were described in the Icelandic sagas, and bronze *lurs* have been found in archeological digs. Today the *lur* is usually made of wood or birch bark. It is played with a mouthpiece, like a trumpet or bugle.

### The *Langeleik*

One of the earliest stringed instruments is the *langeleik*, resembling a dulcimer or zither. It consists of a long, narrow box with eight or nine strings, one of which is a melody string. The others are tuned to a chord. It is played with a plectrum made of bone. The earliest references to the *langeleik* are from the seventeenth century, although it may have come to Norway as early as the 1400s or 1500s. The earliest dated *langeleik* is from 1669 (Selbu), but there are other *langeleiks* in existence that may be even older. An old Danish church tapestry from around 1560, depicts an angel playing a *langeleik*, and an old Icelandic proverb promises: "The angels become happy when they hear *langeleik* music."

The earliest written reference to the *langeleik* in Norway is in connection with a lawsuit against Bishop Arrebo in 1622, where the complaint concerns a song being played on a *langeleik* at a wedding. Another early reference is from around 1660 when the instrument played a role in a witch trial in Finnmark (North Norway). The accused was said to have danced with the devil and played the *langeleik*. This represents quite a contrast from the *langeleik*-playing angel in Denmark mentioned above. By the end of the 1600s, there were several famous *langeleik* players who are mentioned by name in written sources. Written records also describe *langeleik* players by name in the 1820s to the 1840s. The Norwegian folk music collection registry in Oslo lists 22 *langeleiks* that definitely date to the 1700s, plus many undated ones that are probably from that century. During the 1700s, the *langeleik* was known over the entire country, although the golden age of the *langeleik* appears to have ended by second half of the century in most of Norway. By then competition had arrived in the form of the fiddle and other instruments.

Even after the violin and Hardanger fiddle became popular, the *langeleik* was still used for dancing, although the dancers had to dance in stocking feet

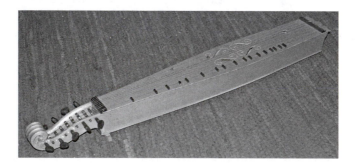

*Langeleik.* The traditional Norwegian dulcimer has nine strings, and is played with a plectrum made of bone. It dates back to the 1500s and is still played today. (Courtesy of the author.)

to permit the soft instrument to be heard. One famous *langeleik* player was Berit Pynten, who lived from 1809 until about 1899. Her little hut still stands on the farm in Valdres. She was famous for her dancing dolls, which were attached by a string to the hand holding the plectrum she used to stroke the strings. When Ludvig M. Lindeman visited Berit Pynten in 1865 on one of his collecting trips, he wrote down 16 of her tunes, including both dance tunes and listening tunes.[7] But an even more famous visitor came in the 1880s: Edvard Grieg. Anders Stilloff, the editor of the Valdres newspaper, published his memories of the visit in 1924:

> Once in the [18]80s, I happened to be traveling with Edvard Grieg through Valdres. Our coach drivers had an irresistible desire to introduce us to Berit Pynten. Edvard Grieg was immediately attracted by the thought, and in the early afternoon we turned onto the country road outside of Berit's artist's residence, which consisted of a small sun-parched hut. Edvard Grieg, who normally walked with his head held high, had to bend over in order to enter. The hut was neat and clean, but Berit was apparently not vain. She was clearly not on intimate terms with soap and water, and her once-black wool skirt, showed many signs of the struggle for survival. Berit had received us out in the farmyard with much pomp and stage presence and shown us into the hut. But when we looked, she had disappeared. Nor were any of the drivers to be seen. But finally Berit appeared, escorted by the drivers, who were bright eyed and well satisfied. There was no mistaking that there had been some of the strong stuff in the storehouse.
>
> The *langeleik* now appeared on the table, and Berit started in determinedly. And how she could play. There was no doubt about that. It didn't take long before Grieg became very interested. He took out a notebook and began writing feverishly page up and page down, while Berit worked her magic on the strings, bringing forth one *springar* and *halling* after the other. Clearly music was neither technique nor profession for her. It was passion, and it brought forth a message from a time long ago when people lived stronger and more personally than now. "You know the notes, too!" Berit shouted as her plectrum continued dancing undisturbed over the strings. Grieg just nodded, smiled warmly, and wrote on with the same speed.
>
> When we left, Berit stood in the farmyard smiling graciously. It had been a big day, certainly more so than she herself realized. It is certainly possible that a *langeleik* player from Valdres hadn't lived in vain, but became a part of what has made Grieg's name great, even if she never appeared on any title page.[8]

By the late 1800s, *langeleik* playing had died out almost everywhere except in Valdres, where the tradition has survived to this day. But even there interest faded after about 1930. In the early 1900s, there was a heated debate over the place of folk music and folk instruments. Many people wrote letters to editors complaining that they were forced to listen to the awful sounds produced by Hardanger fiddles and *langeleiks* on the radio. As a result, there was little activity from about 1930 to about 1970. But since the 1970s and 1980s, there has been an increased interest in the instrument, with courses offered, and instruments constructed and available for purchase.

*Langeleik* tunes are divided into two major groups, dance tunes and listening tunes. *Klokkeslåtter* (bell tunes) and *Huldreslåtter* (troll-girl tunes) are just for listening, and usually have some sort of folktale connected to them. Most *langeleik* melodies, though, are dance tunes such as *halling, springar,* and *ganger,* which will be described later. The tunes are usually learned by rote, by listening and imitating a master player, although some tunes have now been written down, and a couple of instruction books have been published for learning the instrument.

### The Hardanger Fiddle

While the flat fiddle or European violin has traditionally been played in Norway, the most quintessentially Norwegian musical instrument has to be the Hardanger fiddle, or *hardingfele.* The oldest known instrument is from 1651. It immediately became popular as an accompaniment to dance, because it was a more flexible instrument than the *langeleik,* which has rather limited melodic possibilities, and the sound carries much better.

The Hardanger fiddle differs from a violin in several ways. It is richly decorated, with mother-of-pearl inlay in the fingerboard and tailpiece, and

Hardanger fiddles. This traditional Norwegian instrument is richly decorated and has four extra strings running beneath the fingerboard that reverberate sympathetically. It dates from the 1700s. (Courtesy of the author.)

it has a carved dragon head or lion's head as part of the scroll at the end of the peg box and ink decorations on the body of the instrument. Even more significantly, instead of the usual four strings, there are eight or nine strings. The top four strings are played on, and the bottom four or five strings run through the neck and beneath the other strings. They are not stroked, but vibrate sympathetically, giving the instrument its characteristic drone. The bridge is flatter than a regular violin, making it easier to play two or three strings simultaneously. The instrument is usually held lower than a classical violin, with the wrist bent and the heel of the hand in contact with the neck of the instrument. There are many different possible tunings, depending on what melody is being played.

## Dance

The tradition of folk dance is thriving in Norway today. There are four primary types of Norwegian folk dance: song dances, *tur*-dances (figure dances), *gamaldans* (old dance), and rural dances. The rural dances, or *bygdedanser*, are the oldest type of dance surviving in an unbroken tradition and include the *springar*, which is in an uneven 3/4 time, and the *gangar*, which is in 2/4 time. Both have a sequence of different *turer*, or figures, and were normally danced to instrumental accompaniment, first the *langeleik* and later the fiddle. But if one was without instruments, a type of vocal scatting called *slåttestev* could be used.

There are many variants of both *springar* and *ganger*. *Springar* variants include the *pols*, the *springleik*, and the *rundom*. *Gangar* variants include the *halling*, *rull*, and *bonde*. These in turn have regional variations. A *springar* from Valdres has a slightly different rhythm than a Telemark *springar*, for example.

From the mid-1800s, the so-called *runddans* (dance in the round) or *gamaldans* (old dance) began to be popular. These included such dances as waltz, schottische (*reinlender*), polka, and mazurka, and were often accompanied by the accordion, although the regular fiddle and Hardanger fiddle were also used. The song dance was revived around the turn of the twentieth century by Hulda Garborg and Klara Semb, who were interested in promoting Norwegian folk culture. They collected folk dances, taught dancers, and developed a costume for the dancers, inspired by the Hardanger regional dress.

Both folk dancing and folk music are popular today, although not among all Norwegians. Groups and clubs exist to promote both, and competitions, or *kappleik*, are held all over the country. Many professional folk musicians both perform and record regularly. Folk music and dance are also popular in Norwegian-American areas of the United States. The high school folk dancers from Stoughton, Wisconsin, are well known, and have even been profiled on

Norwegian television. Founded in 1983, the Hardanger Fiddle Association of North America has a Web site; a quarterly journal, *The Sound Post*; and an annual meeting. Its mission is to promote the playing of Hardanger fiddle and other folk instruments in the United States and Canada.

## ART MUSIC AND ORCHESTRAL MUSIC

The 1840s marked the beginning of the National Romantic breakthrough in Norwegian art music as well as in literature and visual art. Now that Norway had its own constitution and more autonomy than during its 400-year-long union with Denmark, Norwegians wanted to prove that Norway had its own culture and identity that were different from European culture or even from Scandinavian culture. They finally had their own university, founded in 1811. But there was still no music conservatory, and students had to go to Copenhagen or Leipzig to be trained. Although there had been amateur orchestras in the cities, the first full professional orchestra was formed in 1857 in Oslo, or Christiania, as it was known then.

### Ole Bull

One of the greatest and most famous performing artists of the 1800s was Ole Bull (1810–1880). He wrote more than 70 works, including *Sætergjentens søndag* (Herdgirl's Sunday), although little survives. A child prodigy, he made his debut at age nine as soloist with *Det Harmoniske Selskab* orchestra. Early on he became familiar with Norwegian folk music and was given a Hardanger fiddle. He learned to play from several famous Hardanger fiddle players, and later transcribed a number of tunes, which he used as the basis of some of his compositions. Intending to study theology, he moved to Christiania at age 18. Before long he traveled to Europe, where he met the famous violinist, Paganini, and was inspired by his playing. He married a French woman, with whom he had four children.

Bull began playing concerts in Europe, where he demonstrated his talent at improvisations of local tunes and imitation of sounds. He made his first tour of America in 1843. He was an immediate success in New York, where he played everything from Paganini variations to "Yankee Doodle Dandy." A handsome and charismatic performer, he understood the importance of PR and showmanship. In a letter to his wife he wrote: "it isn't possible to get ahead there—even with the greatest talent. You need some humbug."[9] He became so famous that the P. T. Barnum Circus even featured a violin-playing dwarf named Ole Bull Junior. He even played a concert in Havana, Cuba, where he learned Cuban melodies. During his two years in America, he held more than 200 concerts and earned more than $100,000.

Bull made several more tours of America, and in 1852, inspired by utopian ideals, purchased 11,000 acres in northern Pennsylvania. Intending to establish a colony for Norwegian immigrants, called Oleana, he lured them there with promises of money as well as free food and lodging. Altogether 300 Norwegians, plus a few Danes and Swedes, attempted to settle in Oleana. When the colonists found it difficult to farm the poor soil, they began heading west to Wisconsin and Minnesota. Although Bull got his money back from the land purchase, he lost a fortune from his promise to support the hundreds of immigrants.

He was mocked mercilessly by some in Norway, including journalist Ditmar Meidell who wrote Oleanna, a ballad still sung by Norwegian Americans that poked fun at Bull's folly with verses claiming outrageous promises of beer flowing in the rivers and wheat and corn planting themselves. The song gained extra popularity with a translation by Pete Seeger in the 1950s.

Bull continued his tours of the United States, even sailing to San Francisco by way of the Panama Canal. After his wife's death in 1862, Ole Bull continued touring in Germany, Vienna, Prague, Moscow, Warsaw, and Paris. Between 1867 and 1870, he made several tours of America, including San Francisco, where he was crowned with a gold laurel wreath encrusted with pearls and diamonds. Later he involved himself with good causes among Norwegian Americans, such as raising money to purchase Norwegian books for the University of Wisconsin library and for the celebration of Leif Eriksson.

In 1870 Bull remarried. His new bride was an American, Sara Thorp, daughter of a senator from Wisconsin. Nineteen-year-old Sara had become pregnant during a visit to Bull's home in Norway with her mother. She married the 60-year-old musician in September that year, in Madison, Wisconsin. After only two years, Ole Bull tired of the bourgeois life of the Thorp family and returned to Norway, leaving his wife and daughter Olea behind.

In 1872, he began planning his fairy-tale house at Lysøen near Bergen. The villa, its exterior an unusual blend of Moorish, Arabic, Venetian, and Byzantine styles, is a museum today. The interior, with its 15-meter-long music room, is characterized by equally eclectic styles, and has elaborately twisted pillars and symbols from both the Old and New Testament, as well as the Free Masons. He eventually reunited with his wife and child in 1876, when they joined him at Lysøen. Sara later toured with her husband as his accompanist and business manager.

Always a great self-promoter, Bull climbed to the top of the Cheops Pyramid near Cairo and played På solen jeg ser (I Look at the Sun) only four years before his death in 1880. In 1877 he made his last European tour, but after that he took three more trips to America, where he was viewed as a

Ole Bull's home at Lysøen, near Bergen, completed in 1873. Ole Bull lived here until his death in 1880. Donated in 1974 to the Norwegian Society for the Preservation of Ancient Monuments by Ole Bull's granddaughter, Sylvea Bull Curtis, it is now a museum and concert locale. (Courtesy of the author.)

living legend. He met or was friends with such famous Americans as Henry Wadsworth Longfellow, Harriet Beecher Stowe, and Thomas Edison. Always interested in modern technology, he installed a telephone in his home in Cambridge, Massachusetts.

An active performer until the end, Bull died at Lysøen in 1880. His funeral was a national spectacle. After the service at Lysøen, with Edvard Grieg at the organ, his casket was transported to Bergen, accompanied by a convoy of 14 ships. As his ship sailed into the harbor in Bergen, a choir of more than 1,000 singers had gathered and all the church bells began to chime. Flags waved at half-staff on buildings, markets, and ships. All the newspapers had black-edged front pages, and schools and stores were closed.

Despite the fact that he spent his adult life touring about the world, Ole Bull considered himself a Norwegian patriot and encouraged interest in Norwegian folk music and culture. He encouraged younger talents such as Henrik Ibsen, Bjørnstjerne Bjørnson, Rikard Nordraak, and Edvard Grieg.

At Bull's funeral Bjørnson said: "Ole Bull gave us self-confidence as a nation when we most needed it."[10]

### Bull's Contemporaries

Other well-known composers of the same generation as Bull include L. M. Lindeman (1812–1887) and Halfdan Kjerulf (1815–1868). Lindeman is best known for his arrangements of folk melodies, but he also was a music teacher and organist and composed a number of the hymns that still appear in the Church of Norway hymnal. With his son, Peter, he founded a school for organists in 1883, which became the Music Conservatory in 1895. This remained the only music conservatory in Norway until 1905, when the Bergen Music Academy was founded.

Halfdan Kjerulf (1815–1868), who had had musical training as a child, was supposed to become a civil servant. He began studying law, but after an illness interrupted his legal studies, he traveled to Paris on vacation. There he came in contact with a lively musical scene, and met Berlioz and other early romantic composers.

Unfortunately, when he returned home, he learned that his father had died and that he would be responsible for supporting his family. He worked as a newspaper editor, but still pursued his interest in music. He studied composition on his own and was eventually offered a position as director of a male chorus. Still dissatisfied with his knowledge of music theory, at the age of 33 he was finally able to travel to the music conservatory in Leipzig and complete his education as a composer. He himself felt that he wrote in both a European, German-Romantic style and a style influenced by Norwegian folk music.[11] He is best known for his piano pieces and songs arranged for male chorus. One of his most performed and recorded works is "Ingrids vise" (Ingrid's Song), written to a text by Bjørnstjerne Bjørnson.

### The Golden Age

The second half of the 1800s is often called the golden age of Norwegian music. This period was important for the male chorus, which remains popular to this day. Three of the most important composers of this period are Johan Svendsen (1840–1911), Rikard Nordraak (1842–1866), and Edvard Grieg (1843–1907). Like Kjerulf and Lindeman before him, Svendsen was inspired by Norwegian folk melodies, although they had less direct impact on his music. Born in Christiania, he spent most of his professional life in Copenhagen. A close friend of Edvard Grieg, they were never rivals but rather complemented each other. Svendsen wrote mostly for orchestra, whereas Grieg specialized in chamber music and works for piano and voice. Svendsen was more oriented toward newer European music and composers such as

Berlioz, whereas Grieg had been inspired by the vision of a national music by Rikard Nordraak and Ole Bull. Both studied music in Leipzig.

Svendsen lived for periods of time in Christiania, but spent most of his life abroad. Early on he lived in Leipzig and Paris, working with such composers as Saint-Saéns, Hans Gade, Henri Vieuxtemps, Franz Liszt, and George Bizet, and later in Copenhagen. After he fell in love with the Jewish-American singer, Sarah "Sally" Levett, for a time he moved to the United States where they could be married. While there, he began two new orchestra works: *Sigurd Slembe* and *Carnival in Paris*. Upon his return to Europe he met and was inspired by Richard Wagner and his wife, the daughter of Franz Liszt. On Edvard Grieg's invitation, he returned to Christiania, where he lived and worked for five years, composing and teaching violin and composition. In 1874, both Svendsen and Grieg were granted an annual artist's salary from the Parliament, an honor granted only to the great poets Ibsen, Bjørnson, and Lie. Inspired by Franz Liszt's *Hungarian Rhapsodies*, he wrote four *Norwegian Rhapsodies* for orchestra, using Norwegian folk tunes as their basis.

Svendsen was known to be quite a favorite of the ladies. One evening, after intercepting a bouquet of roses and a love letter from a female admirer, his jealous wife, Sally, burned the manuscript of Symphony No. 3, which he had just completed. This act inspired Henrik Ibsen, whose Hedda Gabler commits a similar deed. This tragedy may also have destroyed Svendsen's desire to compose, because he never again wrote anything significant. He did, however, accept an offer to become the principal conductor of the Royal Theater in Copenhagen. The people in Christiania tried collecting donations to keep him there, but he felt he could not refuse the Copenhagen offer. At his farewell concert in Christiania, King Oscar II was present. The ladies of the city, represented by composer and pianist Agathe Backer Grøndahl and pianist Erika Lie Nissen, presented him with an ivory baton encrusted with gold and diamonds.

Svendsen spent the rest of his career in Copenhagen, and returned to Christiania only rarely. His marriage to Sally ended, and he fathered three children with a young Danish ballerina before his divorce was final and he was able to marry her. He had a successful career in Copenhagen, where he promoted the careers of many young composers. Edvard Grieg considered him to be one of Europe's foremost conductors, although he worried about the loss of Svendsen as composer.[12]

Rikard Nordraak (1842–1866) is best known as the composer of Norway's national song, *Ja, vi elsker dette landet* (Yes, we love this land), which has a text by Bjørnstjerne Bjørnson, Nordraak's cousin. He was born in Christiania, but studied in Berlin and Copenhagen. Returning to Christiania, he came to know Ole Bull and L. M. Lindeman, and was also a friend of Edvard Grieg.

Nordraak's interest in Norwegian folk music was inspired by Bull. He only lived to the age of 23, so he did not leave behind a large body of work.

## EDVARD GRIEG

Edvard Grieg (1843–1907) is doubtless Norway's greatest composer, and had an international reputation during his lifetime. Music historians have not always appreciated him, however, sometimes describing him as a miniaturist and an overly romantic composer who never managed to write a successful symphony. The commemoration in 1993 of the 150th anniversary of his birth and in 2007 of the centennial of his death did, however, bring renewed appreciation for Grieg's work, along with new recordings.[13] Grieg societies have been founded all around the world, and the International Grieg Society holds a conference every second year.[14]

A close friend of Rikard Nordraak, Edvard Grieg was strongly inspired by Nordraak's passion and his desire to create a Norwegian identity and a national music. Hungarian composer Béla Bartók once said that Grieg was one of the first to "cast off the German yoke and turn to the music of his own people."[15] He wrote for piano, solo voice, choir, and orchestra, but is especially known for his *Piano Concerto in A minor* and the *Peer Gynt Suites*, which have been performed and recorded countless times.

Grieg grew up in a musical family in Bergen. His mother was a highly regarded and trained accompanist. She collaborated with Ole Bull, who later encouraged the young Edvard to study music in Leipzig. Bull became a valuable mentor, introducing Grieg to Norwegian folk music while at the same time encouraging him to create his own style. In 1867 Grieg married his cousin, soprano Nina Hagerup, whose mother did not think Grieg had much promise: "He is nothing and has nothing, and he makes music that no one cares to listen to."[16] Perhaps they were not impressed by his small physical size. He was barely 5 feet tall and weighed about 100 pounds, having lost a lung to tuberculosis in his youth. Unfortunately, because Grieg's parents were also opposed to his marrying and taking on the responsibilities of a family, none of the parents were present at the wedding. As an engagement gift to Nina, Grieg wrote *Hjertets Melodier* (Melodies of the Heart, op. 5), with texts by their friend, Hans Christian Andersen. One of these, *Jeg elsker Dig* (I love you) is still often sung at weddings.

Nina and Edvard often performed together, and she was known for her interpretations of his songs. They had only one child, who died at 13 months. In the years following the death of their child, they traveled around Europe performing together and never really had a home base. Their marriage was not without difficulties, which led to a brief separation in 1883. Grieg's good friend Frants Beyer convinced Grieg to reconcile with Nina and encouraged him to build a home. Grieg then bought land south of Bergen and built his villa, which he called Troldhaugen. He spent summers there, hiking in the mountains, and winters in Christiania and Copenhagen, and toured the Continent. Troldhaugen has stood as a Grieg museum since 1928. For years concerts were held inside the house, but in 1985 a small concert hall was built behind the house and then expanded to include a museum building in 1995. Grieg's composer's cabin is also preserved on the estate, and the graves of Nina and Edvard are located nearby in the side of a cliff.

One of Grieg's earliest popular successes was his series of *Lyric Pieces*, which became best sellers all over Europe. They were simple enough to be used in the home and for teaching, but at the same time interesting and appealing, inspired by Norwegian folk music. Between 1864 and 1901 he produced 10 booklets of lyric pieces. He wrote his famous *Piano Concerto in A Minor* while on vacation in Denmark in 1868. This remains one of the most frequently performed piano concertos to this day. After the death of his little daughter in 1869, he began working on arrangements of Norwegian folk music and published *25 Norwegian Folk Songs and Dances* for piano. In the years that followed he began working closely first with author Bjørnstjerne Bjørnson on both poems and plays, and then with Henrik Ibsen, whom he had met on a trip to Italy in 1866. In 1874, Ibsen asked him to write music for his master-piece, *Peer Gynt*, which took more than a year to complete. It was an immedi-ate success, although some modern critics and theater directors feel that the music is too romantic or time bound to be used today. Other music has been written to Peer Gynt, including by Norwegian composer Harald Sæverud, but it is fair to say that none of this newer music has touched the hearts of the public to quite the same degree. Grieg created two concert versions, *Peer Gynt Suites No. 1 and 2*, which he often played on tour. The immense popularity of these works is shown by the fact that two of the best-known pieces, *I Dovregubbens hall* (The Hall of the Mountain King) and *Morgenstemning* (Morning Mood), have even been used in television commercials and movies.

In addition to his orchestral and piano music, Grieg wrote many songs to poetry by Arne Garborg, A. O. Vinje, and Hans Christian Andersen, among others. These works are frequently sung and recorded. Some of his best-known vocal compositions are the *Haugtussa* song cycle, for voice and piano, and *Fire salmer* (Four Psalms) for baritone solo with choir. Grieg traveled widely in Europe and became good friends of composers such as Tchaikovsky, Brahms, Franz Liszt, and Saint-Saens, among others. He is also considered to have influenced such composers as Béla Bartók, Ravel, and Debussy. His piano pieces, *Slåtter*, based on Hardanger fiddle tunes transcribed by Johan Halvorsen, became popular in Europe, and were played by Australian pianist

Percy Grainger, among others. Béla Bartók was so impressed with these tunes that he was inspired to take a six-week tour of Norway. He even brought a Hardanger fiddle home with him to Hungary. Grieg was quite successful in his lifetime, and made a comfortable living from his composing and touring.[17] Today Grieg's music is well represented on iTunes as well as other sources of classical music.

Another of the leading composers of romances, along with Kjerulf and Grieg, was Agathe Backer Grøndahl (1847–1907). She was also a pianist who studied with Franz Liszt and performed with both Ole Bull and Edvard Grieg. On her 1890 tour of England, she even received an enthusiastic review from George Bernard Shaw, who did not particularly care for Grieg's music. Although she was largely forgotten after her death, interest in her music has increased recently. Many of her 250 songs and 150 piano pieces have been recorded and made available.

Two more composers from the late nineteenth and early twentieth century are Christian Sinding (1956–1941), best known for his piano piece, *Frühlingsrauschen*, and Johan Halvorsen (1864–1935), who was considered Norway's best conductor after Johan Svendsen. Halvorsen composed works inspired by Norwegian folk music, including the music for a play called *Fossegrimen* about one of Norway's best-known Hardanger fiddlers, *Myllarguten* (The Miller's Boy). Halvorsen played Hardanger fiddle, and was the first composer to use the fiddle as a solo instrument with symphony orchestra. *Fanitullen*, the most popular movement of *Fossegrimen*, begins with a solo Hardanger fiddle, which gradually is supported by all the violins in the orchestra.

### The Post-Grieg Generation

The generation after Edvard Grieg had the challenge of coming out from under his shadow. They tended to go in one of two directions: either to be inspired by the new directions in Europe or to follow in Grieg's nationalistic footsteps.[18] Two composers who represent these disparate directions are nationalistic composer Eivind Groven (1901–1977), who himself played both Hardanger fiddle and *seljefløyte*, and modernist Fartein Valen (1887–1952), whose radical, atonal music aroused intense debate. Harald Sæverud (1897–1992) was another antiromantic. He wrote new music for Ibsen's *Peer Gynt*. He was also nationalistic, however, in that he was inspired by folk music without actually copying folk tunes. One of his most famous pieces is the anti-Nazi work *Kjempeviseslåtten* (Ballad of Revolt), which he composed in 1942 during the German occupation of Norway and dedicated to the members of the resistance. He originally wrote it as a piano piece and later scored it for orchestra.

Klaus Egge (1906–1979) was a leader among composers, serving as chairman of the Norwegian Society of Composers for 27 years. He began composing in a nationalist tradition, with his piano sonata based on the folk tunes of *Draumkvedet* (The Dream Ballad). In the 1930s he began moving in the direction of neo-classicism, and later in life developed a 12-tone technique. Geirr Tveitt[19] (1908–1981) is one of the most extreme examples of the nationalistic direction of composition in Norway; he was fascinated by Old Norse mythology and heathenism. He did not use folk tunes directly in his compositions, but rather was inspired by the characteristics he found in Norwegian folk music. Unfortunately 80 percent of his work was destroyed in a fire on his farm in 1970, although it has been possible to reconstruct some of the pieces thought to be lost. He was devastated by the loss, and it marked the end of his active composing. One of his most popular songs is *"Vi skal ikkje sova burt sumarnatta"* (We Shall not Sleep Away the Summer Night), written to a poem by Aslaug Låstad Lygre. This song has entered the canon of popular folk songs and is familiar to all.

## Church Music

Knut Nystedt (1915–), choral composer and organist, is one of the few Norwegian composers today who is performed worldwide. He studied with Aaron Copland, among others. Founder and conductor of The Norwegian Soloists' Choir from 1950 to 1990, he toured with them internationally. The recording *Immortal Nystedt* (2005) was nominated for two Grammy Awards in 2007, including Best Choral Performance.[20]

Egil Hovland[21] (1924–), also an organist, is one of Norway's most productive contemporary composers. Like Knut Nystedt, he also studied with Aaron Copland. In addition to his composing, he has been involved in updating the liturgy of the Church of Norway, and has contributed many hymns, choral works, and organ accompaniments used by the church.

## Theater

Although most cities had local theaters as early as the 1780s and amateur theater can be documented as far back as the 1500s, productions used the Danish language and often Danish actors. Ole Bull started a Norwegian theater in Bergen, *Den nationale Scene*, in 1850. His application to *Stortinget* (Parliament) for a subsidy was denied, but he found support among university students in Christiania, who raised 300 *spesiedaler* (unit of money used from 1560 to 1875) for the theater. One of these students was dramatist Henrik Ibsen, who spoke out in support of Bull's theater. In 1851, Bull invited Ibsen to Bergen where he worked as dramatist and theater director until 1857. Ibsen was succeeded by Bjørnstjerne Bjørnson, who also learned the basics of theater during his stint in Bergen. The theater had a hard time financially, however, and after raising money for the theater by playing concerts on several occasions, Bull finally left the theater to its board. After leaving the Bergen theater, Ibsen served as artistic director at *Christiania norske Theater* (The Christiania Norwegian Theater) until it went bankrupt in 1862. He was consultant for the Christiania Theater in Oslo from 1862 to 1864.

Theater finally came to be seen as an important part of nation building, and theaters began receiving public support. *Den nasjonale scene* (The National Theater), Bergen, the oldest professional Norwegian theater in Norway, held its first performance in 1876. *Trondhjems norske teater* came in 1861, and The National Theater, Oslo, followed in 1899.

In 1912, *Det Norske Teatret* (The Norwegian Theater) was founded in Oslo by Hulda Garborg, who served as the first chair of the board. She wanted to start a theater that would perform in the language of the people, which is to say *Nynorsk* (New Norwegian), the language created by Ivar Aasen based on rural dialects. It was quite a bold move to establish a *Nynorsk* theater in the middle of Christiania, which was the stronghold for the Dano-Norwegian language.

The first performance was *Jeppe på Bjerget* (Jeppe on the Hill), by Danish-Norwegian playwright, Ludvig Holberg, and translated into *Nynorsk* by poet Arne Garborg, the husband of Hulda Garborg. Although the performance was attended by King Haakon VII as well as the prime minister, a week later organized riots and protests lasting six days began against the use of *Nynorsk* in the theater. The opposition only served to strengthen the resolve of the actors, who saw their work as part of the movement toward Norwegian identity and nationalism. The theater is going strong today, producing plays written originally in *Nynorsk* as well as ones translated from *Bokmål* and other languages. In 1985 a new building was opened, and it remains the largest and most modern theater in Norway.[22]

In addition to theaters in major cities like Oslo, Bergen, Trondheim, and Stavanger, there are small theaters all over the country, often working with amateur companies or hosting *Riksteatret*, the touring company from Oslo.

### Bringing Theater to Rural Norway

*Riksteatret*, like the mobile cinema, was started in the late 1940s with the aim of bringing culture to rural areas. While people in cities such as Oslo, Bergen, Trondheim, and others have had theater for hundreds of years, this new endeavor was intended to bring theater, and later modern dance, to the 75 percent of the population who live outside the larger cities. With 12–14 productions and 600 performances a year, it currently reaches 100,000 to 130,000 people annually. *Riksteatret* and the regional theaters combined receive about 25 percent of the national funding for theater in Norway. The remaining 75 percent goes to theaters in the cities.

## Opera and Ballet

Because Norway had neither a royal court nor an aristocracy, it does not have the long tradition of opera found elsewhere in Europe. In the 1800s, both Bjørnson and Ibsen experimented with music written to their plays. Bjørnson had planned to write an opera, but it was never completed. A few operas were staged at the Christiania Theater and later National Theater in Oslo each year beginning in the 1880s, and a few other efforts were made in the early 1900s. Norway did not, however, have sufficient public interest in opera to support regular performances. It was not until 1950 that the Norwegian Opera Society was formed. It arranged for a number of performances and tours until finally in 1959 the Norwegian Opera was founded, with the world-famous soprano Kirsten Flagstad (1895–1962) as its first director.

Norwegian ballet has a similar history. In 1948 the New Norwegian Ballet, the first independent ballet company, was formed. In 1953 it joined the Opera Society, and they have remained together ever since. For many years they both performed in the *Folketeater* building at Youngstorget in Oslo, built in the 1930s, but finally in 2008 a beautiful new opera house was opened on the Oslo harbor. Since its opening, not only have the opera and ballet played to sold-out houses but also attending live broadcasts of world opera in movie theaters has become popular. Despite the growth in popularity of opera and ballet in recent years, according to 2008 statistics (predating the opening of the new opera house), only about 7 percent of the population reported attending an opera during the last 12 months while about 13 percent have attended a ballet or dance performance.[23]

## Choirs

The male chorus has had a long history in Norway. Many of the best composers, including Grieg, Kjerulf, and Svendsen wrote songs to poetry by Wergeland, Welhaven, Bjørnson, and Ibsen for male choruses. There was no tradition of mixed choir until the late 1870s. Once women's emancipation began to flower, women's choruses as well as mixed choirs were founded. Choirs popped up everywhere, among students, labor unionists, and churches. Perhaps the popularity of choirs in Norway at the time the Norwegian-American colleges were founded explains why the tradition is so strong at colleges such as St. Olaf, Concordia, and Luther, where the tradition of Norwegian-American choir conductor and composer F. Melius Christiansen lives on.

Choirs remain popular in Norway, with student choirs, mixed choirs, male choirs, and boys' choirs. The male chorus in the northern Norwegian village of Berlevåg was made famous, after the documentary *Heftig og begeistret* (Cool and Crazy) came out in 2001. The Norwegian Broadcasting Company's boys choir, *Sølvguttene*, has made numerous recordings, and both the Oslo Chamber Choir and the Oslo Gospel Choir have recorded extensively and toured internationally. The latter choir was the best-selling Norwegian musical group in the 1990s and has sold more than a million records.[24]

## JAZZ

There is an active jazz scene in Norway. In 1953 the Norwegian Jazz Forum was formed, a membership and interest organization designed to promote jazz in Norwegian society. Today it is publicly funded and consists of about 25 jazz festivals, 60 jazz clubs, 90 big bands, 450 professional jazz musicians, 80 jazz students, and 5 regional jazz centers in Oslo, Bergen, Trondheim, and Bodø in the north, and Arendal in the south. In 2005, the Jazz Forum established the National Jazz Stage in Oslo. The Forum also owns a record company, Odin, and publishes the journal *Jazznytt* (Jazz News).[25] Some of the best-known jazz musicians include saxophonist Jan Garbarek, pianist Kjetil Bjørnstad, tenor sax and goat horn player Karl Seglem, and guitarist and composer Terje Rypdal.

## POPULAR MUSIC

Popular music in Norway runs the gamut from folk to rock, punk, hip-hop, country and western, and metal. If a band has international ambitions, it usually means they must record in English. Some internationally known singers and bands are a-ha, Sissel Kyrkjebø, Lene Marlin, Sondre Lerche, DumDum Boys, Thomas Dybdahl, Kings of Convenience, Maria Mena, and Marion Raven, and also black metal groups such as Turbonegro, Satyricon, Dimmu Borgir, Gluecifer, and Mayhem.[26]

### Pop Rock

a-ha, with members Morten Harket, Magne Furuholmen, and Paul Waaktaar-Savoy, is probably the Norwegian pop-rock band with the greatest international success, having sold more than 70 million records since its debut in 1985. Its first album, *Hunting High and Low*, sold more than 8 million copies and was released in 2010 in an updated version. The hit single "Take on me," hit the top of the pop charts in 27 countries, including the Billboard Hot 100 in the United States where it remained for 23 weeks. It is the only Norwegian band ever to achieve this level of success in the United States. It was undoubtedly aided by its cutting edge music video, which won six MTV Video awards in 1986. Its ninth studio album, *Foot of the Mountain*, released in 2009, was their most successful international album in 20 years.

It hit the top of the charts in Germany, second place in Norway, and fifth in Britain.[27] Nonetheless a-ha is splitting up. Its farewell tour commenced in October 2009 in Cologne, Germany. The tour covered Europe, Asia Australia, South America, Canada, and the United States with a final concert on December 4, 2010, in Oslo.

Other pop and rock bands include Røyksopp, Postgirobygget, D. D. E., de Lillos, and Tre små kinesere. Electro rock band Datarock, founded in 2000, is perhaps the most recent success. It has had songs featured on commercials for iPod and Coca Cola, in addition to some video games such as the Sims 2 and FIFA 09 and 10.

### Country and Western

American country and western music has had a special place in Norway because of the 1960s, when all things American were popular. Norwegian country artists such as Bjøro Håland also traveled to the United States and performed at such venues as Norsk høstfest, an annual Norwegian-American music and cultural festival in Minot, North Dakota.

### Folksinging

In the 1970s, a number of young artists were inspired by American artists such as Pete Seeger. Beginning in the 1970s and continuing until today, singer/songwriters like Erik Bye, Alf Cranner, Finn Kalvik, Lars Klevstrand, Lillebjørn Nilsen, Jan Eggum, Øystein Sunde, and Halvdan Sivertsen have written and performed music that has entered the canon and appears in song-books used in schools. The songs are often written in dialect and are usually accompanied by folk guitar.

Another type of folk music is based on traditional Norwegian folk music. Several groups have appeared who have taken the traditional music and re-created it with more modern instrumentation, rhythms, and style. Some of these groups are Folque, Dvergmål, and Bukkene Bruse.

### Black Metal

Black Metal is Norway's claim to international fame in modern popular music. It constitutes the biggest musical export for Norway. Black Metal is heavily influenced by Speed Metal and Thrash Metal. There are several sub-genres, including Death Metal, Viking Black Metal, and Ambient Black Metal. Black Metal bands typically consist of two electric guitars, electric bass, and a drum set. They also feature one or more vocalists, and occasionally key-board. The music is characterized by speed and brutality, with abrupt tempo changes as well as sudden key and time signature shifts and complex guitar and drum work. The first band to define the genre in Norway was Mayhem, formed in 1984. Another internationally known band is Turbonegro (1988–1998; 2002–).[28]

### Sámi Music

The language, culture, and music of the indigenous Sámi people were repressed for generations by the majority Norwegian culture. The 1970s, with Norway's first vote against joining the European Community, introduced a period of cultural pride among all Norwegians, including the Sámi. Among other things, they began a revival of the traditional Sámi vocal music, the *joik*. Traditionally, the *joik* was never intended to be performed in public, but rather each *joik* is composed for a specific purpose, inspired by a person, thing, or something in nature. A *joik* written about a person is very personal, and considered to belong to the subject of the *joik*, not to the composer.

Things began to change in the 1970s when the group *Tanabreddens ungdom* (The Youth of the Tana Riverbank) produced three albums that combined traditional *joik* with modern western music, accompanied by percussion, bass, and guitar. For the first time *joik* music was created to be performed and disseminated, and was owned by the composer rather than the subject of the *joik*. The music of *Tanabreddens ungdom* became so popular that one of their records reached the top of the pop charts in Norway.

Even greater success has been enjoyed by Sámi artist Mari Boine, who combines traditional *joik* with elements of jazz, rock, and electronica. Born in 1965 into a deeply religious Laestadian family, she was raised to believe that the *joik* was the devil's work. As she grew older, she began using her music to fight for her culture as well as for other issues such as women's liberation and the environment. Her breakthrough album *Gula gula* (1989) was released internationally, and she has toured widely.[29] In 1994, she was invited to perform at the opening ceremonies of the Winter Olympics held in Lillehammer, Norway. She declined, however, saying she had no wish to be the sole representative of the Sámi.[30]

### MUSIC AND THEATER AWARDS

The *Spellemannprisen*[31] has been award annually since 1973 by the Norwegian music industry. It has the following categories: best male and female performers, pop group, electronica, contemporary music, rock, blues, country, hip-hop, traditional folk music/dance, dance band, jazz, classical, folk songs, children's music, composers, lyricist, music video, newcomer, hit of the year, and *Årets Spellemann* (Musician of the Year). The theater prize, the *Heddapris*, has been awarded since 1998 in 11 categories. The decisions are made by a jury of experts.

## THEATER AND MUSIC FESTIVALS[32]

Festivals are enormously popular during the summer months in Norway, although some take place during the winter. Virtually every little town or community has a festival, so there are literally hundreds every year.

For music and arts festivals, the largest include:

- The Bergen International Festival. *Festspillene i Bergen* is the largest festival of its kind in the Nordic countries, with more than 150 events in 15 days. It includes music, literature, theater, dance, opera, and visual art.
- *Festspillene i Nord-Norge.* Held in June each year in Harstad in North Norway, it includes concerts, theater and dance performances, art exhibitions, literary and film events, and a variety of seminars.
- The Molde International Jazz Festival. It has been going strong every July since 1961.
- *Øyafestivalen.* The largest pop and rock festival in Norway. Held each August in Oslo.
- Risør Chamber Music Festival. It is held every June.
- ULTIMA Oslo Contemporary Music Festival. Held in September/October.
- *Riddu Riddu.* The International Indigenous People's Festival is held annually in July in northern Norway.

Some of the largest theater festivals are:

- *Spelet om heilag Olav.* Produced each year in July at Stiklestad, where Saint Olav's last battle took place. This enormous production is put on with professional actors assisted by local volunteers.
- *Kristin Lavransdatter.* Held in July near Otta in Gudbrandsdalen. Set in fourteenth-century Norway, it is based on the Nobel-Prize-winning historical novel by Sigrid Undset.
- Peer Gynt Festival. Produced in early August each year in Gålåvatnet, Gudbrandsdalen.

## PUBLIC SUPPORT FOR THE ARTS[33]

The most important funding for the arts comes from the government, although in recent years additional sponsorship has been provided by private foundations and advertisers. Public funding is allocated through the Ministry of Cultural Affairs and the Norwegian Cultural Fund and is disbursed at three levels—state, county, and local municipality. Although public support of the arts began in the 1800s as part of the creation of the Norwegian national identity, it was not really until after World War II that a systematic cultural policy was developed to spread culture to the people by decentralizing and democratizing it. Community halls and regional arts centers were established all over the country. Culture was now defined much more broadly than previously and, as mentioned elsewhere, touring theater, concerts, art exhibits, and cinema began to travel the country. Artists in Norway are unionized and politically influential, thus ensuring that the arts are a legitimate topic of political debate.

The Fund for Performing Artists supports projects involving professional performing artists living and working in Norway, and also recordings made in Norway. Users of copyright-protected materials must pay a fee to Gramo, a collecting agency for musicians, performing artists, and record producers, and to the Fund for Performing Artists for noncopyright-protected recordings. Artists can receive money from both sources: remuneration for use of their work and as grant support for projects and travel.[34] In addition, there are numerous stipends available through the state-funded Government Grants for Artists.[35]

## Notes

1. http://www.eurovision.tv/event/artistdetail?song=24699&event=1481. Accessed 10/7/09.

2. http://www.dagbladet.no/nyheter/2009/05/16/575207.html. Accessed 10/7/09.

3. http://www.frikar.com/. Accessed 10/7/09.

4. *Store norske leksikon.* http://www.snl.no/.nbl_biografi/Olea_Cr%C3%B8ger/utdypning. Accessed 10/9/09.

5. Ådel Gjøstein Blom, *Folkeviser i arbeidslivet* (Oslo: Universitetsforlaget, 1977), pp. 177–179.

6. Information from the Music Information Centre, Norway. http://www.mic.no/mic.nsf/doc/art2002092015073189958342. Accessed 10/8/09.

7. http://www.snl.no/.nbl_biografi/Berit_Skjefte/utdypning. Accessed 10/11/09.

8. *Valdres,* March 6, 1924. http://valdreskvelven.no/historie/langeleik.htm. Accessed 10/11/09. Translation by author.

9. Knut Hendriksen, *Ole Bull* (Oslo: Cappelen. 2000), p. 191. Translation by author.

10. Einar Haugen and Camilla Cai, *Ole Bull: Norway's Romantic Musician and Cosmopolitan Patriot* (Madison: The University of Wisconsin Press, 1993), p. xxvi.

11. Nils Grinde, *Norsk musikkhistorie: Hovedlinjer i norsk musikkliv gjennom 1000 år* (Oslo: Universitetsforlaget, 1971).

12. Arvid O. Vollsness, ed., *Norges musikkhistorie. 1870–1910* (Oslo: Aschehoug, 1999), pp. 103–145.

13. http://www.nytimes.com/2007/09/16/arts/music/16tomm.html?pagewanted=1&_r=1. Accessed 10/26/09.

14. Web site of the International Grieg Society. http://www.griegsociety.org. Accessed 10/26/09.

15. Vollsness. p. 22. Translation by author.

16. Ibid.

17. http://www.griegsociety.org/default.asp?kat=1024&sp=2. Accessed 10/27/09.

18. http://www.mic.no/mic.nsf/doc/art2002092309385020803845. Accessed 11/3/09.

19. Arvid O. Vollsness, ed., *Norges musikkhistorie. Inn i middelalderen: 1914–50* (Oslo: Aschehoug. 2000).

20. http://www.mic.no/mic.nsf/doc/art2002100809284116531471. Accessed 11/3/09.

21. http://www.mic.no/mic.nsf/doc/art2002101119070951262531. Accessed 11/3/09.

22. http://www.detnorsketeatret.no/OMTEATRET/Historia/tabid/80/Default.aspx. Accessed 10/29/09.

23. http://www.ssb.no/norge_en/kultur_en.pdf. Accessed 11/2/09.

24. http://www.ogc.no/en/index.php. Accessed 10/28/09.

25. http://www.jazzforum.no/about-norsk-jazzforum. Accessed 10/29/09.

26. http://bandindex.no/. Accessed 10/14/09.

27. http://www.aftenposten.no/kul_und/article3322202.ece. Accessed 10/19/09.

28. http://www.mic.no/mic.nsf/doc/art2002092311413114817578. Accessed 11/4/09.

29. http://www.mic.no/mic.nsf/doc/art2002101417564968599221. Accessed 11/4/09.

30. http://www.mariboine.no/biography.php. Accessed 11/4/09.

31. http://www.spellemann.no/. Accessed 10/21/09.

32. http://www.norwayfestivals.com/index.cfm?setlanguage=3. Accessed 1/4/10.

33. http://www.culturalprofiles.net/norway/Directories/Norway_Cultural_Profile/-2191.html. Accessed 11/5/09.

34. http://www.ffuk.no/about-the-fund-foThr-performing-artists.70865.en.html. Accessed 11/5/09.

35. http://www.kunstnerstipend.no/english/. Accessed 11/5/09.

# 10

## Art and Architecture/Housing

### ART

The earliest examples of art in Norway are visible today in the Stone Age rock carvings found in about 70 different locations in various parts of the country, more than anywhere else in Europe.[1] Stone Age carvings comprise both naturalistic and stylized animals connected to hunting, and are usually placed in locations far from settlements. "*Helleristninger*," or rock carvings, were also made by Bronze Age people. These carvings have much more variety. They show warriors, ships, wagons, farm animals, and fertility symbols, and are often found on flat rocks in fertile fields. *Rødøymannen*, a 4,000-year-old stone age carving from Nordland, depicts a skier, and served as inspiration for the symbols for events in the 1994 Winter Olympics, held in Lillehammer, Norway. An impressive collection is found in Alta, north of Tromsø, where a walkway carries museumgoers over a large field of carvings.

Examples of weapons, jewelry, and other ornamental objects have been found in Norway from the Bronze Age, which began around 2000 BCE and ended abruptly around 500 BCE. These objects had only geometric decorations, never figures or organic motifs.

### Viking Art

While rune stones have been found in Norway, the most significant evidence of the art of the Vikings (ca. 793–1066) was found in the ship burial mounds that were excavated in southern Norway. In 1880 the Gokstad ship was unearthed, and in 1904 the iconic Oseberg ship, with its wooden cart,

Rock carvings at Alta, first discovered in 1972. The main site contains about 3,000 individual carvings, the oldest of which date to 4200 BCE. It is a UNESCO World Heritage Site. (Courtesy of the author.)

sledges, beds, and many other personal and household objects, was excavated. Unfortunately, medieval grave robbers had already removed all the jewelry that presumably would have been buried with the women—probably Queen Åsa and her servant—found in the Oseberg grave. But there remained a treasure trove of wooden objects. The ship itself is richly decorated with carved animal figures, intertwined and flowing gracefully up the prow and the stern. Rich carving is also found on sledges and bedposts, which display ferocious-looking animal heads with gaping mouths. These ships, along with the less well-preserved Tune ship, are displayed at the Viking ship museum in Oslo.

Several different styles of carving and decoration have been identified, used not only in wood, but also in metal jewelry, weathervanes, and stone slabs. While many of these styles are clearly Norwegian, for some one must look to the other Scandinavian countries to find a significant number of examples. There was clearly much contact among these countries as well as with the rest of Europe through both trade and plundering. Oseberg style, named after the ship, is characterized by gripping beasts, with their often-elongated bodies, paws grasping themselves, other beasts, or the borders. This style dates to around 900–975 CE and is followed by the Borre style, named for a collection of bronze objects found in a ship grave at Borre, southwest of Oslo, where gilded bronze objects were found. A common Borre motif is a chain consisting of overlapping, braided ribbons. This style also has two types of gripping beasts, the four-legged one with a canine head and a twisting, ribbon-like body, seen from the front, and a more naturalistic animal, in profile, with its head turned back. Also common in this style is a masklike Borre head, with its triangular face, round eyes, and ears. Borre style extends from mid-800s into the 900s, and examples are also found in the British Isles, especially the Nordic stone crosses on the Isle of Man.

Overlapping Borre and Mammen styles, the Jelling style, named for a silver cup found in a grave in Jutland, Denmark, is characterized by s-shaped, ribbon-like animals. It was used from approximately 860 into the 900s. The Mammen style, first identified on a war axe inlaid with silver also found in a gravesite in Jutland, can be interpreted as a further development of the Jelling style, with interlacing ribbons and abstract animal bodies.

The Ringerike style, named for a site in Norway, came into use toward the end of the 900s into the 1000s. It also depicts a large, four-legged animal, but is combined with plant motifs. There would typically be one large animal or bird of prey fighting a serpent or dragon. The plants usually have elongated leaves, forming a lobe at the end.

Finally, the Urnes style is named for the elegant carvings on the stave church in Urnes, on the west coast of Norway. The carved animals are slender and are connected by thin ribbons intertwined in figure eights. In the portal the base is a four-legged animal, probably a stylized lion, portrayed with ribbon-like animals and serpents. This style appeared in the mid-1000s and is also found in Sweden and Denmark.[2]

### Stave Churches

While the architecture of stave churches is dealt with below, the rich decorations both inside and outside many of the churches exemplify medieval art. The oldest existing churches were built as early as the 1100s, but virtually all were expanded and decorated well into the seventeenth and eighteenth centuries. The Urnes style of carving has already been mentioned, but many of the churches are decorated with early carvings and later paintings. About 140 stave church portals or wood-carved entrances exist today, most in an intricate, intertwining style. Some are still located at the original church, while others have been moved to museums or to newer churches.[3]

The origin of the tradition of carved portals cannot be traced, because nothing remains of earlier secular wooden buildings. There is, however, every reason to believe that it was common to decorate these buildings just as ships and other household objects, such as the sledges and wagons found in the Oseberg grave, were ornamented. The roofs were also decorated with crosses on the gable ends and dragon heads sticking out of the tops of the gables. This interesting juxtaposition of Christian and pre-Christian symbolism raises the questions of how thorough Christianization actually was or if Norwegians were attempting to maintain both belief systems in their houses of worship.

## Painting

During the period from the mid-1300s, when Norway was devastated by the Black Plague and fell under the rule of Denmark, to the mid-1800s, little of significance was produced in Norwegian art. In the nineteenth century, National Romanticism begins to be apparent in fine arts as well as in music and literature. Norway, however, lacked the aristocracy and wealth that typically supports the arts. Hereditary titles had been discontinued after 1821, and the upper classes—for example, the civil servant class—were not particularly wealthy. Although the university was established in 1811, there was no arts academy until 1909. A drawing school was started in 1818 and the National Gallery was founded in Oslo (then Christiania) in 1836, but even the state had little money to support the arts.

### National Romantic Painting

The economic situation began changing in the 1800s, with the arrival of industrialization, imported largely from England. The Norwegian shipping industry became established and grew rapidly, and society became more mobile. As mentioned previously, the first half of the 1800s was a time of searching for Norwegian identity, and artists tried to find characteristic elements of Norwegian folk culture that would distinguish Norwegian tradition and culture from European culture and even from that of other Scandinavian countries. These artists were not, however, isolated from Europe. They were educated in the universities and conservatories of Europe, first in Copenhagen, Dresden, and Düsseldorf, and later in Munich and Paris. But an important goal was to find what was typically Norwegian. They found what they were looking for in Norway's magnificent and dramatic nature.

Johan Christian Dahl (1788–1857) is considered the father of Norwegian painting. Born and raised in Bergen, his poor family could not afford to send him to art school. He was, however, apprenticed to a prominent decorative painter and eventually his talent was recognized. Educator and poet, Lyder Sagen, took the initiative to raise the money to send him to the art academy in Copenhagen.[4] Dahl was later named professor at the Academy of Art in Dresden, Germany, where he did most of his painting. There he became a leader of the naturalistic movement. Although he traveled and painted elsewhere in Europe, including Italy, Denmark, and Germany, Dahl traveled to Norway five times between 1826 and 1850 to study the landscape and make sketches. His motifs were mostly of wild mountain landscapes, waterfalls, forests, moonlit nature, and the sea, which he painted in a naturalistic style, depicting nature as it actually appeared. Two of his most famous paintings are *From Stalheim* (1842) and *Birch in Storm* (1849). The birch tree was commonly used as a symbol of Norwegianness. Dahl also played an important role in the founding of the National Gallery, which was established in Oslo in 1842 and contains many of his works.

One of Dahl's most famous students was Thomas Fearnley (1802–1842). He also studied in Copenhagen and Dresden, as well as Stockholm. He traveled widely in Europe, including Rome and Naples, Paris, London, and Amsterdam, and later moved to another popular destination for art students, Munich. He also undertook several study tours to Norway, where he had first met Dahl and decided to study with him. After Fearnley's premature death, it was Dahl who suggested that some of his works be acquired by the Oslo Art Association.[5]

Peder Balke (1804–1887) was another landscape painter and student of J. C. Dahl. In 1844, he also traveled to Norway with Dahl. Son of a poor tenant farmer, and originally named Peder Andersen, he began his artistic career

*Birch in Storm* by J. C. Dahl (1788–1857). Dahl is considered the father of Norwegian painting. Painted in 1849, this piece is a prime example of the National Romantic style. (Bergen Art Museum. Photo: Werner Zellien.)

*The Slindre Birch* (1839) by Thomas Fearnley (1802–1842). Fearnley was one of J. C. Dahl's students, and also used the birch tree as a symbol of Norwegian identity. (The National Museum of Art, Architecture and Design, Oslo. Photo: Jacques Lathion.)

apprenticed to a local painter. The two were hired to decorate the Balke church in Toten, which had been restored. After two years of apprenticeship, young Peder set out on his own, but always wished to return to Toten. In 1826 he moved in with the Anders Balke family, where he was treated like a son and allowed to take the Balke name. Anders Balke and another benefactor encouraged the young artist to move to Christiana to study at the art school (*Tegneskolen*) there.[6] From there he studied in Stockholm, Copenhagen, Dresden, Paris, and London. He also traveled extensively in Norway, including as far north as Finnmark in 1832, before beginning to study with J. C. Dahl in Dresden in 1836. Balke eventually moved away from the naturalistic, National Romantic style of Dahl to his own, more symbolic, late Romantic view of nature. In the late 1840s, he sold two larger paintings of North Cape and Trondheim and about 30 smaller oil sketches of North Norwegian landscapes and seascapes to the French king Louis Philippe. The young prince had traveled to North Norway in 1795 while in exile after the French Revolution, going as far north as North Cape. The aging king fell in love with Balke's paintings. Louis Philippe was deposed, however, before he could order any more. Though long forgotten, in the 1990s the sketches were brought out of storage, restored, and are now on permanent display at the Louvre.

While Dresden had been a popular destination for Norwegian artists, there was never a "school" in the same way that scholars speak of the later Düsseldorf School. Düsseldorf began to gain a reputation in Germany as more modern, moving in a more realistic direction as well as being a pleasant place for young painters to work, learn, and socialize. It was usual for painters to develop specialties—landscapes or people, for example—and also common for them to collaborate. One of the most famous collaborative paintings is *Bridal Procession in Hardanger*, painted by Adolph Tidemand (1814–1876), who painted the wedding party, and Hans Gude (1825–1903), who was responsible for the landscape. It was a commission for the great Tableau, performed at Christiania Theater in 1849, which also included a male chorus singing a song by Halfdan Kjerulf and Andreas Munch. Tidemand and Gude were both home in Norway because of the revolutions in Europe at the time.

*Bridal Procession in Hardanger* (1848) by Adolph Tidemand (1814–1876) and Hans Gude (1825–1903). Tidemand painted the wedding party and Gude the landscape. (The National Museum of Art, Architecture and Design, Oslo. Photo: Jacques Lathion.)

Unlike many Norwegian painters before him, instead of studying at the art school in Christiania, Tidemand had gone first to Copenhagen where his family had connections. He studied there for five years. He then began his tour of the Continent, visiting Düsseldorf, Munich, and Rome before returning to Christiania where he tried to establish himself as an artist. Although Tidemand eventually returned to Düsseldorf and lived there the rest of his life, he made frequent trips to Norway. In Norway he was especially fascinated with rural peasant life, and became a specialist in genre painting, or depictions of ordinary people in everyday life. One of his best-known paintings is *The Haugians* (1852), which depicts a meeting of members of the pietistic, lay-church movement led by Hans Nielsen Hauge.

Landscape painter Hans Gude arrived somewhat later in Düsseldorf, after he had studied under Danish landscape and folk-life painter Johannes Flintoe (1787–1870) in Christiania. Gude is considered a typical representative of the Düsseldorf School's position in the transition from Romanticism to Realism.[7] While Tidemand did not teach or accept pupils, Gude became a professor at

*The Haugians* by Adolph Tidemann (1814–1876). Painted in 1852. This painting depicts a meeting of followers of pietist Hans Nielsen Hauge. (The National Museum of Art, Architecture and Design, Oslo. Photo: Jacques Lathion.)

the academy when he was only 29, and was known to be an excellent teacher and mentor, even supporting young artists financially later in his career. He traveled extensively in Norway, particularly in the 1840s, and eventually left Düsseldorf.[8] His work became increasingly realistic beginning in the mid-1850s, and he began to choose different motifs. Gude's earliest paintings were usually mountain scenes from Norway, but later he became more interested in the coast and seascapes, not only from Norway but also Germany, Scotland, and Wales. He also moved away from oils, and began using watercolor and gouache. He lived in Britain for a time, where he learned to paint outdoors. Until then, all Norwegian painters had done their work in a studio, basing their paintings on sketches made during their trips home during the summer. Gude was critical, however, of the British type of realistic painting, which he considered merely copying what could be seen, without asking why.[9] In 1863, he was offered a professorship at a newly established art school at Karlsruhe where he attracted a large following of Norwegian painters, including Kitty Kielland, Eilif Peterssen, Otto Sinding, Christian Krohg, and Frits Thaulow. Gude later moved to the Berlin Academy of Art, where he worked the rest of his life. He did, however, find it difficult to cope with the new interest in modernism and symbolism.

### The 1870s: Historicism and Realism

In these years the younger generation was moving more consistently toward realistic painting but was also divided into two factions, both oriented more toward Paris than Germany. One group, later called the Lysaker Circle, was liberal politically but nationalistic in theme. It was led by Erik Werenskiold (1855–1938). Active in painting, drawing, and graphic arts, Werenskiold is perhaps best known for his illustrations of Asbjørnsen and Moe's Norwegian folktales, which he made together with Theodor Kittelsen (1857–1914). These two are responsible for creating the mental image most Norwegians have of a troll. Other members of the more nationalistic camp are Christian Skredsvig (1854–1924), Eilif Peterssen (1852–1928), and Kitty Kielland (1843–1924), who all were landscape painters. Peterssen, also known for his portraits and historical paintings, started an art school for ladies in Munich before he left for Rome and Venice. Two other artists of this school were interiors painter Harriet Backer (1845–1932), who studied with Kitty Kielland under Peterssen in Munich before moving to Paris, and Gerhard Munthe (1849–1929), who painted realistic landscapes but also harked back to Norwegian medieval and folk art in his tapestry designs.[10]

The other group, which was more radical and internationally oriented, was led by Christian Krohg (1852–1925), part of a group often called the Kristiania Bohemians. This was a reference to their nonconformist lifestyle and hours spent in the cafes of the Norwegian capital city. Trained as a lawyer, Krohg was a journalist and author, as well as a painter, and was a social critic in both media. He studied in Karlsruhe and Berlin for a period before returning to Kristiania for two years, spending summers in Skagen, Denmark. Finally, in 1881 Krohg went to Paris. Although he was only there for six months before returning to Norway, there seems to be significant French influence in his work.[11]

In the 1880s, Krohg produced mainly polemical paintings in three categories: the seamstress pictures, depicting a young, exhausted seamstress who has fallen asleep over her work; the Albertine pictures, showing a young prostitute; and a series depicting the struggle for survival. In 1886 he also wrote a novel about Albertine, exposing the exploitation of young girls in prostitution, which at the time was legal and controlled by the police. (Publicly supported prostitution was to be banned some years later.) The novel was confiscated when it first came out, and Krohg was charged and fined for offending common decency.

Krohg was married to impressionist Oda Krohg (1860–1935), whom he had met in Paris. She never studied art formally, but painted many original and lively portraits of their children. In 1889 the Krohgs left Kristiania. They lived in a number of places, including Paris for several years. In 1909 they returned to Kristiania, where he was offered a position as professor at the newly established Royal Academy of Art and Design.

### Modern Art

Edvard Munch (1863–1944) is Norway's most famous painter. He had a difficult childhood, suffering from poor health as a child. His deeply religious father, though a doctor, never earned much money, so the family ended up moving frequently from apartment to apartment. He lost both his mother and beloved sister to tuberculosis, and another sister suffered from mental illness. These formative experiences are reflected in some of his works, including *The Sick Child, The Dead Mother and Child*, and *Melancholy, Laura*.

While Munch had little formal training, he studied under Christian Krohg for a time. In his early years, Munch experimented with naturalism and impressionism. Participating actively in the art community in Kristiania in the 1880s, he debuted in the Fall Exhibition of 1883. In 1885, he received his first stipend for a short trip to Paris. This experience moved him away from naturalistic painting toward a more expressionist approach in which he sought to communicate emotions and experiences, rather than depict reality. Finally, in 1889, after a successful one-man show in Kristiania and upon the recommendation of his artist colleagues, he was awarded a state stipend, and departed for Paris. He spent the next 20 years of his life living abroad, although he spent summers in his little house in Åsgårdsstrand in southern Norway. In 1892, Munch was invited to put on a one-man show in Berlin at an exhibition of the *Verein Berliner Künstler* (Berlin Artists' Association). His unconventional themes and techniques created a scandal. The exhibition was closed prematurely, and Munch's paintings were removed. However, all the commotion and international attention it gained him pleased Munch and benefited his career.

A central theme of his works is seen in the title of a cycle of paintings, called *Frieze of Life —A Poem about Life, Love and Death*. Munch experimented with various media, including watercolor, drawings, and prints, and often made multiple versions of the same motif. His most famous painting is *The Scream*, from 1893, depicting a man standing on a bridge, his hands held on either side of his head, with brilliant orange and black swirls in the sky behind him. This image has become a ubiquitous representation of the anxiety of

*The Scream* (1893) by Edvard Munch (1863–1944). Munch's most famous painting, it exists in two painted versions. This one was painted in tempera and pastel on cardboard and hangs in the National Gallery in Oslo. The other, which was damaged in a robbery, is oil on canvas and is at the Munch Museum in Oslo. (The National Museum of Art, Architecture and Design, Oslo. Photo: Jacques Lathion. © 2010 The Munch Museum/The Munch-Ellingsen Group/Artists Rights Society (ARS), NY.)

modern society, and has been seen in everything from newspaper cartoons to inflatable dolls and automobile commercials.

After a nervous breakdown in 1908, Munch settled in Oslo, where he continued to work. Some of his best-known works include murals for the cafeteria of the Freia chocolate factory as well as farm scenes and self-portraits. After some controversy, his paintings were selected to decorate the festival hall (the Aula) at the University of Oslo in 1912.[12] After his death in 1944, the bulk of his works was bequeathed to the City of Oslo. In 1963, the city built a special museum to house the approximately 1,100 paintings, 4,500 drawings, and 18,000 prints Munch left. The museum has been expanded, and more recently security was greatly tightened after thieves made off with *The Scream* and *Madonna* in a daring daylight armed robbery in 2004. The paintings were recovered, but not without significant damage. Plans are under development to build a new Munch museum on the waterfront near the new opera house, which was completed in 2008.

A contemporary of Munch, Harald Sohlberg (1869–1935) was among the landscape artists who learned from Erik Werenskiold and Eilif Peterssen, as well as Harriet Backer. A neo-romantic, he is best known for his paintings and prints of *Summer Night* (1899) and *Winter Night in Rondane* (1914, and other versions).

Nikolai Astrup (1880–1928) was considered to have some of the same mystical, symbolic relationship to nature as Sohlberg.[13] Born and raised in Jølster, in western Norway, he returned there after living and traveling abroad to run a small farm, which can be visited today. Many of his paintings depict life and nature around the farm during various seasons and moods. He is especially known for his woodcuts and is, along with Edvard Munch, considered one of Norway's best graphic artists.

### Other Twentieth-Century Artists

In the first decades of the twentieth century, the conflict continued between the proponents of the Lysaker circle and the followers of Christian Krohg, although both groups had moved away from a realistic copying of nature. The period was characterized by independence from Sweden, along with an economic upturn, which also benefited the art world. The position of director was added to the National Gallery, and, as mentioned previously, the State Academy of Art was established in 1909.

Henrik Sørensen (1882–1962) was one of Matisse's students. While in Paris he also became familiar with Cezanne, Degas, and van Gogh, who all influenced his work.[14] Also known for his paintings of Jesus Christ, Sørensen painted altarpieces for churches in Vinje, Notodden, Steinkjer, and Hamar. He was also selected to paint one of the large murals in Oslo City Hall. Norwegian painters

*Winter Night in Rondane* (1914) by Harald Sohlberg (1869–1935). Twenty different versions of this painting exist in oil or water color, in addition to the color lithographs. This one is oil on canvas and hangs in the National Gallery in Oslo. (The National Museum of Art, Architecture and Design, Oslo. Photo: Jacques Lathion.)

continued their close connection to the European art world, and other Norwegian pupils of Matisse were Jean Heiberg, Per Krohg, and Axel Revold.

Kai Fjell (1907–1989) debuted in 1932, but had a sensational breakthrough in a one-man show at *Kunstnernes Hus* (The Artists' House) in Oslo in 1937, and was proclaimed the new Edvard Munch. Fjell was known for his surrealistic, individualistic paintings, with a use of familiar symbols. His long career extended until his death at age 81. In addition to his smaller paintings, he also was responsible for large murals in the government building in Oslo, the old Fornebu airport, and a church, as well as book illustrations and stage decorations for the National Theater.

Arne Ekeland (1908–1994) was a student of Axel Revold, but spent considerable time in Paris and Italy, where he was influenced by Picasso and Georges Braque, as well as the German expressionists. His breakthrough came in 1940 at a one-man show at *Kunstnernes Hus*. He was a political painter, believing that humans could create a society that would bring an end to war, poverty, and exploitation. Several of his paintings hang in the *Storting*.

Nonfigurative art gained greater popularity in the late 1950s, with Jakob Weidemann (1923–) a prime example. He is considered a modernistic interpreter of the Norwegian obsession with landscape and nature.[15] He captures the sense of nature through color and shape, but abstractly, not figuratively. Weidemann also created spectacular stained glass works for two churches in Steinkjer, where light became a religious symbol. Another popular artist, Karl Erik Harr (1940–), from northern Norway, represents a more figurative style in his many paintings, book illustrations, and graphics of North Norwegian nature.

In the 1970s many artists turned their attention to politically inspired art, producing both paintings and graphic art. Two of the most common topics were protests against the U.S. war in Vietnam and Norway's application for membership in the European Economic Community. These artists also created art in public spaces, such as metro stations, and graphic art gained in popularity and influence. As in the literature of the time, Mao Zedong and Che Guevara were the heroes of the young artists, who were fighting against what they perceived to be the capitalistic establishment of the older generation.[16]

Odd Nerdrum (1944–) is a contemporary Norwegian painter who has enjoyed international recognition, although he is controversial at home. His works are displayed in the Hirshhorn Museum and Sculpture Garden in Washington, D.C.; the Metropolitan Museum in New York; the San Diego Museum in California; the Walker Art Museum in Minneapolis, Minnesota; and the Gothenburg Museum in Sweden, as well as the National Gallery in Oslo.[17] He employs old-world techniques, mixing and grinding his own pigments. Unlike the more abstract, nonfigurative painting popular in Norway today, Nerdrum paints still-life works and portraits, often of people dressed in skins and cloaks from another time, and large allegorical works, also from another, unspecified time. He has called himself the "king of kitsch." One critic claims that while Nerdrum paints in the style of the Old Masters, his themes are thoroughly modern. His characterization of Nerdrum's work: "imagine the result if Rembrandt had painted the sets of *The Road Warrior*."[18]

Another young artist who has received international attention is Vebjørn Sand. He is best known for the Keplar star (Norwegian Peace Star) at the Oslo airport, Gardermoen, and the Leonardo bridge project. He successfully convinced Norwegian highway authorities to build a bridge based on Leonardo da Vinci's sixteenth-century design over the highway linking Oslo and Stockholm.[19] Sand has also participated in the debate over art training in Norway. Like Nerdrum, he supports classical training, with its emphasis on technical mastery.

## Sculpture[20]

Conditions for sculptors in nineteenth-century Norway were even more difficult than they were for painters. Most sculptors had to earn a living as wood-carvers or decorators. The situation changed for the better in the second half of the 1800s with the increased interest in monuments all over Europe. In Norway there was particular interest in monuments of important historical events supporting Norwegian national identity. Another opportunity for sculptors was to work on the reconstruction of the Nidaros Cathedral in Trondheim, with its many sculptures both inside the building and on the façade.

One artist who worked on the cathedral was Gustav Vigeland (1869–1943), arguably Norway's most important sculptor. Before settling in Oslo he studied in Copenhagen and Paris, where he was inspired by the works of Rodin. During his career Vigeland completed nearly 100 portrait busts of famous Norwegians such as Henrik Ibsen, Camilla Collett, and Henrik Wergeland. His best-known project is the Vigeland Sculpture Park located in the 80-acre Frogner Park in Oslo. Consisting of 212 bronze and granite sculptures and several wrought iron gates, it represents more than 20 years of Vigeland's work.[21] Depicting his vision of the human struggle from birth to death, he created sculptures of nude people of all ages, showing a variety of emotions and relationships. The most spectacular piece is the Monolith, which towers over the middle of the park. It consists of 121 individual figures carved into a single granite block nearly 56 feet tall. Completed after his death, the stone was carved by three stone masons working for 14 years. Vigeland lived and worked in his studio near the park from 1924 until his death in 1943. The studio, which was supplied by the City of Oslo in exchange for ownership of the originals of all his past and future works, now serves as a museum dedicated to Vigeland. The park was completed after his death.

Dyre Vaa (1903–1980) is well known for his public statues in Oslo, including the four fairy tale motifs on Anker Bridge, the swans in front of the City Hall, and the statue of eighteenth-century writer Ludvig Holberg beside the National Theater. He also created the statue of St. Olav at the site where he fell at Stiklestad and one of Henrik Ibsen in his hometown of Skien.

## FOLK ARTS

Norway is known for its folk arts, such as wood carving, silver and gold jewelry, rosemaling, weaving, and knitting. The term "folk" art is used to describe the practical and decorative arts that were thought to originate among rural people, or *folket*. It began to be especially prized during the 1800s when the urban elite was searching for examples of specifically Norwegian culture that they could use to support the idea of Norwegian identity.

*The Monolith* by Gustav Vigeland, located in Vigeland Park, Oslo. This sculpture was made of a single block of granite 56 feet tall, and consists of 121 individual figures. (© 2010 The Vigeland Museum/Artists Rights Society (ARS), New York/ BONO, Oslo. Photo by author.)

The most distinctively Norwegian of all the folk arts is often considered to be *rosemaling*, or rose painting, although similar painting is found all over Europe. Rosemaling became popular in the 1700s once the chimney came into common use in rural Norway. Before then, the smoke escaped through a hole cut into the ceiling of the hut, resulting in extensive soot accumulation on the walls. With the new chimney, in addition to greater economic prosperity, people began decorating walls and furniture, as well as plates, bowls, and cups with the vine-like foliage and flowers of rosemaling. Styles of rosemaling vary considerably from one part of the country to another, with differences in color, motif, and design. The Telemark area, in southern Norway, is especially known for its

Rosemaling, the traditional Norwegian decorative painting, used on furniture, walls and household objects. Examples shown are of Telemark style (box and bowl) and Valdres style (bellows). (Courtesy of the author.)

C and S-shaped tendrils and more asymmetrical design, where Hallingdal tends to have a symmetrical design, with a large flower in the middle surrounded by leaves.

Rosemaling was heavily influenced by baroque and rococo styles popular in Europe. Sometimes religious motifs were used, and stave churches (see below) were often decorated with rosemaling. Many famous rosemalers produced works that are prized today. While the tradition was strongest between about 1750 and 1850, it has recently enjoyed a renaissance, both in Norway and among Norwegian Americans. Mostly cheap mass-produced rosemaling is found in the tourist shops in Norway, but talented artists also produce beautiful rosemaling both in Norway and the United States. Skogfjorden, the Concordia College Norwegian Language Village, imported two well-known Norwegian rosemalers, Nils Ellingsrud and Sigmund Aarseth, to decorate the dining hall and the staff lounge at the facility near Bemidji, Minnesota. Rosemaling workshops and competitions are offered at Skogfjorden; Vesterheim Museum in Decorah, Iowa; and elsewhere.

Although rosemaling is better known, wood carving actually began earlier, probably in the 1600s. One type of carving is called *karveskurd*, or chip carving, and is found on furniture as well as other small wooden objects like boxes, mangle boards (for pressing cloth), caskets, and chests. Chip carving consists of square, triangular, circular, or star-shaped geometric patterns made with ruler and compass. The design elements are chipped out of the flat surface using a small knife or chisel.

Other carving is inspired by Renaissance style, in low relief. It consists of vine tendrils, or acanthus, but also flowers, which were sometimes painted as well as carved, and is found on wooden objects such as tankards and mangle boards, but also on furniture, supporting posts, door frames and pillars, pulpits, altar-pieces, and baptismal fonts in churches. This type of carving was especially well developed in Valdres, Hallingdal, and Telemark in southern Norway.[22]

## APPLIED ART

Norway is also known for contributions to the applied arts, including glass, textiles, silver and enamel, ceramics, porcelain, and furniture. Norwegian glass design often is inspired by natural materials such as pine needles or snow. While not as well known as Swedish glass, Norwegian Hadeland glass is distributed internationally. The factory, founded in 1762, is open for visitors, who can view glassblowing demonstrations and purchase glass at the factory outlet. Silver- and goldsmithing dates back to pre-Viking days, and today some of the most beautiful silver filigree is inspired by Viking techniques. The Norwegian folk costumes, or *bunader*, are ornamented with intricate filigree-work brooches, or *søljer*, with their hanging dangles, made of gold or silver, belts, buttons, and shoe buckles. Some famous jewelers from the 1800s still have jewelry stores named after them, including David Andersen and Jacob Tostrup. Andersen and Tostrup also specialized in enameling of jewelry and other objects. Both attracted attention at the World Exhibitions in Paris in 1889 and Chicago in 1893.[23]

Norway's oldest porcelain factory, *Porsgrund porselænsfabrik* AS, was founded in 1885. Many well-known Norwegian artists have created designs, including Theodor Kittelsen, Gerhard Munthe, Jakob Weidemann, and Odd Nerdrum. Porsgrund is known for special occasion plates, especially Christmas plates, and fine china, including Hearts and Pines Christmas china and its traditional farmer rose pattern. The company has struggled financially in recent years, suffering layoffs and the shift of production offshore, and is threatened with closure.

### The Husflid Movement

In 1867, the scholar Eilert Sundt wrote the book *Om Husfliden i Norge* (About Hand Crafts in Norway) in which he argued that contrary to popular opinion, rural Norwegians were surprisingly good at all manner of handcrafts, ranging from carpentry and wood carving to boat-building, knitting, and sewing. He compared their cleverness with their hands favorably to the book learning of the urban, educated elite. They could make the necessities of life with their own hands, and were even able to produce a bit more than they required for their own use, which they could sell to earn some cash. In time an ideological movement developed, the *Husflid*-movement. In its earliest phase, the 1800s, *Husflid* was creative, making new designs and products. By the 1930s, the focus had shifted to preservation of traditional styles, with innovation being looked down upon. Today it has again become popular to take the old ideas, techniques, and materials and to create something new with them. In

Kristenteppe tapestry woven by Marit Anny Tvenge from Valdres. This tapestry is traditionally used during christenings, as well as weddings. (Courtesy of the author.)

addition to the *Husfliden* stores, which exist in most towns and cities in Norway, there are also museums of applied arts in Oslo, Bergen, and Trondheim.

Other commercial forms of applied art that Norway is known for include furniture and textiles—weaving and knitted garments, in particular. Knitting is treated in Chapter 6.

### Furniture

There is a long Norwegian tradition of furniture building, dating back to the Viking age of the tenth and eleventh centuries. Dragon style (historicism), with its characteristic dragon and serpent heads, became especially popular after the Oseberg Viking ship was found in 1904. Built-in carved cupboards, beds, tables, benches, and chairs are all examples of the work of rural wood carvers and carpenters. In the cities, Norwegian carpenters were hired to make much of the furniture in the royal palace built in Christiania for the Swedish king as well as in the small summer palace, Oscarshall. Neo-rococo and neo-renaissance styles were popular, but classical motifs were also commonly used. In the late 1800s non-European influences, such as Chinese, Japanese, Indian, and Turkish, can also be seen.[24] In the twentieth century, commercial furniture production was especially concentrated in the Møre and Romsdal region of western Norway, with well-known producers such as Ekornes, with its Stressless chairs, and Hellegjerde. While Ekornes continues to produce furniture in Norway, tough economic times have caused layoffs, and some furniture manufacturers have moved production offshore to countries with cheaper labor, such as Poland, Lithuania, Thailand, and China.

## ARCHITECTURE[25]

After the end of its period of greatness, which lasted from approximately 1217 to 1319, Norway was a poor country, under the control of Denmark from 1380 to 1814 and Sweden from 1814 to 1905. With the center of power located in Copenhagen for 400 years and Stockholm for nearly 100 years, there was no tradition of feudalism, and no castles surrounded by villages of peasants, only small, scattered farming communities. There were few noble families who might commission architects to design manor houses. Even after the first university was established in 1811, there was no school of architecture or building design. Of course buildings were constructed in Norway, but their design was influenced by the availability of locally available materials, mostly wood and stone, and the knowledge of how best to use these materials.

### Viking and Early Medieval Period

The oldest known remains of houses have been found on the west coast, near Stavanger. Houses from the Iron Age (Migration period: 350–550 CE), made of readily available stone, sod, and log, were constructed to provide shelter for both humans and animals. Evidence of Viking age dwellings has been found at Borg, in Lofoten,[26] Kaupang, along the west side of Oslo Fjord,[27] as well as in Iceland, Lance aux Meadows (North America), and England. Both archeological evidence and descriptions from the sagas tell us that longhouses generally consisted of one large room with benches around the walls for sitting or sleeping. The houses were made of logs, where those were available, laid horizontally and notched at the ends. The walls were self-supporting, and also carried the roof, which was made of turf.[28] A central fire provided warmth for heating and cooking, and a hole in the roof allowed the smoke to escape. Because little remains of the actual wood superstructure of these houses, the best evidence of the wood-working skill people had at the time is found in buried Viking ships that have been preserved (see above).

### Stave Churches

The most important examples of wood construction from the medieval period are the stave churches, built from approximately 1100 into the 1300s. While at one time there were as many as 2,000 of these churches, only 28 remain today, all located south of Trondheim. Some of the rest were demolished deliberately after the Reformation (1537) or after 1851, when a law was passed establishing a minimum size for churches. Many others were burned accidentally or simply dismantled by unappreciative landowners and sold for the lumber. Others were the victims of wind, weather, rot, or landslides. In 1723, the king claimed the right to sell churches to the highest bidder. These private owners did not always maintain the churches properly. By the time the municipalities began buying these churches back in the mid-1800s, many were in poor condition. Several stave churches were moved to museums, including the Norwegian Folk Museum in Oslo, Fantoft in Bergen, and Maihaugen in Lillehammer.

For some the rescue was last minute. The stave church at Vang in Valdres was in the process of being torn down when painter J. C. Dahl happened upon the project and managed to stop the demolition. He was unable to find anyone in Norway to buy the church, but he finally convinced the King of Prussia to purchase it and set it up in what is now Karpacz, Poland.[29] It still stands today, although greatly modified. Fortunately, one of Dahl's students made careful measurements and sketches, which have survived. The Garmo stave church at Maihaugen was torn down in 1882 and its parts scattered among various farms in the community. Anders Sandvig, founder of Maihaugen Museum, managed to recover nearly all the pieces and had it reconstructed and consecrated in 1920–1921 at the museum in Lillehammer.[30]

Fantoft stave church in Bergen, which also had been rescued and moved from its original location on the Sognefjord in 1883, was burned down in the early 1990s along with several other churches. The deed was allegedly committed by black metal artist Varg Vikernes, also known as *Greven* (The Count), and other Satanists. A reproduction of the Fantoft stave church has been built on the same site.

Although there is quite a variety among stave churches, the name "stave church" refers to the structure, which all have in common. The load-bearing structure consists of poles or staves around the nave, which support both the walls and the roof. These poles rest on sills, which themselves lie on a stone foundation, which serves to keep the wood off the ground. The walls are made of vertical planks, which fill in the spaces in the framework. The roofs are covered with wooden shingles, and pine tar is applied to the wood as a preservative. While some stave churches are small and simply constructed, others are richly decorated with acanthus (vine and tendril) carving around the doors and dragon heads extending from the roof. These decorations are said to frighten away evil spirits.

The Urnes stave church is the oldest existing example and is listed on UNESCO's cultural heritage list. Although it is believed to have been built and rebuilt at least twice, and thus is difficult to date, most scholars believe it was first constructed from twelfth into the thirteenth centuries. The best-preserved and most authentic stave church is Borgund, from the 1100s. The surviving churches were expanded over the centuries to meet the needs of the congregations. The structures of some churches that were torn down are preserved in architectural drawings made in the 1700s and 1800s.[31]

### Stone Churches

While in the rest of Europe wooden churches were replaced by stone churches, this was not the rule in Norway. Many rural churches are built of wood even today. Building in stone was unknown in Norway before the arrival of the Christian church. It was more expensive to build in stone, partly because the expertise needed had to be imported from abroad. As a result, although many stone churches were constructed during this period, they were mainly built in the cities. Examples include the cathedral in Stavanger (1125), Old Aker church in Oslo (1100s), and Maria Church in Bergen (Romanesque/Norman 1180), which was used between 1360 and 1754 by the German merchants who were part of the Hanseatic League. The most impressive early church is the Romanesque/Gothic Nidaros cathedral in Trondheim (1070–1300), the largest stone cathedral in Scandinavia. It was built on the site of St. Olav's grave, and during the Middle Ages it became a destination for pilgrims from all over northern Europe.[32]

Borgund Stave Church, built in the 1100s, is one of 28 surviving stave churches. Located in western Norway, at the eastern end of Sognefjord. (Courtesy of the author.)

At one time there were as many as 300 stone churches in Norway, but only about 160 remain today. Most were constructed between 1100 and 1320 and were often built on the sites of earlier wooden churches. Some, particularly churches on royal farms and monasteries, were demolished after the Reformation, as they were considered remnants of Catholicism. Others were destroyed in wars. The stones were often reused in other projects. The Hamar cathedral ruins are now covered in protective glass and used for concerts. The ruins of Hovedøya monastery and Margaretha Church in Oslo are preserved and are also used for public events.

### Houses from the Fifteenth to Eighteenth Centuries

In the late medieval and early modern periods, the houses of most ordinary people were made of logs lain horizontally, with notches cut in the ends allowing them to be stacked up neatly, like Lincoln Logs. The technique dates back to the Viking age. Unlike the crude log cabins found in the frontier of the United States, these houses were constructed with a v-shaped groove in the underside of each log, allowing each one to rest securely over the one beneath, with no gaps. This technique permitted the structure to remain tight, even after the logs dried and the house settled. Many examples of these houses are preserved today in open-air museums in Norway. The oldest houses, called *årestuer*, consist of one room; later ones have more than one. They have a high threshold and low doorway to keep the heat in, and the earliest ones continued the traditional practice of an open hearth in the middle of the floor with a hole in the ceiling for smoke to escape. Some of these were used as late as the mid-1800s, although in many places chimneys came into use in the 1600–1700s, providing a much cleaner and healthier environment.

A typical building seen even today on Norwegian farms is the *stabbur*, or storehouse. It is also made of logs, and usually is placed on pillars, with steps not attached to the building in order to keep animals out of the food supply. The bottom story is usually smaller than the top, and the doorways are often richly carved. This type of storehouse dates back to the Middle Ages and is even mentioned in the Gulating Law from 900 CE.

### Trading Towns

The most striking old trading town was in Bergen, where you can still see the old *Bryggen*, or Hanseatic wharf. While the buildings that exist today were constructed in the 1700s, they were built according to original patterns and methods of construction predating the founding of a Hanseatic *Kontor*, or trading office, in 1360. The wooden structures, with their long rows of houses and storerooms along a common passageway, are characteristic of local architecture as far back as the 1200s. The 61 surviving buildings are included on UNESCO's World Heritage List and are the only existing example of a Hanseatic office in Europe.[33] The front building in each row was reserved for the merchant with the most seniority; those with less were housed farther back. No heat or fire was allowed in the buildings, for fear of fire, so the rooms were cold and dark, especially in the wintertime. Meals were cooked and served in special buildings called *Schøtstuer* behind the rows of merchant houses.

### Danish Period: 1380–1814

The population of Norway was decimated during the Black Plague, which began in 1349. In 1397, a politically weakened Norway entered a union with Sweden and Denmark; after Sweden withdrew from the union in 1523, Norway gradually fell under Danish control. All government power and activity was then centered in Copenhagen. Several fortresses were built or expanded, mainly to defend against the Swedes. These included Akershus in Oslo (1300–1660), Fredriksten, in Halden on the Swedish border (1640–1645), Kristiansten Fortress in Trondheim (1682–1684), Bergenhus Fortress in Bergen (completed ca. 1700), and Vardøhus Fortress in northern Norway (originally built in early 1300s, and expanded in 1738).

In 1624 the city of Oslo, which had been built almost entirely of wood, burned down. Christian IV, the king of Denmark and Norway from 1588 to 1648, declared that the city should be reconstructed in a new location, beneath Akershus Fortress. He declared furthermore that all buildings should be constructed in brick or stone and that the streets should be broad and laid out in a quadratic fashion, that is, at right angles to each other. This section of Oslo still bears the name of *Kvadratur*. The new city was then renamed in his honor: Christiania. Christian IV also founded the city of Kongsberg in 1624, after silver was found there and made a similar quadratic plan for the south coast city of Christianssand (now called Kristiansand) in 1641.

Other well-preserved historic cities from this period include Fredrikstad, from the 1600s, which is a complete garrison town, and the city of Røros, near the Swedish border in Trøndelag, which was founded in 1644 when copper mining began. The buildings that exist today are from the 1700s and are included on the World Heritage List.[34] Both Røros and Kongsberg have beautiful churches built in 1784 and 1761. Wooden houses from the 1700s to the 1800s are preserved in Old Bergen and Old Stavanger.

The nobility was not large in Norway and no royal palaces were built, so only a few impressive residences and manor houses were constructed in this period. Some of the best known, which can be visited today, are Rosendal Barony, western Norway (1665); Jarlsberg, near Tønsberg (1699); Bogstad, near Oslo (1700s); and Ulefoss, in Telemark (1807). Stiftsgården, the largest wooden structure in Norway, was built in Trondheim between 1774 and 1778. It was built by Danish nobility, and eventually purchased by the state. Today it serves as the royal residence when the royal family is in Trondheim.

### Nineteenth-Century National Romanticism

As mentioned earlier, the early decades of the 1800s were characterized by the effort to define a specifically Norwegian culture, in architecture as well as in music, art, and literature. In the late 1800s, *Sveitserstil* (Swiss chalet style) became popular for wooden buildings. Swiss chalet style architecture, which actually originated in Germany, is characterized by steeply sloped roofs with gables; decorative carving, especially along the roof edges; high-ceilinged rooms; large, tall windows; balconies; and a raised stone foundation.[35] It often has cupolas and towers. Many train station buildings were constructed in this style because railroads were being built during this period.

In the 1890s, Norwegian dragon elements were added to the Swiss style, creating a particularly Norwegian-romantic style. The Frognerseteren restaurant in Oslo, built in 1890, is a prime example, although the style was also used in furniture, homes, and hotels such as the historic Union and Kviknes (Balestrand) hotels on the west coast of Norway.

### After 1905: Independence from Sweden

The city of Ålesund in western Norway is extraordinary architecturally because it is unique in the consistency of its design. After a fire destroyed 80 percent of the buildings in the city in 1904, it was rebuilt during the next three years in *Jugendstil*, or Art Nouveau. More than 600 buildings were constructed in the same style during that three-year period. The architects had been educated abroad, but because Norway was in the process of gaining its independence from Sweden in 1905, they were especially interested in creating a Norwegian architecture. Today there is some controversy about preservation of the buildings. Some feel it is sufficient to preserve the facades of the buildings, while others stress the importance of preserving authentic interiors as well.

### Oslo—Mid-1800s to 1930

Oslo, both the largest city in Norway and its capital since the reign of Haakon V (1299–1319), has a particularly interesting architectural history, one closely connected to its social and economic history. Already in the 1800s people were flooding to the city in search of employment. In response to the housing shortage, large blocks of tenements were erected, especially on the east side of Oslo near the factories. In the early part of the twentieth century, owners of some factories, including Freia chocolate and Nitedal matches, began providing better housing for their workers.

In the second half of the nineteenth century, small suburbs began to crop up around Oslo. Single-family homes and smaller apartment buildings were built for the new, growing middle class of civil servants and university professors to the west of the city. These people wished to distinguish themselves from the tradesmen class, who lived and worked in the same buildings. This new middle class desired to separate work from leisure. While these areas are now considered neighborhoods within the city of Oslo, at the time areas such as Briskeby and Homansbyen were located far outside the city borders.

The Homan brothers, who began building in the 1850s, can be thought of as the first commercial housing developers. They were inspired by the English villa cities in their planning.[36] Some of the streets were named after Swedish/ Norwegian royalty: Josefinesgate, Oscarsgate, and Gustavsgate. Others were named after the original owners of the land: Uranianborg terasse and Under-haugsveien. Strict covenants controlled the height of fences and the size of both houses and gardens, which were to be large and airy, with gravel paths as well as fountains and flower beds, and be protected from unnecessary noise or commercial activity. Fruit trees were planted in the gardens. The houses were built of brick, stone, or stucco.

In the early twentieth century, inspired by Ebenezer Howard's concept of garden cities, the Christiania municipality decided to build Norwegian versions, called *hagebyer*, outside the city limits of the day. The first one, Ullevaal Hageby, was built between 1915 and 1922. These were originally intended for working-class families, but because they turned out to be so expensive, they became homes for upper-middle-class families and represented an economic loss for the city of Oslo. In a way these garden cities were ideological forerunners of the *drabantbyer*, the post–World War II housing in Oslo (see below). The idea was that all should have sunlight, nature, and fresh air, and that these neighborhoods were to be self-contained units located outside the central city.

From the 1920s and until the beginning of World War II, functionalism (*funkis*) came into vogue. This style of architecture stresses the value of function over form and also emphasizes the belief in progress, science, and modernity.[37] French architect le Corbusier is viewed as the inspiration for functionalistic ideas in Norway. One modern notion was increased differentiation of room functions. Separate rooms were to be used for leisure, sleeping, and cooking, and parents and children should have separate bedrooms. The importance of light, fresh air, and nature was emphasized, a notion that permeates Norwegian architectural philosophy to the present day. While traditional houses continued to be built all through this period, many houses in Oslo are built in *funkis* style. A number of larger buildings, most notably Ekeberg restaurant, which has recently been restored and reopened after many years of decline, and the Ingierstrand beach pavilion were in this style, and so were many apartments, office buildings, and stores that can still be seen in Oslo.

*Funkis* buildings can be identified by their flat roofs, large, flat surfaces, curved walls, geometric shapes, horizontal bands of windows, flexible interiors, and lack of excess decorations. *Funkis* apartment buildings are often tall and narrow, in order to allow light into all the rooms. Technology was in fashion, and buildings were often equipped with elevators.

Functionalism also inspired contractors and builders of prefabricated houses, creating a style one author has called *folk funkis*.[38] One type of *folk funkis* house is called "a skirt and blouse house" because the ground floor and second floor were painted different colors, with vertical siding on one floor and horizontal siding on the other.

Arne Korsmo (1900–1968) was a leading functionalist architect and professor at the technical university in Trondheim. He designed 50 homes in the Oslo area, including Villa Stenersen for art collector and businessman Rolf Stenersen. The iconic Oslo City Hall was designed by architects Arnstein Arneberg and Magnus Poulsen. Begun in 1931, it was not completed until 1950 because construction was interrupted by the occupation. The exterior

Villa Stenersen in Oslo designed by Arne Korsmo, 1938. This house is a prime example of the Funkis style of architecture popular from the 1920s to 1940s. It was built for businessman and art collector Rolf E. Stenersen. (Courtesy of the author.)

is decorated with reliefs depicting Norse mythology, a statue of Viking king Harald Hardråde, and sculptures of the craftsmen who built the hall. Inside the walls are richly decorated with murals depicting Norwegian history and culture. Many well-known artists are represented, including Henrik Sørensen, Alf Rolfsen, Axel Revold, Edvard Munch, Dyre Vaa, Dagfin Werenskiold, and Per Krohg.

### Post–World War II Housing Crisis

Virtually, no housing was built during the German occupation because any construction that occurred was in support of the German war effort. In addition, the northernmost county of Finnmark and also northern Troms were totally destroyed in 1944. The Germans employed a scorched-earth policy as they withdrew before the advancing Russian army: forcibly evacuating the population and destroying every building they found. The housing in the rest of the country was also in poor shape because much of it had been requisitioned to house the occupying forces. These factors as well as the tendency of people to move to Oslo to find work and to get married and have children in much greater numbers led to a critical shortage of housing in the capital city. In addition, when economic conditions improved in Norway,

Oslo City Hall, completed in 1950. Designed by architects Arnstein Arneberg (1882–1961) and Magnus Poulsen (1881–1958). (Courtesy of the author.)

people began to have higher expectations for housing standards. While the old tenement apartments on the east side of Oslo may have had one room and a kitchen, no running water or bath, and an outhouse in the courtyard, this was no longer acceptable to people.

In 1948, the city of Oslo annexed the surrounding area of Aker. With one stroke of a pen, the physical size of the city was multiplied by 26. Oslo suddenly became the fourth largest city in the world in terms of area, although much of this new land included the extensive forests to the north and east of the city. Now came the difficult work of procuring building sites and planning future construction. Most of the old Aker area at that time was farmland. In this time of housing crisis, new housing needed to be built as efficiently as possible to keep it affordable. City planners were strategic in their approach. They did not extend city services to new areas until after the land had been purchased, because the price per acre was lower for farmland than it would be for developed land. Many farmers resisted selling their land because it meant the end of a life style for them and their descendents. Others sold happily, and either bought new farms elsewhere or simply retired. Some farmers sold their acreage, but negotiated to keep the farmhouse and a few acres

Oslo City Hall interior. *Work, Administration, Celebration*, by Henrik Sørensen (1882–1962). This enormous mural takes up the entire south wall of the great hall and contains both allegorical and realistic depictions of the Norwegian people and various aspects of life. (Courtesy of the author.)

around it. This meant that many new apartment complexes were constructed next to a tiny farmhouse. These farmhouses still exist, and some have been converted to community gathering centers.

There are several different periods of construction after World War II. The earliest apartment buildings were built closer to the center city, and were the precursors to the *drabantbyer*, sometimes translated as satellite towns. In 1952 Lambertseter, the first true *drabantby*, was built. Similar projects were begun in Bergen, Trondheim, and other cities. The philosophy behind the *drabantbyer* was the familiar desire to provide working-class families with housing that was full of light, fresh air, and green surroundings. Each apartment was to offer separate bedrooms for the married couple and their children, and the kitchens should be small so that no one would be tempted to convert it into a sleeping space. Initially each *drabantby* was intended to be a self-contained neighborhood, with schools, day-care centers, and shops all within walking distance. Unfortunately, the housing shortage after the war was so acute that construction of housing units was prioritized, and other services were put on the back burner. This meant that the stay-at-home mothers were often stuck at home with the children, while the fathers headed off to work in the city. People had to travel long distances by inadequate public transportation to buy groceries and to send the children to school. The earliest *drabantbyer* were constructed with traditional building techniques, laying brick by hand, and generally consisted of complexes of four-story block buildings. Despite the drawbacks, these apartments were immensely popular. The only way a family could manage to purchase one was through a lottery system among members of OBOS, *Oslo Bo- og Sparelag* (Oslo Housing and Savings Association). Years of seniority in the association were necessary to reach the top of the list. Parents even signed their infant children up for membership in the hope that by the time they were old enough to buy an apartment, they would have sufficient seniority.

Beginning in the 1960s, building became more mechanized. More use was made of slabs of prefabricated walls put into place by enormous cranes. The requirement that any building more than four stories have an elevator encouraged the construction of buildings with 10 or 12 stories. Therefore during the 1960s, massive apartment complexes were built, farther and farther from the center of Oslo. The old farms that were replaced are commemorated in the names of these *drabantbyer:* Lambertseter, Ammerud, Kalbakken, and Bøler.

The *drabantbyer* came to be a target of criticism, particularly by the political left. This was ironic in a way because it was a social-democratic political philosophy that drove the project from the beginning. The belief was that everyone should have the opportunity to have equality in housing. In fact equality was stressed to such a degree, that every apartment had a balcony—even those on the ground floor. According to the critics, the *drabantbyer* had been planned from the top down, with no input from the people who would be living there. The complexes were said to be monotonous, boring places for young people to live, and poorly designed. The critics ignored polls indicating that most people who lived in *drabantbyer* were generally happy with their lot. They were pleased to have apartments of a much higher standard than those left behind in the east side tenements. These new apartments had two or three bedrooms, running water, and bathrooms. The residents even loved the laundry cellars, which were equipped with modern washing machines and drying rooms.

A turning point came at the end of the 1960s, when an extensive report was published evaluating the *drabantby* project at Ammerud. The authors of the report maintained that the planning process had been undemocratic and rigid, and failed to consider future changes and development. They claimed that the people who would live in the apartments had no input into the choices that were made. A couple of years later a follow-up report was issued.

This time the authors interviewed people who lived in the development. These interviews revealed that while the residents had many complaints about lack of local services, crowded schools, and expensive apartments, most were reasonably happy living there because the conditions were so much better than they had experienced before.

As a result of this debate, however, the direction of development changed beginning in the 1970s. For the first time, quality would be prioritized over quantity, the buildings would have no more than four stories, and planners would return to the original ideals of offering closeness to nature and pleasant, local neighborhoods with all the necessary facilities.[39] The first concrete result of the new thinking was Romsås, which was finished around 1975. The housing shortage was still a major challenge for Oslo, and long seniority in OBOS was required in order to buy an apartment in the complex. With this new project, planned to house 10,000 inhabitants, planners wanted to avoid building just another bedroom community. One goal was to ensure that the infrastructure, including roads, public transportation, schools, day-care centers, and other services, would be complete when people moved in because

Romsås Drabantby, built in the mid-1970s. The plan was to build an apartment complex with comfortable, modern units, which were affordable and close to nature as well as to public transportation. The design made it more convenient to get around on foot than by car, and kept the automobile away from the central areas. (Courtesy of the author.)

that had been one of the major criticisms in the Ammerud report. Many of these public buildings were actually built first, used by the contractors during the construction phase, and then converted to their permanent functions. An elaborate system of roads, trails, and walking paths was created with the express goal of keeping motor traffic out of the central living areas. Parking garages were constructed around the perimeter, along a ring road, and public buildings were placed along the walking paths to actually make it more convenient to reach places such as schools or shopping on foot than to drive a car.

As a result of the Oslo housing policies, today more than 70 percent of Oslo residents live in apartments, according to the 2001 census. The percentage, however is not typical for all of Norway; nearly two thirds of all Norwegians live in single-family homes.[40] So there is significant variation across the country. While in Oslo only 12 percent of residences are single-family homes, in the small community of Sigdal, not far from Oslo, the number is 96 percent (Figure 10.1).

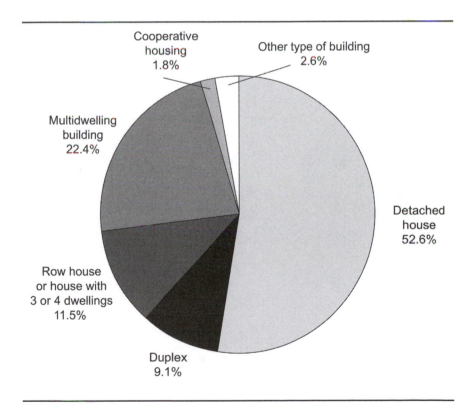

**Figure 10.1**
Number of dwellings by type of building, 2009. (Statistics Norway.)

## Contemporary Architects

Sverre Fehn (1924–2009) was the grand old man of modern Norwegian architecture. He was responsible for designing numerous public and private buildings in Norway, including the glacier museum at Fjærland, the Ivar Aasen museum in Ørsta, the museum building at Maihaugen in Lillehammer, and the National Museum of Architecture, located inside the old Bank of Norway building in Oslo. In 1997 he won the Pritzker Prize, the top international award for architecture. The jury's citation says: "he has broken new ground in giving modern architectural form to elements of his native Norwegian landscape, northern light, grey stone and verdant green forest blending fantasy and reality into buildings that are both contemporary and timeless."[41]

Of the contemporary architectural firms that have made their mark both in Norway and abroad, Snøhetta is probably the most prominent. Among other international commissions, it was hired to design the library in Alexandria, Egypt (2001), the University of the Gambia (2008), and the museum building of the September 11 Memorial in New York, scheduled for completion in 2011. In Norway its projects have included the opera house in Oslo (2008) and the new Holmenkollen ski jump (2010), among others.

Maihaugen Museum Building, Lillehammer. This building houses a variety of exhibits, both permanent and temporary. The rest of the museum contains houses and other buildings from the Middle Ages to the twentieth century. Designed by Sverre Fehn and built in stages from 1955 to 1994. (Courtesy of the author.)

Oslo Opera House, 2008, designed by Snøhetta. It is the home of the Norwegian National Opera and Ballet. In April 2009, it was declared the winner of the 2009 Mies van der Rohe award, the European Union prize for contemporary architecture. The building's roof is a popular place to walk and enjoy the view of Oslo fjord on a nice summer day. (Courtesy of the author.)

### Contextualized Architecture and Conservation

Both Norwegian art and architecture are characterized by a self-consciousness of Norwegian identity and a desire to incorporate the Norwegian love of nature and natural materials into the design. Obviously the easy availability of wood and stone made these popular building materials. The roofs of houses were often made of slate, tile, or grass. Today turf roofs are enjoying a comeback. They are "green" in all sorts of ways, providing good insulation and a natural appearance, especially for mountain cabins, and also replicate traditional building styles.

Although earlier in the twentieth century it was common to tear down older buildings, during the last 30 years that attitude has changed dramatically. In the 1980s, a proposal to tear down large sections of apartment buildings in the Grønland–Grünerløkka areas in Oslo was stopped because of public protest. More recently the old Oslo post office (1913–1924) was converted into apartments. Similar conservation and contextualizing efforts are apparent in cities all over Norway. In Bergen, the new SAS Hotel (1982) was built in a style that mirrored the adjacent Bryggen. In Trondheim, the

Oslo Opera House Interior. The interior emphasizes wood and glass. It contains 1,100 rooms, including the main auditorium, stage 2, and a rehearsal stage, as well as gift shop, banquet space, restaurants, and bars. (Courtesy of the author.)

design of the Royal Garden Hotel (1984) was inspired by the old warehouses along the Nid River. And when a large fire in Trondheim consumed an entire city block in 2002, the intense debate that ensued over how to rebuild the area is typical for Norway today. Should the new construction replicate the old or instead be something that honors the old and looks to the future? The latter argument prevailed.

## Notes

1. Knut Berg, "Fra helleristninger til dyreornamentikk," in *Norges kunsthistorie 1: Fra Oseberg til Borgund* (Oslo: Gyldendal Norsk Forlag, 1981), p. 16.

2. http://akershus.kulturnett.no/Historie/arkeologi/Artikler/stilarter_jernalder .html. Accessed 10/13/08.

3. Erla Bergendahl Hohler, "Stavkirkene, Den dekorative skurd," in *Norges kunsthistorie 1*, p. 253.

4. http://www2.skolenettet.no/kunstweb/bilde/kunstnere/dahl.html. Accessed 10/5/08.

5. Magne Malmanger, "One Hundred Years of Norwegian Painting," in *The Art of Norway 1750–1914* (Minneapolis Institute of Arts and Regents of the University of Wisconsin, 1979), pp. 92–93.

6. http://www.mjosmuseet.no/museene/balke_senteret. Accessed 4/30/10.

7. Magne Malmanger, "Maleriet 1814–1870, Fra klassisisme til tidlig realisme," in *Norges kunsthistorie 4: Det unge Norge* (Oslo: Gyldendal Norsk Forlag, 1981), p. 231.

8. Magne Malmanger, "One Hundred Years of Norwegian Painting," p. 95.

9. Malmanger, "Maleriet," p. 239.

10. Malmanger, "One Hundred Years," pp. 96–99.

11. Knut Berg, Nils Messel, and Marit Lange, "Maleriet 1870–1914," in *Norges kunsthistorie 5: Nasjonal vekst* (Oslo: Gyldendal Norsk Forlag, 1981), p. 173.

12. Munch Museum. http://158.36.77.168/munch/content2.aspx?id=100&lang=en&mid=. Accessed 11/11/08.

13. Knut Berg, "Naturalisme og nyromantikk 1870–1900," in *Norges malerkunst* (Oslo: Gyldendal, 1993), p. 496.

14. Marit Lange and Nils Messel, "Inn i et nytt århundre 1900–1914," in *Norges malerkunst: Vårt eget århundre* (Oslo: Gyldendal, 1993), p. 48.

15. Hans-Jakob Brun, "Maleriet 1940–1980," in *Norges kunsthistorie 7* (Oslo: Gyldendal, 1983), p. 147.

16. Jan Askeland, *Norsk malerkunst*, p. 313.

17. http://www.oddnerdrum.com/frame_odd.htm. Accessed 2/9/09.

18. Paul Cantor, *ArtCyclopedia*. http://www.artcyclopedia.com/feature-2004-02.html. Accessed 1/21/10.

19. Vebjørn Sand Web site, http://www.vebjorn-sand.com/thebridge.htm. Accessed 1/21/10.

20. Tone Wikborg, "Norsk skulptur i en brytningstid," *Norges kunsthistorie 5*, p. 309.

21. http://www.vigeland.museum.no/en/. Accessed 1/4/10.

22. Trond Gjerdi, "Folk Art," in *The Art of Norway*, pp. 27–88.

23. Jan-Lauritz Opstad, "Silver and Enamel," in *The Art of Norway*, pp. 179–183.

24. Inger-Marie Lie, "Furniture," in *The Art of Norway*, pp. 184–186.

25. Elisabeth Seip, manager of the Norwegian Architecture Museum, Oslo. "Architecture in Norway." http://www.reisenett.no/norway/facts/culture_science/architecture_in_norway.html. Accessed 1/4/10.

26. http://www.lofotr.no/Engelsk/engUtgravningene_31.html. Accessed 1/4/10.

27. http://www.kaupang.uio.no/eng/index.html. Accessed 1/4/10.

28. Peter Anker, *The Art of Scandinavia* (New York: P. Hamlyn, 1970), pp. 158–159.

29. Håkon Christie, "Stavkirkene – Arkitektur," *Norges kunsthistorie 1*.

30. http://www.stavkirke.org/stavkirker/garmo.html. Accessed 1/4/10.

31. Håkon Christie, "Stavkirkene – Arkitektur," pp. 139–252.

32. http://www.nidarosdomen.no/english/. Accessed 1/4/10.

33. http://www.stiftelsenbryggen.no/. Accessed 1/4/10.

34. http://www.icomos.no/cms/content/view/51/66/lang,english/. Accessed 1/4/10.

35. http://www.husbyggeren.no/sveitser.htm. Accessed 1/4/10.

36. http://home.online.no/~hvel/Homb.Homb.blir.til.html#Homansbyen%20blir %20til.

37. Arne Lie Christensen, "Innledning. Om funksjonalisme, modernisme og modernitet," *Funkis. Funksjonalismen i Oslo og Akershus. Fremtid for fortiden* nr., 3/4-2007, pp. 4-12.

38. Bjørn Kristiansen, "Folkefunkis i Akershus," *Funkis. Funksjonalismen i Oslo og Akershus*, pp. 74–80.

39. Jon Guttu, "Drabantbyen som skyteskive," *Drabantbyen: Fremtid for fortiden* nr., 3/4 2002 (Fortidsminneforeningen: Oslo Akershus), pp. 56–67.

40. Statistics Norway. http://www.ssb.no. Accessed 1/4/10.

41. Pritzker Prize. http://www.pritzkerprize.com/laureates/1997/jury.html. Accessed 1/21/10.

# Glossary

**Æsir:** Nordic gods

**akevit:** Aquavit; liquor made from potatoes

**allemannretten:** right allowing public access to private land

**Amanda:** Norwegian film awards

**arbeidsviser:** work songs

**årestue:** open hearth house

**Ash lad:** Askeladden; youngest brother and underdog hero of folktales

**bacalao:** stew of dried, salt cod, tomatoes, onions, garlic, peppers, etc.

**bånsull:** lullaby

**barnehage:** preschool

**barneskole:** elementary school

**bedehus:** prayer house

**Berlinerkranser:** small white wreath-shaped cookies

**bløtkake:** several-layered sponge cake filled with whipped cream and fruit

**Bokmål:** majority written language, derived from Danish

**brown cheese:** national cheese made from whey cooked down and caramelized

**brunost:** see brown cheese

**bukkehorn:** musical instrument made from a ram's horn

**bunad:** Norwegian national costume

**bygdekino:** mobile cinema; traveled around in rural areas with movies

**Christiania:** name for Oslo from 1624 to 1925 (Kristiania from 1877)

**drabantbyer:** post–World War II high-rise apartment complexes

**draug:** creature of the sea

**Draumkvedet:** dream ballad, medieval ballad

**dugnad:** custom of volunteer group projects

**ERASMUS:** EU student exchange program

**EU:** European Union

**European Economic Area (EEA):** treaty Norway has with EU

**fjord:** long, narrow inlet of sea water, reaching as far as 126 miles inland. Very deep with steep sides

**flatbread:** thin, flat bread, usually baked on a griddle

**folkehøgskole:** folk high school. One-year, non-academic program

**folketrygden:** national insurance scheme

**Forest Finns:** one of five national minorities; originated in Finland and settled in southeastern Norway

**fossegrim:** waterfall sprite that can teach one to play the fiddle

**friluftsliv:** outdoor recreation

**funkis:** Functionalist architecture

**futhark:** runic alphabet

**fylke:** administrative district similar to a county

**gamalost:** "old cheese"; firm, brownish-yellow cheese made of skim cow's milk

**gangar:** dance; 2/4 time

**geitelokk:** song for calling goats

**geitost:** see brown cheese

**gløgg:** spiced wine, served with almonds and raisins

**gravlaks:** cured salmon

**grunnskole:** obligatory school; now 10 years

**hagebyer:** garden cities

**halling:** athletic dance for men; 2/4 time

**Hardanger fiddle/hardingfele:** richly decorated Norwegian fiddle, with four or five resonating strings under the four that are played on

**Heddapris:** theater prize

**heimbrent:** home-distilled liquor

**Heimskringla:** history of Norwegian kings, written in thirteenth-century Iceland

**heks:** witch

**helleristninger:** pre-historic rock carvings

**hjaling:** Norwegian yodeling

**hulder:** beautiful troll-girl with cow's tail

**huldrefolk:** supernatural creatures who live underground or in the mountain

**huldreslått:** troll-girl tune

**hurtigruta:** Coastal Express passenger line

**husflid:** handcrafts

**huv:** Norwegian yodeling

**hytte:** cabin, cottage

**Janteloven:** see Law of Jante

**joik:** Sámi vocal music

**jøssing:** anti-Nazi Norwegian during World War II

**julebord:** literally Christmas table; pre-Christmas party

**julebukk:** tradition where children visit neighbors between Christmas and New Year's Eve to get cookies and treats

**julekalender:** Advent calendar

**julenek:** sheaf of grain for the birds at Christmas

**julenisse:** Christmas elf, Santa Claus figure

**juleøl:** Christmas beer

**juletrefest:** children's Christmas party

**kappleik:** folk music competition

**karamellpudding:** Norwegian flan; custard with caramel sauce

**karveskurd:** chip carving

**kebab:** fast food pita sandwich; introduced to Norway by immigrants

**kjempevise:** heroic ballad

**klippfisk:** fish dried on flat rocks

**klokkeslått:** bell tune for fiddle

**klubb:** potato dumplings

**koldtbord:** smorgasbord; buffet

**kransekake:** wreath cake made of a tapered tower of marzipan rings

**krone/crown:** Norwegian unit of currency; worth about 15 cents

**krumkake:** thin, cone-shaped cookie baked on an iron

**kulokk:** song for calling cows

**kumler:** potato dumplings

**kvadratur:** quadratic area of streets in old Oslo; designed by Christian IV

**kven:** one of five national minorities; originated in Finland

**kvikaker:** pancake-type cake

**Laestadians:** followers of Lars Laestadius who worked among the Sámi

**laling:** Norwegian yodeling

**Landsmaal:** original name for Nynorsk

**lånekassa:** Norwegian State Educational Loan Fund

**langeleik:** Norwegian dulcimer

**Law of Jante/Janteloven:** "law" stating that you are no better than anyone else

**lefse:** round, flat bread, baked on griddle; made for special occasions

**likhet:** equality; similarity

**lompe:** small potato tortilla often wrapped around a hot dog

**lur:** long, wooden horn

**lusekofte:** Norwegian patterned sweater

**lutefisk:** fish; dried fish soaked in lye-solution before cooking

**Marshall Plan:** U.S. assistance to European countries during reconstruction after World War II

**matpakke:** packed lunch; open-faced sandwiches, fruit, or vegetable

**medisterkaker:** pork meatballs

**nasjonal samling:** the Norwegian Nazi party, led by Vidkun Quisling

**NAV:** Norwegian Labor and Welfare Administration

**nisse:** small gnome-like creature

**nøkk:** creature of lakes or ponds

**nøkkelost:** semi-hard yellow cheese flavored with cumin, caraway seeds, and cloves

**NRK/Norsk Rikskringkasting:** State-owned broadcasting station

**Nynorsk:** minority written language; derived from dialects

**OBOS:** Oslo Housing and Savings Association

**omgangsskoler:** ambulatory schools; taught by traveling teachers

**oskorei:** air spirits

**Oslo accords:** peace agreement brokered by Norwegians between Israelis and Palestinians in 1994

**pannekaker:** large, thin pancakes rolled up with jam

**pappapermisjon:** paternity leave

**pepperkaker:** gingerbread cookies

**PRIO:** Peace Research Institute of Oslo

**rakfisk:** cured fresh-water fish

**raspeballar:** potato dumplings

**rekeaften:** casual supper of shrimp in the shell, which guests peel to build open-face sandwiches with bread and mayonnaise

**ridderost:** soft cheese

**Riksmaal:** old name for Bokmål; Dano-Norwegian

**Riksteatret:** touring theater company

**risengrynsgrøt:** rice porridge

**Roma:** also known as Gypsies; one of five national minorities

**Romani:** the travelers; one of five national minorities

**romjul:** period between Christmas and New Year

**rømmegrøt:** sour cream porridge

**rosemaling:** decorative painting; rose painting

**rusbrus:** alcopop

**russ:** graduating seniors

**russetog:** parade for graduating seniors on May 17 (National Day)

**saga:** Old Norse story of heroes, kings, or families

**samboer:** cohabitant (unmarried partner)

**samboerskap:** cohabitation (two unmarried people)

**samfunnshus:** community meeting hall

**Sámi:** indigenous people

**sandkaker:** Christmas cookie, small tart

**Schengen:** security agreement among 25 European countries providing for open borders

**Selburosa:** eight-pointed star common in knitwear; from Selbu, Norway

**seljefløyte:** willow flute

**sjømannskirke:** Norwegian mission to Seamen; church for Norwegian sailors abroad

**skillingsbolle:** sweet bun

**slåttestev:** fiddle tunes sung for dancing

**smalahove:** smoked lamb's head

**smørbrød:** fancy open-faced sandwich

**sølje:** silver brooch for bunad

**spekemat:** dried, cured meat

**Spellemannprisen:** music awards

**springar:** dance in uneven 3/4 time

**stabbur:** store house farm building

**stave church:** medieval wooden church

**stavkirke:** stave church

**stev:** short folk song or verse

**Stortinget:** parliament

**sveler:** pancake-like cake folded in half and filled with sweet filling

**Syttende mai:** Norway's national day; May 17

**tagging:** graffiti

**tatere:** travelers; also called Romani

**t-bane:** light-rail, subway system

**tettsted:** area of low to moderate density housing

**tørrfisk:** dried fish; usually air-dried on racks outdoors

**trikk:** electric streetcar; tram

**troll:** supernatural creature that is large, stupid, and ugly

**trolldom:** magic

**trollvise:** supernatural ballad

**tussefløyte:** Norwegian wooden recorder (flute)

**ungdomshus:** youth meeting hall

**ungdomsskole:** lower secondary school

**videregående skole:** upper secondary school

**Viking:** raiders, traders, seafarers from 800 to 1066 CE

**vinmonopolet:** state-run liquor store

**wienerbrød:** Danish pastry

# Bibliography

GENERAL

## Books

Heidar, Knut. *Norway: Elites on Trial*. Boulder, CO: Westview Press, 2001.

Kiel, Anne Cohen. *Continuity and Change: Aspects of Contemporary Norway*. Oslo: Scandinavian University Press, 1993.

Maagerø, Eva, and Birte Simonsen, eds. *Norway: Society and Culture*. Kristiansand: Portal Books, 2005.

Su-Dale, Elizabeth. *Culture Shock! Norway*. Singapore: Times Media Private Limited, 2003.

*This Is Norway*. Statistics Norway. Available on http://www.ssb.no.

## Web sites

The Anti-Racist Centre in Norway. http://www.antirasistisk-senter.no/english/news/index.html

Countries and Their Cultures: Norway. http://www.everyculture.com/No-Sa/Norway.html

Cultural Profile of Norway. http://www.culturalprofiles.org.uk/norway/Directories/Norway_Cultural_Profile/-1.html

Facts about Norway. http://www.ssb.no/english/subjects/00/minifakta_en/en/

Gateway to the Public Sector in Norway. http://www.norway.no/

Global Peace Index: Norway. http://www.visionofhumanity.org/gpi/results/norway/2008/

International Peace Research Institute (PRIO). http://www.prio.no/
Norway: The Official Site in the United States. http://www.norway.org/
Norwegian Defense Official Website. http://www.mil.no/languages/english/start/
Norwegian Institute of International Affairs. http://english.nupi.no/
Norwegian Online Telephone Directory. http://www.gulesider.no/tk/
The Royal Family. http://www.kongehuset.no/english/vis.html
Statistics Norway. http://www.ssb.no/english/

## CHAPTER 1: LAND, PEOPLE, AND POLITICS

### Books and Journals

Ingebritsen, Christine. *The Nordic States and European Unity*. Ithaca, NY: Cornell
    University Press, 1998.
———. *Scandinavia in World Politics*. Lanham, MD: Rowman & Littlefield
    Publishers, 2006.
*Jewish Life and Culture in Norway. Wergeland's Legacy*. New York: Abel Abrahamsen,
    2003.
Maagero, Eva, and Birte Simonsen, eds. *Norway: Society and Culture*. Kristiansand:
    Portal, 2005.
Riste, Olav. *Norway's Foreign Relations—A History*. Oslo: Universitetsforlaget, 2005.
*Scandinavian Review*, 2005, Vol. 92, No. 3. Special Issue devoted to 100 years of
    Norwegian independence.

### Web sites

Eriksen, Thomas Hylland. "Being Norwegian in a Shrinking World." http://
    folk.uio.no/geirthe/Norwegian.html
Introduction to the Sámi People. http://boreale.konto.itv.se/samieng.htm
The Oslo Center for Peace and Human Rights: http://www.oslocenter.no

## CHAPTER 2: HISTORY

Abrahamsen, Samuel. *Norway's Response to the Holocaust: An Historical Perspective*.
    New York: Holocaust Library, 1991.
Ferguson, Robert. *The Vikings*. New York: Viking, 2009.
Kjeldstadli, Knut, and Grete Brochmann. *A History of Immigration: The Case of
    Norway 900–2000*. Oslo University Press, 2008.
Lovoll, Odd S. *The Promise of America*. Rev ed. Minneapolis: University of Minnesota
    Press, 1999.
Nordstrom, Byron J. *Scandinavia since 1500*. Minneapolis: University of Minnesota
    Press, 2000.
Stokker, Kathleen. *Folklore Fights the Nazis: Humor in Occupied Norway, 1940–1945*.
    Madison: University of Wisconsin Press, 1997.

## CHAPTER 3: RELIGION AND THOUGHT

Crossley-Holland, Kevin. *The Norse Myths*. New York: Pantheon Books, 1989.

Davidson, H. R. Ellis. *Gods and Myths of Northern Europe*. Baltimore: Penguin Books, 1964.

———. *Scandinavian Mythology*. New York: Hamlyn Publishing Group, 1969.

DuBois, Thomas A. *Nordic Religions in the Viking Age*. Philadelphia: University of Pennsylvania Press, 1999.

Graham-Campbell, James. *The Viking World*. London: Francis Lincoln, 2001.

Haywood, John. *Encyclopaedia of the Viking Age*. London: Thames & Hudson, 2000.

———. *Penguin Historical Atlas of the Vikings*. New York: Penguin, 1996. Detailed maps of Viking settlements in Scotland, Ireland, England, Iceland, and Normandy.

Lindow, John. *Handbook of Norse Mythology*. Santa Barbara, CA: ABC-CLIO, 2001.

———. *Norse Mythology: A Guide to the Gods, Heroes, Rituals, and Beliefs*. Oxford and New York: Oxford University Press, 2002.

Molland, Einar. *Church Life in Norway 1800–1950*. Trans. by Harris Kaasa. Minneapolis: Augsburg Publishing House, 1957.

O'Donoghue, Heather. *From Asgard to Valhalla: The Remarkable History of the Norse Myths*. London: I. B. Tauris, 2007.

Orchard, Andy. *Cassel's Dictionary of Norse Myth and Legend*. London: Cassell, 2002.

Williams, Gareth, "Viking Religion." http://www.bbc.co.uk/history/ancient/vikings/religion_01.shtml.


## CHAPTER 4: MARRIAGE, GENDER, FAMILY, AND EDUCATION

Facts about education in Norway. http://www.ssb.no/english/subjects/04/02/facts/facts2009.pdf

Gender in Norway. http://www.gender.no/

*Men and Women in Norway*. Statistics Norway. http://www.ssb.no

NOKUT (Norwegian Agency for Quality Assurance in Education). http://nokut.no/en/


## CHAPTER 5: HOLIDAYS AND LEISURE ACTIVITIES

Culture and Media Theme Page, Statistics Norway. http://www.ssb.no/english/subjects/07/media_en/

Norway.com: sports. http://blog.norway.com/category/sports/

Norwegian Trekking Association. http://www.turistforeningen.no/english/


## CHAPTER 6: CUISINE AND FASHION

### Cookbooks

Brimi, Arne, and Bengt Wilson. *A Taste of Norway*. Oslo: Norwegian University Press, 1987.

Scott, Astrid Karlsen. *Authentic Norwegian Cooking*. Olympia, WA: Nordic
    Adventures, 2000.
Viestad, Andreas. *Kitchen of Light: The New Scandinavian Cooking*. New York:
    Workman Publishing, 2003.

### Fashion

### Books

Bøhn, Annichen Sibbern. *Norwegian Knitting Designs*. Oslo: Grøndahl & Søn, 1965.
McGregor, Sheila. *Traditional Scandinavian Knitting*. New York: Dover Publications,
    1984.
Noss, Aagot. "Rural Norwegian Dress and Its Symbolic Functions" in *Norwegian
    Folk Art. The Migration of a Tradition. The Museum of American Folk Art,
    New York and The Norwegian Folk Museum, Oslo*, 1995. New York: Abbeville
    Press.
Sundbø, Annemor. *Setesdal Sweaters. The History of the Norwegian Lice Pattern*.
    Kristiansand, Norway: Torridal Tweed, 2001.
Vanberg, Bent, and Karin Hybbestad Schwantes. *Norwegian Bunads*. Oslo: Hjemmenes
    forlag, 1991.

### Web sites

The Bunad and Folk Costume Council. http://www.bunadraadet.no/
Norwegian Design Council. http://www.norskdesign.no/?lang=en_US
Norwegian Fashion. http://www.norwegianfashion.no/

## CHAPTER 7: LANGUAGE AND LITERATURE

### Works in Translation

### Folktales

Asbjørnsen, Peter Christen, and Jørgen Moe. *Norwegian Folk Tales*. Trans. Pat Shaw
    Iversen. New York: The Viking Press, 1960.
———. *Norwegian Folk Tales 2*. Norway: Dreyer, 1990.

### Crime Fiction

#### Kjell Ola Dahl (K. O. Dahl): Detectives Frank Frølich and Inspector Gunnarstranda

*The Fourth Man*. Trans. Don Bartlett. London: Faber & Faber, 2007 (2005 original).
*The Man in the Window*. Trans. Don Bartlett. London: Faber and Faber, 2008 (2001
    original).
*The Last Fix*. London: Faber and Faber, 2009 (2000 original).

#### Karin Fossum: Inspector Sejer Series

*Don't Look Back*. Trans. Felicity David. New York: Harvest Books, 2005 (1996 original).

*He Who Fears the Wolf.* Trans. Felicity David. New York: Harvest Books, 2006 (1997 original).

*When the Devil Holds the Candle.* Trans. Felicity David. New York: Harvest Books, 2007 (1998 original).

*The Indian Bride* (*Calling Out for You* in Britain). Trans. Charlotte Barslund. New York: Mariner Books, 2008 (2000 original).

*Black Seconds.* Trans. Charlotte Barslund. New York: Mariner Books, 2009 (2002 original).

*The Water's Edge.* Trans. Charlotte Barslund. Boston: Houghton Mifflin Harcourt, 2009 (2007 original).

### Anne Holt: Vik/Stubø Series

*What Is Mine.* Trans. Kari Dickson. New York: Grand Central Publishing, 2008 (2001 original).

*What Never Happens.* Trans. Kari Dickson. New York: Grand Central Publishing, 2008 (2004 original).

### Jo Nesbo: Harry Hole Series

*The Redbreast: A Novel.* Trans. Don Bartlett. Brattleboro: Harper Paperbacks, 2009 (2000 original).

*Nemesis: A Novel (Harry Hole Mystery).* Trans. Don Bartlett. Brattleboro: Harper Paperbacks, 2010 (2002 original).

*The Devil's Star: A Novel.* Trans. Don Bartlett. New York: Harper, 2010 (2003 original).

*The Redeemer (A Harry Hole Mystery).* Trans. Don Bartlett. New York: Harper Paperbacks, 2009 (2005 original).

*The Snowman.* Trans. Don Bartlett. Random House of Canada, Limited, 2010 (2007 original).

### Kjersti Scheen

*Final Curtain.* Trans. Louis Muinzer. London: Arcadia Books, 2004 (1994 original).

### Gunnar Staalesen: Varg Veum Series

*Yours until death.* Trans. Margaret Amassian. London: Arcadia, 1993 (1979 original).

*At Night All Wolves Are Grey.* Trans. David McDuff. London: Arcadia, 1986.

*The Writing on the Wall.* Trans. Hal Sutcliff. London: Arcadia, 2004 (1983 original).

*The Consorts of Death.* Trans. Don Bartlett. London: Arcadia, 2010 (2006 original).

### Selected Other Literature

Ambjørnsen, Ingvar. *Beyond the Great Indoors.* Trans. Don Bartlett and Kari Dickson. London: Black Swan, 2005.

Christensen, Lars Saabye. *The Half Brother.* Trans. Kenneth Steven. New York: Arcade Pub., 2004.

Faldbakken, Knut. *Sweetwater*. Trans. Joan Tate. London and Chester Springs, PA: Dufour Editions, 1994.

Hamsun Knut. *Hunger*. Trans. Sverre Lyngstad. Edinburgh: Rebel, 1996.

Hoel, Sigurd. *Meeting at the Milestone*. Trans. Sverre Lyngstad. New York: Green Integer, 2001.

Hoem, Edvard. *Ave Eva: A Norwegian Tragedy*. Trans. Frankie Shackelford. Las Cruces, NM: Xenos Books, 2000.

Kjærstad, Jan. *The Seducer*. Trans. Barbara J. Haveland. London: Arcadia, 2003.

———. *The Conquerer*. Trans. Barbara Haveland. Rochester, NY: Open Letter, 2007.

———. *The Discoverer: A Novel*. Trans. Barbara Haveland. Rochester, NY: Open Letter, 2009.

Loe, Erlend. *Naive. Super*. Trans. Tor Ketil Solberg. Edinburgh: Canongate Books, 2005.

Lønn, Oystein. *According to Sofia*. Trans. Barbara J. Haveland. London: Maia, 2009.

Ibsen, Henrik. *Four Major Plays (Oxford World's Classics)*. London: Oxford University Press, 2008.

Petterson, Per. *Out Stealing Horses: A Novel*. New York: Picador, 2008.

Ragde, Anne B. *Berlin Poplars*. Trans. James Anderson. London: Harvill Secker, 2008.

Sandel, Cora. *Alberta and Freedom*. Trans. Elizabeth Rokkan. Chester Springs, PA: Dufour Editions, 2008.

Skram, Amalie. *Constance Ring (European Classics)*. Translated ed. Evanston: Chicago: Northwestern University Press, 2002.

———. *Under Observation*. New York: Women in Translation, 1992.

Solstad, Dag. *Shyness and Dignity*. Saint Paul, MN: Graywolf Press, 2006.

Ullmann, Linn. *A Blessed Child*. Trans. Sarah Death. New York: Alfred A. Knopf, 2008.

———. *Before You Sleep*. Trans. Tiina Nunnally. New York: Viking, 1999.

———. *Grace: A Novel*. Trans. Barbara Haveland. New York: Knopf: 2005.

Undset, Sigrid. *Kristin Lavransdatter*. Trans. Tiina Nunnally. New York: Penguin, 1997–2000.

Vesaas, Tarjei. *The Birds*. Trans. Torbjørn Støverud and Michael Barnes. Chester Springs, PA: Dufour Editions, 1995.

Wassmo, Herbjørg. *The House with the Blind Glass Windows*. Trans. Lloyd, Roseann, and Allen Simpson. Canada: Seal Press, 1995.

———. *Dina's Book*. Trans. Nadia M. Christensen. New York: Arcade Publishing, 1994.

## Anthologies

Gaski, Harald, ed. *In the Shadow of the Midnight Sun: Contemporary Sámi Prose and Poetry*. Seattle: University of Washington Press, 1998.

Hanson, Katherine, ed. *Echo: Scandinavian Stories about Girls*. New York: Women in Translation, 2000.

————. *An Everyday Story: Norwegian Women's Fiction*. New York: Women in Translation, 1995.

## Secondary Resources

Ibsen.net Web site: http://ibsen.net/index.gan?id=83

Kolloen, Sletten Ingar. *Knut Hamsun: Dreamer & Dissenter*. New Haven: Yale University Press, 2009.

Maagerø, Eva, and Birte Simonsen, eds. *Norway: Society and Culture*. Chapter 13: "The Norwegian Language—Democracy in Practice?" by Eva Maagerø; Chapter 14: "Norwegian Myths and Tales," by Elise Seip Tønnessen; Chapter 15: "Norwegian Literature," by Elise Seip Tønnessen; Chapter 16: "Children's Literature," by Elise Seip Tønnessen.

Naess, Harald. *A History of Norwegian Literature* (Histories of Scandinavian Literature). Lincoln and London: University of Nebraska Press, 1993.

Norwegian Children's Literature. Brochure published by NORLA (Norwegian Literature Abroad). http://norla.no/index.php/content/download/4079/70324/file/NORLA-brochure.pdf. Accessed 11/24/09.

Zagar, Monika. *Knut Hamsun: The Dark Side of Literary Brilliance (New Directions in Scandinavian Studies)*. Seattle: University of Washington Press, 2009.

## CHAPTER 8: MEDIA AND CINEMA

### Norwegian Film History

Soila, Tytti, et al. *Nordic National Cinemas*. New York: Routledge, 1998.

### Web sites

"A Brief History of Norwegian Film." http://www.norway.org/aboutnorway/culture/film/A_Brief_History_of_Norwegian_Film/

Database of all films shown at Norwegian cinemas. http://film.medietilsynet.no/Filmdatabase

Film & kino. http://www.filmweb.no/filmogkino/english/

Nordic film cooperation. http://www.scandinavian-films.org/about.htm

Pan-Scandinavian cooperation, Scandinavian Films. http://www.scandinavian-films.org

## CHAPTER 9: PERFORMING ARTS

### Norway: Cultural Profile

http://www.culturalprofiles.net/norway/Directories/Norway_Cultural_Profile/-1.html

Norwegian Band Index. http://bandindex.no/

### Folk Dance and Folk Music

Hardanger Fiddle Association of America. http://www.hfaa.org/
Norwegian Traditional Music Agency. http://www.folkmusic.no/

### Ole Bull

Haugen, Einar, and Camilla Cai. *Ole Bull: Norway's Romantic Musician and Cosmopolitan Patriot.* Madison: University of Wisconsin Press, 1993. English-language biography of Ole Bull.

### Edvard Grieg

Benestad, Finn, ed. *Letters to Colleagues and Friends: Edvard Grieg.* Trans. by William H. Halverson. Columbus, OH: Peer Gynt Press, 2000.
Benestad, Finn, and William H. Halverson, eds. and trans. *Edvard Grieg: Diaries, Articles, Speeches.* Columbus, OH: Peer Gynt Press, 2001.
"Grieg 2007." http://eng.grieg07.no/
Grimley, Daniel M. *Grieg: Music, Landscape and Norwegian Identity.* Woodbridge, Suffolk, UK: Boydell Press, 2006.
Jarrett, Sandra. *Edvard Grieg and His Songs.* Aldershot, Hants, England, and Burlington, VT: Ashgate, 2003.

### Jazz

Norwegian Jazz Archive. http://www.jazzarkivet.no/
Norwegian Jazz Base. http://www.jazzbasen.no/index_eng.html

### CHAPTER 10: ART AND ARCHITECTURE/HOUSING

Anker, Peter. *The Art of Scandinavia.* New York: Hamlyn Publishing Group, 1970.
Berg, Knut. "Nordic Art at the Turn of the Century." In *Dreams of a Summer Night. Scandinavian Painting at the Turn of the Century.* London: Hayward Gallery, 1986.
Bjørnstad, Ketil. *The Story of Edvard Munch.* Trans. Torbjørn Støverud and Hal Sutcliffe. London: Arcadia, 2005.
Buchhart, Dieter, ed. *Edvard Munch: Signs of Modern Art*/Foundation Beyeler. (English edition edited by Christopher Wynne.) Ostfildern: Hatje Cantz; [Riehen]: Fondation Beyeler; [Schwäbish Hall]: Kunsthalle Würth, 2007.
Cantor, Paul. "The Importance of Being Odd: Nerdrum's Challenge to Modernism." *ArtCyclopedia.* http://www.artcyclopedia.com/feature-2004-02.html.
Malmanger, Magne. *One Hundred Years of Norwegian Painting.* Oslo: Nasjonalgalleriet, 1988.
Nelson, Marion, ed. *Norwegian Folk Art: The Migration of a Tradition.* Museum of American Folk Art, New York, and The Norwegian Folk Museum, Oslo, 1995. New York: Abbeville Press.
Schulz-Norberg, Christian. *Modern Norwegian Architecture.* Oslo: Norwegian University Press, 1986.

Varnedoe, Kirk. "Northern Light." In *Nordic Art at the Turn of the Century.* Yale University Press, 1988.

———. *Northern Light: Realism and Symbolism in Scandinavian Painting, 1880–1910.* Brooklyn, NY: Brooklyn Museum, 1982.

**Web sites**

Architecture in Norway. http://www.reisenett.no/norway/facts/culture_science/architecture_in_norway.html

Vigeland Sculpture Park. http://www.vigeland.museum.no/en

# Index

**About the Author**

MARGARET HAYFORD O'LEARY, PhD, is professor and chair of the Norwegian Department at St. Olaf College in Northfield, MN, where she has taught since 1977. She also teaches courses on language, culture, and society regularly at the International Summer School at the University of Oslo. She has co-authored *Norsk i Sammenheng* (McGraw Hill, 1992) a textbook for intermediate Norwegian, and *KlikkNorsk* (Skandisk, 2003), an interactive computerized grammar. In addition she has translated a novel, *The Four Winds*, by Gerd Brantenberg (Women in Translation, 1995) and several short stories from Norwegian, and published articles on Norwegian literature and language pedagogy.